The Imagined Conflict

The Imagined Conflict

On Science and God

Sverre Holm

WIPF & STOCK · Eugene, Oregon

THE IMAGINED CONFLICT
On Science and God

Copyright © 2025 Sverre Holm. All rights reserved. Except for brief quotations in critical publications or reviews, no part of this book may be reproduced in any manner without prior written permission from the publisher. Write: Permissions, Wipf and Stock Publishers, 199 W. 8th Ave., Suite 3, Eugene, OR 97401.

Wipf & Stock
An Imprint of Wipf and Stock Publishers
199 W. 8th Ave., Suite 3
Eugene, OR 97401

www.wipfandstock.com

PAPERBACK ISBN: 979-8-3852-5763-8
HARDCOVER ISBN: 979-8-3852-5764-5
EBOOK ISBN: 979-8-3852-5765-2

VERSION NUMBER 11/20/25

Revised version of Norwegian original with title:
Den innbilte konflikten: Om naturvitenskap og Gud
Lunde forlag / Veritas imprint, Oslo, Norway, 2021.

Unless otherwise noted, Scripture quotations are taken from The Holy Bible, New International Version®, NIV®. Copyright © 2011 by Biblica, Inc. Used with permission of Zondervan. All rights reserved worldwide. www.zondervan.com.

Scripture quotations marked (NRSVUE) are taken from the New Revised Standard Version Updated Edition. Copyright © 2021 National Council of Churches of Christ in the United States of America. Used by permission. All rights reserved worldwide.

Scripture quotations marked (DRA) are from the Douay-Rheims 1899 American Edition and are in the public domain.

For my grandchildren, Eline, Filip, Ada, and Fredrik,
with a hope and a prayer that you and your generation
will overcome the myth of the imagined conflict.

Contents

List of Figures | ix
Preface | xiii

Introduction | 1
1   God's Two Books | 12
2   The Amazing Creation | 31
3   Serious Science in the Middle Ages and the Unwavering Galileo | 52
4   The History of Life and the Universe | 103
5   Philosophy of Science | 141
6   Evolution and Purpose | 164
7   Man and Evolution | 196
8   The Perceived and the Real Conflict | 223

Appendix: The Bible and Science | 239
Afterword | 263
References | 265
Index | 281

List of Figures

Figure 1. Peter Waage (1833–1900) was a professor of chemistry at the University of Oslo. Early in his life, in an award-winning student essay from 1857, he quoted "God has arranged everything according to measure, number, and weight" in Greek. He also quoted it near the end of his life in a speech in Stockholm in 1898 at the memorial marking fifty years since the death of the chemist Berzelius. | 3

Figure 2. Stephen Hawking (1942–2018), English theoretical physicist, cosmologist, and author. | 8

Figure 3. Albert Einstein on a boat trip in the Oslo Fjord in 1920 with the geologists Heinrich Goldsmith and Jakob Schetelig. | 9

Figure 4. God, who is the source of all truth as shown in the two books of nature and grace, is above the horizontal line, while our incomplete understanding in science and theology is below the line. | 13

Figure 5. Uppsala University's seal: Truth in grace and nature. | 17

Figure 6. Blaise Pascal (1623–1662), mathematician, physicist, philosopher, and author. | 24

Figure 7. Magnetic resonance image (MRI) of the head and speech organ during the pronunciation of *s*. | 33

Figure 8. The FOXP2 gene is located on the long arm of chromosome 7 at position 31. | 35

LIST OF FIGURES

Figure 9. A water molecule consists of two hydrogen atoms (H) and one oxygen atom (O). In other similar molecules, the atoms are typically arranged at right angles to each other. The unique angle in water of 105 degrees allows the molecules to easily assemble into crystals (regular tetrahedrons), such as in ice. | 37

Figure 10. James Clerk Maxwell (1831–1879), Scottish physicist best known for Maxwell's equations from 1865. | 39

Figure 11. *Earthrise*, photo taken from Apollo 8 on December 24, 1968. | 40

Figure 12. Image of Earth alongside Saturn's rings, taken July 19, 2013, by the Cassini spacecraft. | 41

Figure 13. Cosmic evolution. | 44

Figure 14. William Thomson, first Baron Kelvin (1824–1907), was a Scottish-Irish physics professor. One of the seven base units in the International System of Units (SI) is named after him: Kelvin (K), the unit for absolute temperature. | 46

Figure 15. The cover of Riccioli's *Almagestum Novum*, 1651. Copernicus's model is on the left and Tycho's model on the right. The Earth-centered model of Ptolemy lies defeated on the ground. Note that the scale tips in favor of Tycho. | 62

Figure 16. Timeline of important events in the development of the heliocentric model. | 64

Figure 17. The view of antiquity with the earth in the center. Shown here are the spheres for the inner celestial bodies, the Moon, Mercury, Venus, and the Sun. | 67

Figure 18. The outer planets Mars, Jupiter, and Saturn and their spheres in the ancient worldview. Note how the epicycles, the small secondary circles, for these planets are almost a mirror image of the Sun's orbit around the Earth. | 69

Figure 19. Copernicus's model with the Sun in the center. The distances between all the nearest planets up to and including Mars are to the correct scale, while Jupiter and Saturn are too close to Earth in this figure. The outermost circle of fixed stars is not part of today's model. | 73

Figure 20. Illustration from Riccioli's book, 1651. When a cannon ball is fired toward the north (*E*), the earth's rotation causes it to go sideways and instead end up at point G. Such bending does not happen if the cannon is fired toward the east (B). | 75

Figure 21. Tycho's geoheliocentric model. It is like Copernicus's model in all essential respects, except that the earth is stationary relative to the stars. | 77

Figure 22. Kepler's elliptical orbits shown in correct scale. The corresponding circular paths are shown with dashed lines. The difference is greatest for Mercury and Mars. The most important effect is the displacement of the center of the path, not that the path is no longer round, because that would not have been visible here. The displacement of the center is also included in Ptolemy's model. | 78

Figure 23. Kepler found the relationship between orbital period and distance from the Sun for the planets. Earth appears here as any other planet, and that is a strong indication that Copernicus's Sun-centered universe is correct. | 81

Figure 24. *Left*, Copernicus's model with the Earth in summer position. The farthest star appears to be to the left of the nearest star when viewed from Earth. *Right*, in winter, the farthest star appears to be to the right of the nearest star when viewed from Earth. | 98

Figure 25. Caricature drawing of William Buckland in the hyena cave drawn by geologist, paleontologist, and priest William Conybeare in 1822. | 117

Figure 26. Nicolas Steno (1638–1686) or Niels Steensen, which was his Danish name. As an anatomist, he found the outlet duct of the parotid gland, which used to be called ductus stenonis. He also laid the foundations for geology. This also led him to study crystals, and he formulated Steno's law, which states that the angles are the same in all crystals from the same mineral. | 119

Figure 27. Mary Anning grew up in a Dissenter congregation. Even without an education, she became an outstanding fossil hunter and paleontologist, and she was known for her ability to assemble bone remains into complete skeletons. She handed them over to other researchers, such as Buckland, without initially getting much credit for it. In 2010, she was on the list of the ten most important female researchers in Great Britain. | 122

Figure 28. Georges Lemaître in priestly garb in the early 1930s. | 130

Figure 29. The Cathedral of Chartres; construction began in 1045 and was completed around 1220. Guillaume (William) de Conches (ca. 1085–1154) came from Conches in Normandy but worked at the cathedral school in Chartres and possibly also in Paris. He wrote about how Plato could be reconciled with the Bible. | 146

Figure 30. Charles Darwin (1809–1882), English naturalist who proposed the theory of evolution in the book *The Origin of Species* in 1859. *The Descent of Man*, published in 1871, also deals with human origins. | 166

Figure 31. Gregor Mendel (1822–1884), Augustinian monk who worked in the St. Thomas Monastery in Brno, which is today in the Czech Republic, at that time part of Austria. Between 1856 and 1868, he conducted hybridization experiments with pea plants, which he presented as "Versuche über Pflanzen-Hybriden" (Experiments on plant hybrids) in 1865. His work remained almost unknown until it was rediscovered in the early twentieth century. | 172

Figure 32. The major evolutionary transitions in biology depicted as a progression leading to humans. | 176

Figure 33. Extinct mammoth with tusks and hair, from cave painting in Font-de-Gaume in the South of France, dated to approximately 17,000 BC. | 198

Figure 34. Levels of biological classification. | 200

Figure 35. Functional MRI (magnetic resonance imaging) of the brain during testing of short-term memory. | 203

Figure 36. The silicon chip in a 6502 processor of size 3.9 x 4.3 mm. It contains about thirty-five hundred transistors, while modern processors have tens of billions of transistors. | 205

Figure 37. The symbol for the number pi. | 210

Figure 38. Dualism and three forms of monism. | 213

Figure 39. A bird swarm emerging from individual starlings as a response to a bird of prey in the upper right. | 216

Figure 40. William Blake's Newton (1795). | 224

Figure 41. Newton's notes on the Jewish temple based on the book of Ezekiel containing Hebrew writing. Date 1675–1685. | 226

Preface

WHEN ONE READS POPULAR science literature it is hard to avoid the impression that the conflict perspective is the dominant one. This perspective says that science since the seventeenth century developed in conflict with the Christian faith and is about to conquer it. The conflict perspective also implies there was a sharp break with the ideas of the Middle Ages and an introduction of a new way of thinking about how nature works where there is little or no place for God.

At the same time, many Christian scientists, this author included, do their science happily without experiencing any conflict in their daily scientific work. This paradox intrigued me, and this book is the result of the struggle to make sense of it. The book comes out of decades of trying to complement my training in engineering and physics with a study of the history of these subjects.

I discovered that among historians of science the simple, one-dimensional conflict perspective had been abandoned a long time ago. Instead, one can find statements to the effect that the Christian church and the Christian worldview helped scientific investigations. I also found that many of the most important scientists such as Kepler, Pascal, Newton, Ampère, Maxwell, Kelvin, and Lemaître combined their faith in God and science without experiencing much conflict.

This book presents the results of these studies. It is also based on experience from presenting science-God questions in many different settings over the years. The message is that the conflict story promoted by many of the celebrity scientists of our time is based on an imagined conflict.

The book has three unique perspectives. The first one is historical. Here I will clarify misunderstandings about the role of the Christian faith in the history of science. It turns out that the Middle Ages laid the foundation for today's science, before the Scientific Revolution, despite the many who believe that this period was "dark." History also shows how the concept of "natural law," which was so prominent in the seventeenth century, initially seemed unthinkable without a lawgiver. This connection is forgotten in our time. The idea of a beginning, the big bang, has also led to physics and cosmology being more open to a belief in a creator today than before.

The second perspective is scientific. An example is how the Galileo conflict is seen in a new light when the limitations of science at its time are understood. It is important to let the science of the past speak on its own terms and not interpret it based on today's theories, as many natural scientists may be tempted to do. Another example is how vague science is when faced with the question of human consciousness. Yet, many have strong opinions on how human beings originated. But how can we know that when we cannot even agree on what consciousness is?

The third perspective is philosophical. The relationship between the big bang and the need for a creator is partly a scientific question, but, even more, it raises the deeper question of why anything exists at all. Issues related to evolution are often reduced to scientific questions as well. Here, I argue that the philosophical approach is just as fruitful, as it helps to distinguish what science actually says from what some scientists may think it says when they are instead promoting philosophical worldviews influenced by positivism and scientism.

To make some of the topics simpler to grasp, the book uses illustrations throughout. Another unique feature that sets it apart from many other books is that it discusses all those aspects of science that have been viewed as controversial when it comes to the science-God question, from the big bang, life's long history on Earth, the Galileo affair, evolution and Darwinism, to the question of human consciousness. The ambition is to provide a broad and thorough justification for how classical Christian faith can coexist with science. Some may be skeptical that this is possible. Others may feel that it is unproblematic, but they cannot justify why. This may particularly apply to the topics of evolution and the origin of humanity. It should not be underestimated that there are some issues here that may be difficult to resolve. Therefore, the ambition is to discuss this in depth and propose solutions. In the process, I relate my own personal struggle with these questions. Later, in the introduction and in chapter 1, I also tell the story of how I came to embrace the Christian faith despite my background, where almost everything related to technology and science alone.

The book is also intended to encourage more young Christians to pursue a scientific career without fear of having to compromise their faith. A part of that is to highlight the limitations of natural science. Just as science cannot be used to "prove" Christian faith, neither can it be used to defend materialism and atheism. On the contrary, the book ends with some remarks on where the real conflict lies—namely, in the poor justification of science that a naturalistic view of nature and man can provide.

The English version has come about at the suggestion of John Lennox. He has read the entire manuscript, and I have very much appreciated discussions with him on aspects of some of the chapters. Special thanks also to David Cranston who has read through and commented on the English of every chapter. I am also grateful to the editorial team at Wipf and Stock for their pleasant cooperation during the publishing process.

In writing the original version of this book,[1] I have enjoyed many interesting discussions. Special thanks go to Bjørn Are Davidsen, Bjørn Hinderaker, and Thomas Holm, who have commented on most of the chapters. The following individuals have also reviewed one or more chapters and provided comments that have helped improve the book: Torleif Elgvin, Lise Holm, Daniel Joachim Kleiven, Arve Kråkenes, Ben David Normann, Frode Randgaard, and Arnt Inge Vistnes. Thanks to Knut Hegna at the University Library at the University of Oslo, who made me aware of all the historical books the university possesses. Thanks also to Katrine Masvie at Lunde/Veritas Publishing for valuable input and for improving many of my formulations.

I received support from the Norwegian Non-Fiction Literary Fund (NFFO) for writing the original version. Naturally, none of the individuals mentioned here are responsible for the content of any of the chapters.

---

1. Holm, *Den innbilte konflikten: Om naturvitenskap og Gud*.

Introduction

> The scientific revolution outshines everything since the rise of Christianity and reduces the Renaissance and Reformation to the rank of mere episodes, mere internal displacements, within the system of mediaeval Christendom.
>
> HERBERT BUTTERFIELD, *ORIGINS OF MODERN SCIENCE*

AS THE QUOTE SUGGESTS, two major upheavals have greatly influenced our culture, one attributed to Christianity and the other to science. Science emerged during what is known as the early modern period, approximately 1500–1789. The defining years of this period mark the end of the Middle Ages and the French Revolution respectively. Central to this is the publication of Isaac Newton's great scientific work, *Principia*,[1] from 1687. It is commonly believed that Newton's work ended a long process where nature went from being a place where humans could find God's intentions, to becoming a type of mechanism. Despite this, the early natural philosophers still held steadfastly to the idea that this mechanism was initiated and driven by God, and that there was a purpose behind nature. It was precisely this belief in God that inspired them to believe in the possibility and value of natural science.

Today, the picture seems to have completely changed. Rather than thinking that Christian faith can stimulate scientific work, belief is perceived as an obstacle and something that has hindered science over the

---

1. *Philosophiæ naturalis principia mathematica* or *The Mathematical Principles of Natural Philosophy*.

years. The success of science has led to its way of thinking influencing almost all areas, and, for many, natural science has become a "theory of everything" and a replacement for religious faith. In this book, I pose the question of how this came to be and whether this is actually an imaginary conflict.

GOD HAS ARRANGED ALL THINGS

The statement that "you have arranged all things by measure and number and weight" has long been a source of inspiration for me.[2] It was frequently quoted in the Middle Ages, and Professor Peter Waage (1833–1900) at the University of Oslo must have had it as his motto (figure 1). He is known for Guldberg and Waage's law of mass action in chemistry, dating from 1864. At its 150-year anniversary it was stated that "the law has had an impact on chemistry, biochemistry, biomathematics, and systems biology that is difficult to overestimate."[3]

Waage had the quote about measure, number, and weight painted on the ceiling of his office at the University of Oslo. His chemistry book from 1897 quotes it when he talks about how all chemical compounds have an unchanging, specified composition.[4] I have been surprised at how much more influenced the history of science is by ideas from the Bible than I originally thought, as Waage's example shows. My assertion is that the high standing of the Bible in European culture contributed to science advancing as far as it did precisely here, even if the Bible is not the sole cause.

Other factors may include favorable climate, well-developed agriculture that could sustain a large population, healthy competition between the many European states, and Latin as a common language. The latter is due to the church, which has influenced history both with bullies and saints.[5]

---

2. Wis 11:20 (NRSVUE). The Wisdom of Solomon is one of the deuterocanonical books, which are writings from the time between the Old and New Testaments. Some include them in the Bible, including the Catholic Church.

3. Voit et al., "150 Years," 1.

4. From Waage, introduction to *Det daglige livs kjemi* [Chemistry of daily life].

5. From the title of Dickson, *Bullies and Saints*.

Figure 1. Peter Waage (1833–1900) was a professor of chemistry at the University of Oslo. Early in his life, in an award-winning student essay from 1857, he quoted "God has arranged everything according to measure, number, and weight" in Greek. He also quoted it near the end of his life in a speech in Stockholm in 1898 at the memorial marking fifty years since the death of the chemist Berzelius. He was the first chairman of the Norwegian Christian Youth Federation (now YWCA-YMCA Norway), where he served from 1880 to 1900.[6]

Some of the most prominent natural philosophers and scientists have become almost like friends during the process leading up to this book, and I look forward to introducing them here. You will become acquainted with Galileo Galilei, Blaise Pascal, Isaac Newton, William Buckland, James Maxwell, Lord Kelvin, Pierre Duhem, and Albert Einstein, among others. Most of them are Europeans, but we will also briefly visit Indian Nilakantha Somayaji, Persian Ibn Sahl, and Chinese Zu Chongzhi. Some of the researchers also contributed to the philosophy

6. "Portrett av kjemikeren Peter Waage," by Ludvig Forbech, National Library of Norway, Wikimedia Commons.

of science, and here we find that both the experimental method and the idea of natural laws have theological justifications.

Many books have been written about the supposed conflict between Christian faith and science, and historians, theologians, and philosophers have all contributed. I write as an active researcher in physics and believe that this can provide a valuable and different perspective. This is important when it comes to understanding how new scientific knowledge is found, and how new, exciting, and fashionable scientific theories may not necessarily stand the test of time. However, with today's strong specialization in science, I am also aware of the limitations when I venture into areas that differ from my own. I am thinking particularly of biological evolution and theories of consciousness, which are now so central to the shaping of the relationship between God and natural science.

I have had to delve into fields such as history, philosophy, and theology. It is relevant to note how current historians criticize a specific type of historiography exemplified in how historians of the Enlightenment did not judge a historical phenomenon based on its own terms, but according to their own rationalist metrics. The treatment of the church in particular suffered from this perspective.[7] I therefore make an effort here to understand the past on its own terms. It is, of course, not entirely negative to use the present to understand the past, but I try to avoid it because this type of history often leads to a categorization into heroes depending on whether they stood on the "right side" or not. This interpretation of history in light of the present is referred to as presentism, and Butterfield was one of its earliest critics.[8]

Such a choice of perspective sometimes plays a decisive role, for example, in understanding Galileo. Because he turned out to be right in the end, it is easy to make him a greater hero than he actually was, as is frequently done. My ambition is to understand Galileo's science from the perspective of the time when he lived, as opposed to what we consider correct science in hindsight.

My selection from the history of science is, of course, not exhaustive. I deliberately chose the areas most associated with conflict, such as astronomy, cosmology, paleontology, and evolution. As a result, important areas such as medicine and chemistry are hardly mentioned. My starting point is that the alleged conflict between science and God has

---

7. Kjeldstadli, *Fortida er ikke hva den en gang var* [Past is not what it once was], 57.
8. Butterfield, *Whig Interpretation of History*.

been made more significant than it actually is. This is not really about apologetics, but about returning to the constructive interaction that, for the most part, has always existed.

There is a great need to point this out. For example, a recent Norwegian high school textbook claimed that Galileo pointed his telescope toward the skies and observed that Copernicus's theories were correct. In reality, both he and others knew that observing planets like he did was not sufficient to establish the theory; it was necessary to observe the motion of stars. Galileo is also described as someone who served as a role model as he was always willing to reformulate his hypotheses and assumptions if observations and experiments didn't support them. Perhaps the author was influenced by Einstein, who called Galileo "the father of modern science," when in this way he was creating "his own" Galileo.[9] The real Galileo, who avoided reporting observations of double stars that were unfavorable for his own hypothesis, does not support the image of him as a role model. Unfortunately, many textbooks contain idealizing examples that promote an imagined conflict perspective. Thus, in this book, I consciously avoid terms like *father of science* because they so easily lead to unrealistic hero narratives.

Another example comes from *The King's Mirror*, a philosophical and pedagogical text from the mid-thirteenth century. It was written by an unknown author in old Norse and is considered to be Norway's most important literary work from the Middle Ages. It is a dialogue where a king gives his son education in politics and morality. *The King's Mirror*, or *Speculum regale*, belongs to the European speculum genre that was popular between the twelfth and the sixteenth centuries with the ambition to be encyclopedic, but more often served as a set of instructional manuals.

The King's Mirror contains several examples of scientific ideas of its time, which I will give examples of in later chapters. It is a pity that in an introductory essay to the Norwegian edition published in 2000, an artificial conflict is presented regarding the ancient division of the spherical Earth into five belts or zones.[10] Since it was too cold in the far north and south and likely too hot around the equator, only the two temperate zones, one in the north and one in the south, were considered inhabitable. At the time, it was unknown to Europeans that humans inhabited the southern temperate zone, like in Australia and South America. It is

---

9. Einstein, *Ideas and Opinions*, 271.
10. Bagge, introduction to *Kongespeilet* [*King's Mirror*].

true that the church, according to the best science of the time, was skeptical to the claim that there could be a human population in the southern temperate belt, as it was thought impossible to cross the hot area around the equator.

The King's Mirror only comments that "if people live as near the cold belt on the southern side as the Greenlanders do on the northern, I firmly believe that the north wind blows as warm to them as the south wind to us."[11] In passing, it should be noted how obvious it is to the author that the Earth is not flat, despite the myth to the contrary. In the introductory essay, however, it is claimed that the author of *The King's Mirror* here is exploring dangerous ideas, and that in the early 1300s, Peter of Abano, a medical professor in Padova, and Cecco d'Ascoli, an astronomer in Bologna, were burned by the Inquisition for claiming that such a human population existed.

Respected historians of science, however, say that no scientists ever lost their lives because of their scientific views.[12] This needs clarification. It turns out that Peter (or Pietro) d'Abano, who was also an astrologer, was charged with fraud, heresy, and magical arts, but acquitted. He was, however, charged again and sentenced after his death. The astrologer, not astronomer, Cecco d'Ascoli was first warned after casting the horoscope of Jesus Christ and claiming that the fate of God's Son was determined by the stars and not by God.[13] When he would not let go of his claim, he was later convicted and burned for heresy. A closer look, therefore, shows that neither of the two cases had anything to do with science, and that the conflict is contrived. Today, of course, we find these sentences unheard of, but they may be more understandable if we compare the medieval view of theology with how we view the practice of medicine today. We are quick to crack down on quackery if anyone without a formal education claims to be a doctor.[14]

The emphasis on history and philosophy in addition to science means that there is a great degree of interdisciplinary work behind a book like this. Interdisciplinarity is something the Austrian physicist

11. Larson, *King's Mirror*, 16.

12. See the first page of the introduction in Lindberg and Numbers, *When Science and Christianity Meet*.

13. These accounts of conflict are presented in 1896 without reference to any source in White, *Warfare of Science with Theology*, and are mentioned in 1889 in Kretschmer, *Einleitung* [Introduction], 59, so they go far back in time.

14. Hannam, *Genesis of Science*, 119–23. Hannam has also written a thesis on this topic, "Church Discipline of Natural Philosophers."

Erwin Schrödinger encouraged. He received the Nobel Prize in 1933 for important work in quantum mechanics but had interests far beyond his own specialization. In the preface to a book that would turn out to inspire molecular biology, he comments on the expectation he met that he should not write about anything other than his own field of expertise. At the same time, he observes that everyone has a craving for unified and comprehensive knowledge. To avoid the fragmentation of knowledge, someone must be willing to bring together facts and theories from many areas. This is true even if we only have secondhand and incomplete knowledge and even if there is a risk of making fools of ourselves, says Schrödinger.[15] Similarly, that is the chance I take here.

My own journey began with a desire to understand how things are connected. It started with opening clocks, radios, and engines and trying to put them back together without too many leftover parts. I grew up in a residential area where all our neighbors worked in the research institutes that are located just north of Oslo. The neighborhood where I lived for my first eighteen years was called Research Garden,[16] and already in junior high school I was determined to study technology. This led me to what I have been working on almost my entire life—namely, making things work better, whether it was to create better images of the Earth from a satellite or to see the human body with medical ultrasound. At the same time, my curiosity has led me to pursue questions on both how and why things work. When ultrasound waves enter the body, interact with cells and tissue, are reflected, and can be used to create images that can provide medical diagnoses, what is the physics behind that?[17]

Little by little, I have been struck by a side of science that we do not talk about so much—namely, the creative, wondering, and almost mystical aspect. It is common to emphasize rational methods for testing ideas and hypotheses. This can make natural science seem dry, rule bound, and a bit boring. But natural science also requires creative imagination, built on a foundation of in-depth knowledge of the state of the art in the field. Einstein also mentions that there is no logical way to formulate natural laws, "only intuition."[18] When it comes to art and other "creative" professions, this goes without saying, but intuition is also a very important part of science.

15. Schrödinger, introduction to *What Is Life?*
16. The Norwegian address was Forskerhagen.
17. Eventually this became a book: Holm, *Waves with Power-Law Attenuation*.
18. Einstein, *Ideas and Opinions*, 226.

THE BIG QUESTIONS

One aspect of creativity is the ability to ask questions that can be so complicated that we cannot expect to find answers to them. The fact that we are even asking these questions shows something about our humanity and God-given curiosity. The physicist Stephen Hawking, for example, wondered what it is that "breathes fire into the equations and makes a universe for them to describe."[19] Fire is associated with the ancient four elements: water, earth, air, and fire. Fire can be dangerous, but it will also remove slag from iron, and it may be related to the life-giving Sun. Equations come to life, but how and why? Hawking and I are building on a whole series of natural scientists who have come before us. We are children standing on "the shoulders of giants." Newton is usually associated with this expression, but he borrowed it from Bernard de Chartres who, in the twelfth century, in this way showed his enthusiasm for the Greek giants of antiquity.

Figure 2. Stephen Hawking (1942–2018), English theoretical physicist, cosmologist, and author.[20]

Another of these giants was the Hungarian American Nobel laureate Eugene Wigner. In 1960, he wondered why the language of mathematics

19. Hawking, *Brief History of Time*, 174.
20. "Stephen Hawking," by NASA, Wikimedia Commons.

fits physical laws and said that this is a miracle and a wonderful gift, which we neither understand nor deserve.[21] Why are there natural laws? They cannot be scientifically justified but are something we assume or believe. Further, what is it that makes equations, which express abstract ideas in our minds, work so well to express how tangible nature works? Is it not strange that Wigner received a Nobel Prize for contributions to the theory of the atomic nucleus and the elementary particle that was based on a tool he did not understand, and which he regarded as a miracle?

Albert Einstein thought along similar lines when he said that "the eternal mystery of the world is its comprehensibility," and that "the fact that it is comprehensible is a miracle."[22] Einstein links the mystery to the properties of humans in saying that it is as if our intellect was made to understand the world. Like Wigner, one can say that Einstein expressed his theory of relativity with a tool shrouded in mystery.

Figure 3. Albert Einstein on a boat trip in the Oslo Fjord in 1920 with the geologists Heinrich Goldsmith (*left*) and Jakob Schetelig (*right*).[23]

21. Wigner, "Unreasonable Effectiveness of Mathematics," which even has its own Wikipedia page.

22. Einstein, *Ideas and Opinions*, 292–93. These quotes are often shortened to "The most incomprehensible thing about the world is that is comprehensible," which is one of Einstein's best known quotes.

23. Photo: Halvor Rosendahl/Museum of University History, University of Oslo.

Barrow and Tipler are also puzzled by the laws of nature, but just as much by the fundamental constants of nature that are involved in them. "As yet," they say, "we have no explanation for the precise numerical values taken by these unchanging dimensionless numbers."[24] An example is Newton's law of gravity, where the strength of gravity itself is such a constant of nature. If it had been much weaker, we would probably have achieved a new world record in high jumping, but the Sun would have had to be much larger to avoid collapsing. Such a Sun, however, would not have emitted life-giving light and heat, but rather radio waves that carry too little energy to sustain life.[25] On the other hand, if gravity were just a little stronger, matter could collapse in on itself. This would make stars, galaxies, and planets extremely small. Barrow and Tipler continue to say that "the fortuitous nature of many of their numerical values is a mystery that cries out for a solution."

Other puzzles which many believe have been more or less solved are pointed out in an introduction to evolution: "Two other major and largely unsolved problems in evolution, at the opposite extremes of the history of life, are the origin of the basic features of living cells and the origin of human consciousness."[26]

Adding the mystery of the origin of the universe to that, there are therefore at least three major unsolved, and perhaps even insoluble, scientific questions: how the world came into existence, how life began, and how our consciousness came to have the properties that it has. The latter is what enables us to ponder these questions at all.

The most fundamental question was probably posed by the German philosopher and mathematician Gottfried Leibniz in the early 1700s when he wondered why "there is something rather than nothing, as after all, nothing is simpler and easier than something." This question goes far beyond technology, physics, and biology to creation and God.[27]

This book begins in chapter 1 with the idea of God's two books, nature and the Bible. This is an idea with deep roots back in time. Chapter 2 discusses the creation and how good, beautiful, and surprising it is. Here I could choose many different topics, but I start with something that I have encountered in my own research—namely, the remarkable ability of

---

24. Barrow and Tipler, *Cosmological Anthropic Principle*, 31.
25. Lewis and Barnes, *Fortunate Universe*, 106.
26. Charlesworth and Charlesworth, *Evolution*, 125.
27. Leibniz's question—and answer—is in Leibniz, *Principles of Nature and Grace*, §7–8.

humans to communicate complex ideas. Chapter 3 is about the church's alleged opposition to the rise of science throughout history. This is about trying to understand the Middle Ages in its own light and not as a "dark" detour on the way to our own "enlightened" times. I also delve into the conflict surrounding Galileo Galilei of the seventeenth century and why Tycho Brahe's model of the solar system was considered the best for a long time. Chapter 4 is concerned with how both life and the universe had a beginning. A new understanding of fossils from the late eighteenth century led to a complete reassessment of the age of the Earth and life. Eventually, the idea emerged that life is neither eternal, as the Greeks believed, nor created in a few days. Instead, life has both a beginning and a long history, and different life forms are interconnected. Furthermore, the beginning of the universe with the big bang was established as sound science.

The second half of the book is about evolution and the uniqueness of humans, particularly when it comes to consciousness. Here, a foundation in the philosophy of science is important, and chapter 5 is dedicated to that, including thinking about what the limits of science can be. Chapter 6, on evolution, first discusses what is not part of the theory of evolution but what many people mistakenly think is, such as the origin of life. I mainly examine philosophical arguments to distinguish between evolution as a science and evolutionism as a worldview, but also present some scientific arguments. Chapter 7 is about what a human being is and how unique it is in nature. I was particularly surprised by how little science has to say when it comes to understanding what human consciousness actually is, as noted. I conclude in chapter 8 by discussing the origins of the conflict myth.

This book can be read in different ways. Chapters 3–8 largely build upon what I have written in chapter 2 about our place in the universe and cosmic evolution. There, I paint the big picture and show the wonder of how the big bang 14 billion years ago led to intelligent humans. Chapter 3 is about astronomy in Galileo's time and is the most demanding in terms of science. Although it is central, some parts can be skipped. The philosophy of science in chapter 5 is a necessary background to understand evolution in chapters 6 and 7, and these three chapters are best read together.

The appendix contains reflections from someone who is not a theologian on how the ideas presented—in particular in chapters 3, 4, 6, and 7—relate to the Bible in an attempt to understand how the Bible and natural science can be understood together.

1

God's Two Books

> We conclude that God is known first through Nature, and then again, more particularly, by doctrine, by Nature in His works, and by doctrine in His revealed word.
>
> GALILEO GALILEI, 1615, AFTER TERTULLIAN (160–220)

THE IDEA OF GOD'S two books has been with the Christian church from the very beginning as the quote indicates. The two books refer to God's world and God's word, and the first book, general revelation, is found in nature and creation. The second book, or special revelation, is often called grace. It is where God, through the Bible, shows us what we cannot discover in any other way—such as God's goodness, the triune image of God, God becoming human, Jesus's death to reconcile the world with God, and Jesus's resurrection.

The special revelation also influences our approach to nature. Among the important aspects for science is God's faithfulness, or immutability, which gives us the expectation that nature and the laws of nature are unchangeable.[1] A second aspect is God's omnipotence, which means that God was free to create the world as he wanted to. Therefore, we cannot simply

---

1. This was important for Albert Einstein, as will be seen later in this chapter.

use logic to deduce how the world behaves because we do not necessarily understand God. Experiments and observations are necessary.[2]

The relationship between general and special revelation is illustrated in figure 4. Above the horizontal line, we see how God is the originator of both books. This represents an objective truth, or "true truth," as theologian and philosopher Francis Schaeffer expressed it.[3] By that, he meant that this truth is not just something I subjectively believe to be true as postmodernism will have us believe, but it is something that is true independent of us. True truth represents how the world truly is. The figure also illustrates how all truth, no matter its source, is God's truth.[4] We, who are below the horizontal line, only have limited insight, shown here by dotted lines. In philosophical terms, what is above the line deals with ontology, and what is below deals with epistemology.[5]

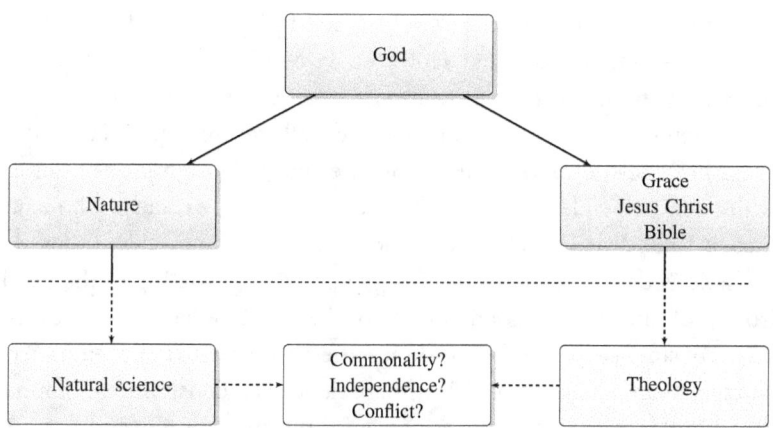

Figure 4. God, who is the source of all truth as shown in the two books of nature and grace, is above the horizontal line, while our incomplete understanding in science and theology is below the line.

2. Isaac Newton used this argument, as will be clearer in chapter 5.

3. The expression "true truth" is from ch. 2 in *Escape from Reason*, book 2 in Schaeffer, *Trilogy*, 218.

4. "All truth is God's truth" is a paraphrase of "let every good and true Christian understand that wherever truth may be found, it belongs to his Master" from Augustine, *On Christian Doctrine*, bk. 2, ch. 18.

5. Ontology is the study of what exists, from the Greek *ontos*, "being," and *logia*, "the doctrine of." Epistemology is the doctrine of knowledge, from the Greek *episteme*, "knowledge."

Regarding theology, we "know in part" (1 Cor 13:12). Yet, some claim that the Bible is so clear that there is no need for interpretation. Doesn't that demonstrate a shortsightedness on behalf of the speaker? It is as if I, coming from the capital where most people live, were to believe that I am the only one who speaks my native language "correctly" and that those from other areas of the country speak with an accent, when in reality we all have accents, whether it is common or not.

All natural scientists probably agree that nature tends to hide itself, as Heraclitus, the Greek philosopher who lived around 500 BC, may have been the first to state. A common view in natural science is what we call scientific realism. The starting point is that there is an objective world, which most scientists would agree to. Again, theology gives the surest way to justify its objectivity, with the idea that it is not us who have created the world, but God. Scientific realism means that we acknowledge that there are truths about nature that are independent of us, but our knowledge of them is limited. However, we believe that we can approach the truth with better theories and more knowledge.

Therefore, intellectual work and great efforts are required to understand both science and theology. But we can make significant progress with a few principles such as unity and coherence. For science, it means that independent branches of science must agree with each other. An example is dating of life from biology and zoology, dating of the Earth from radiometric dating, and dating of the universe based on measurements of star velocities. If, for instance, the universe was to be found to be younger than the Earth, it is clear that science is inconsistent and immature. Similarly, an important principle for interpretation of the sixty-six books of the Bible is that they speak with divine inspiration, truthfulness, and authority.[6] Thus, they speak with a single voice, since the Bible is a unity given to us by God. Another principle is a willingness to follow it, as expressed by Augustine: "Your best servant is the one who is less intent on hearing from you what accords with his own will, and more on embracing with his will what he has heard from you."[7]

Realistically, we must acknowledge that both theology and science can only have a limited perspective. Here, I emphasize the historical development of the relationship between the two and examine how this

---

6. As, for example, stated in the Lausanne Movement, "Lausanne Covenant."
7. Augustine, *Confessions*, bk. 10, ch. 26.

relationship has changed over time. There is no reason to believe that it will not change in the future as well.

As noted in the epigraph of this chapter, the early church fathers agreed that God reveals himself in nature.[8] They based this belief, for instance, on the creation story where God says, "Let there be lights in the vault of the sky to separate the day from the night, and let them serve as signs to mark sacred times, and days and years" (Gen 1:14). Also, note how one of the creation psalms uses active verbs to describe nature: "The heavens declare the glory of God; the skies proclaim the work of his hands. Day after day they pour forth speech" (Ps 19:1–2).

When Jesus was hailed on Palm Sunday, some wanted to silence his followers. But Jesus replied, "If they keep quiet, the stones will cry out" (Luke 19:40). When the testimony from Jesus's followers has been less clear, and our time may be such a time, only the testimony of creation remains. It is for a good reason that many find spirituality in nature. Furthermore, since Jesus was on his way to Jerusalem, he may have been thinking about more than just natural stones. Perhaps that is what we witnessed when the fire in Notre-Dame Cathedral in Paris in 2019 created grief far beyond the ranks of churchgoers?

One could be tempted to think that nature by itself is enough to form a complete picture of God. But special revelation states that more is needed, for "by faith we understand that the universe was formed at God's command, so that what is seen was not made out of what was visible" (Heb 11:3). Central to the Bible's testimony of the character of God is the person of Christ who said that "anyone who has seen me has seen the Father" (John 14:9). This makes Christian revelation different from the revelation in, for instance, Islam, where the book of the Quran is claimed to be the revelation. Therefore, it is so important to read the Quran in its original Arabic language. In contrast, in the Christian faith, revelation primarily refers to the person of Jesus Christ.

Natural science and theology can interact in several ways, as shown at the bottom of figure 4.[9] There can be commonality and harmony, or complete independence, or there can be conflict between them. Toward the end of this chapter, we will see that the relationship between them can be characterized in as many as seven different ways.

---

8. Harrison, *Territories of Science and Religion*, 57–63.

9. I deliberately say *natural sciences* and not *science* here, to make it clear that humanities and social sciences are not necessarily included.

There are often clashes when representatives from either field give in to the temptation to go beyond their own areas of expertise. Unfortunately, both natural scientists and theologians have done this throughout history, and, moreover, it has happened so frequently that many now see nothing but conflict. Nevertheless, it is more accurate to say that, throughout history, there have been all sorts of relationships, and today's historians of science will primarily say that the relationship between natural science and theology is marked by complexity.[10] But since general and special revelation come from the same God, we should strive to understand the deep connection between them. I consider this work to be in accordance with the message of the challenging statement from Jesus's Beatitudes that "blessed are the peacemakers, for they will be called children of God" (Matt 5:9).

Francis Bacon was one of the first to formulate the scientific method, despite not being a scientist himself. The two-book metaphor was clearly something he had in mind when he said, "Let no man upon a weak conceit of sobriety or an ill-applied moderation think or maintain that a man can search too far or be too well studied in the book of God's word, or the book of God's works, divinity or philosophy."[11] To the surprise of many, Charles Darwin endorsed this view and quoted Bacon in the epigraph of the *Origin of Species* in all editions from the first in 1859 until the final one in 1876. Bacon could have taken this idea from the medieval universities.

A good example is found in the seal of the oldest university in Scandinavia, Uppsala University in Sweden, as shown in figure 5, saying "Truth in grace and nature" (*Gratiae veritas naturae*). Like many of the medieval universities, Uppsala University was established in 1477 by a papal decree, issued by Pope Sixtus IV. In the university's seal, we see that nature from below and grace from above unite in truth.

---

10. Complexity as a characterization is from Brooke, *Science and Religion*, 5.
11. Bacon, *Advancement of Learning* 1.3.

Figure 5. Uppsala University's seal: Truth in grace and nature.[12]

Not only the Middle Ages were marked by special revelation. It characterizes our time to the highest degree as well. British historian Tom Holland recently admitted how wrong he had been about Christianity. Holland is known for his popular portrayal of Greek and Roman history, and now he has realized that his own values and morality are neither Greek nor Roman, but thoroughly Christian.[13] The idea that we are all equally valuable permeates Western culture. But this idea does not originate in science. Nor is it self-evident and obvious, even though many would like to believe so. The idea of equality is a consequence of the notion that we are created in God's image, and that Christ died for high and

---

12. "Uppsala Universitets Sigill," Wikimedia Commons.

13. Holland's book on the shaping of the Western mind is well worth reading: Holland, *Dominion*.

low, poor and rich. This affects all Western culture, whether we believe in God or not, says Holland, and these values are given to us from the Bible.

In this book, I build on the assumption that there exists an almighty and personal God independently of us. This is not one of the limited gods of the Greek or Norse pantheons. Neither is God like in pantheism, where there is no distinction between the world and the deity, nor is God an imagined deity that only exists in our minds. There are many good arguments for why an almighty and personal God exists, but this is not within the scope of this book to present. We can to some degree find out something about him by looking at ourselves or nature.

In addition, I assume that God has addressed us over a long time and through many different people. Their records have been preserved for posterity, and the collection of records is what we call the Bible. God has given us the Bible and preserved it through the ages because of his desire to communicate with us. There are many arguments for the reliability of the Bible, but they will not be presented here. I am going to quote from the Bible because of its unique perspective, but also because it has been extremely influential over time, and much more than we realize of our mindset has been shaped by it.

In sum, I assume that *He Is There and He Is Not Silent*, which is the title of Francis Schaeffer's book from 1972 that had a profound influence on me when it came out.[14]

DOES SCIENCE MAKE RELIGION UNNECESSARY?

Many of the scholars from earlier times would probably have found it difficult to understand the modern view that God's two books—nature and the Bible—can be perceived to conflict with each other. Nature has now assumed a superior role, and, for many, natural science has become the only thing that matters. This may be expressed as scientism, which is the view that science and the scientific method are the only valid ways to find truth.

Those who ask big questions and approach science and life with wonder may find it harder to accept the absolute sovereignty of science. Among practitioners of science, I think I also see a greater understanding of the limitations of science. A study from 2012, which included more than twenty-two thousand researchers from France, Hong Kong, India,

---

14. The third book in Schaeffer, *Trilogy*.

Italy, Taiwan, Turkey, the United Kingdom, and the USA, confirms this.[15] It shows that in all countries surveyed there was only a minority who believed there was a conflict between religion and science. The percentage varied from ten to thirty-five. Most scientists believed the two were independent of each other.

The conflict view that is conveyed by celebrity atheist scientists, such as Richard Dawkins, Laurence Krauss, and Neil deGrasse Tyson, as well as the deceased Steven Weinberg, Stephen Hawking, and Carl Sagan, is very different. They have influenced many people with a view that is not representative of what scientists in general think about these questions.

I think we can see this influence in a survey in Western Europe from 2017.[16] I will give the numbers for the UK with the more secular Norway in parenthesis: 31 (42) percent of all respondents answered that they completely or mostly agreed that science makes religion unnecessary in my life. Among active churchgoers, on the other hand, only 15 (5) percent agreed with this statement, and among nonpracticing Christians 21 (28) percent. On the other hand, as many as 67 (69) percent of those without religious affiliation completely or partly agreed. Compared with the rest of Western Europe, the UK is near the median but Norway is more polarized. A small proportion of Christians believe there is a conflict between faith and science while a much larger proportion of those without religious affiliation believe so. My view is that 31 (42) percent of the two countries' population is mistaken here, and I am supported by 85 (95) percent of the active Christians—and by the majority of those who are themselves engaged in research.

A FAITH TO BE PROUD OF

My personal history is that I have never found it problematic to combine belief in God with science, but I found it difficult to explain why. I suspect that many of the believers who see no conflict feel the same way. Where is the conflict felt most strongly? And why has it become so?

For me, these questions spurred a long study of the history and philosophy of science and how this is related to Christian faith. I was surprised to find that reality testified to the opposite of conflict. Just listen

---

15. Ecklund et al., "Religion Among Scientists."
16. Pew Research Center, *Being Christian in Western Europe*.

to what the renowned historian of science Helge Kragh, who won the Abraham Pais Prize from the American Physical Society in 2019, says:

> I was not brought up in a religious milieu but was (like most Danes) born into the Lutheran-Protestant church. Religion did not play much of a role and when I was in my early twenties I left the church. . . . My interest in religion is of relatively new date and mostly a result of my studies in history of science which showed how important Christian religion has been for the development of science.[17]

I discovered the same, and it became important for me to share what I found.

Our time sends strong signals that religion should be a private matter. It is therefore easy to divide life into separate compartments: work, family, faith, etc. My own story illustrates how these areas should rather form a unity. When I found my way to the Christian faith, I had taken some detours because faith did not have a large place in my childhood home. As a fourteen-year-old, I decided not to be confirmed. I thought there could perhaps be a God, but I could not bring myself to believe in the uniqueness of Jesus Christ and his resurrection. This was applauded by my father. The one who best put into words how I felt at the time was Jimi Hendrix and his fifteen-minute track "Voodoo Chile." Its mystical lyrics, suggesting a melancholic predestination, combined with Jimi Hendrix's expressive and emotional blues/rock guitar, really resonated with me.

Yet, I said yes when a good classmate, Hans Jørgen, invited me to meet a few times to read the Bible with him and his mentor, Bjørn. In hindsight, I have understood that at the time I also had the unconscious notion that something was fundamentally wrong with man. There were several reasons for this, not the least of which was mental illness in my near family. Gradually, I got the impression that the Bible concerned me and that the words we read were unlike the words of other books. It struck me that the Bible gave the most realistic description of humanity I had ever encountered. Humanity is both good and evil at the same time, and the dividing line runs right through all of us.[18]

Soon I also began to have some rare visits or visions. A person whom I perceived to be Christ would come to me almost as a living person, often

---

17. Rocha and Kragh, "Interview: Helge Kragh," 233.
18. Solzhenitsyn, *Gulag Archipelago*, pt. 4, ch. 1.

at night while I lay in bed. I cannot remember anything being said, just a strong presence and peace. I am not saying that this is the only way one can experience Christ, but it became my way. Moreover, Christ seems to be appearing to many Muslims in similar ways these days. Even though I have since spent much time on intellectual arguments for God, it is clear to me that such experiences are extremely convincing. They showed me that there exists an invisible world that influences us, and faced with this, science obviously has its limitations.

When at age sixteen I received a concrete challenge to pray a prayer that invited Jesus Christ to take a central place in my life, I was well-prepared and said yes. This was my teenage rebellion against what my parents and family stood for.

Before this, I had only read the Bible with others; now I read it on my own for the first time. That very evening the Bible became a new book for me. "Were not our hearts burning within us while he talked with us on the road and opened the Scriptures to us?" said Jesus's disciples as Jesus appeared to them after the resurrection on the road to Emmaus (Luke 24:32). Now the same thing happened to me, and I just had to read on. Today, this is still a daily habit.

I realized that Christian faith is not simply an intellectual decision in which I agree to theoretical doctrines. Faith is primarily trust and consists in a relationship with a risen Christ and with God. It may sound presumptuous that I, being just one of many creatures, can say that I know the Creator. Of course, we are not talking about exhaustive knowledge; it is just a small glimpse. This is how we know people around us too. My access to God is, as all witnesses in the New Testament testify to, summed up in the statement that "there is one God and one mediator between God and mankind, the man Christ Jesus" (1 Tim 2:5).

Becoming a Christian meant a whole new orientation in all areas of life. Specifically, it meant that in the following year, I signed up for confirmation together with my younger brother. As a student, it also became a challenge for me that everything, including intellect or mind, should be included in faith. After all, Jesus says that the greatest commandment is "Love the Lord your God with all your heart and with all your soul and with all your mind" (Matt 22:37). This meant a commitment to something bigger than myself and worthy of all my attention—namely, knowing Christ and making him known.[19] That is why it became so crucial for

---

19. Which is also the motto of the Navigators, an organization that was a great help to me in my first ten to fifteen years as a Christian. https://www.navigators.org/.

me to ensure all the pieces of the puzzle related to science and God also should fit together.

I had a longing to see a faith I could be proud of. I believe that Christians should be among the leading intellectuals of our time, as the church fathers were in the first centuries, and some of the scientists highlighted in this book were. They did not promote a faith that defers to others to be accepted, nor a faith that isolates itself, lives in a bubble, and has its own "science" in conflict with established science. I long for a faith that is engaged, visible, and stands for something that can appeal to everyone—from the little child to the most sophisticated intellectual.

TOO MUCH TO DOUBT AND TOO LITTLE TO BELIEVE

The challenge is to combine an intellectual, objective approach to faith and a more subjective one. The objective approach is supported by statements from the Bible, both about conscience and the ability to see God in creation. It is said that "the requirements of the law are written on their hearts, their consciences also bearing witness, and their thoughts sometimes accusing them and at other times even defending them" (Rom 2:15). Moreover, it is said that "what may be known about God is plain to them, because God has made it plain to them" (Rom 1:19). This latter verse is sometimes used to claim that the existence of God can be inferred from creation, and that faith can almost be based on reason alone. This may be going a bit far, but even atheists indirectly tell of the ability to see God in nature. Richard Dawkins writes,

> The complexity of living organisms is matched by the elegant efficiency of their apparent design. If anyone doesn't agree that this amount of complex design cries out for an explanation, I give up. . . .
>
> Our world is dominated by feats of engineering and works of art. We are entirely accustomed to the idea that complex elegance is an indicator of premeditated, grafted design. This is probably the most powerful reason for the belief, held by the vast majority of people that have ever lived, in some kind of supernatural deity.[20]

---

20. Dawkins, *Blind Watchmaker*, xiii, xvi, also quoted in Lamoureux, "Do the Heavens Declare," 26–27.

The rest of Dawkins's book is that there is no design in nature despite appearances, but it is striking that his first impression is precisely that the world is full of design and that this apparent design testifies to a designer.

Antony Flew was a philosopher with a long career as an atheist, but just before he died in 2010, he was struck by the incredible complexity of molecular biology and DNA. He thus changed his mind and became a deist—that is, someone who believes in a creator, but not in a personal God who cares about his creation. The theologian and biologist Denis Lamoureux draws the conclusion from Dawkins's and Flew's examples that we can indeed see an intelligent creator behind nature, but it is not the personal God of the Bible who emerges. It might as well be the god of deism, a god who does not care. In addition, we may choose to ignore what we observe and explain it away. God can thus be sensed objectively through nature, but nature can by no means prove his existence.

The opposite of the objective way is to disengage reason. Einstein believed that "a religious person is devout in the sense that he has no doubt of the significance and loftiness of those superpersonal objects and goals which neither require nor are capable of rational foundation."[21] The lack of rationality describes a "blind faith" or a "faith in faith." This I find difficult to defend. On the contrary, the apostle Paul is careful to record how well testified the resurrection of Jesus was. It was a real event that happened in a concrete location and at a defined moment in time. Paul said that Jesus Christ "was raised on the third day according to the Scriptures, and that he appeared to Cephas, and then to the Twelve. After that, he appeared to more than five hundred of the brothers and sisters at the same time, most of whom are still living, though some have fallen asleep. Then he appeared to James, then to all the apostles, and last of all he appeared to me also" (1 Cor 15:4–8).

Blaise Pascal (see figure 6) captured the middle ground between subjectivity and objectivity well. He said that in creation one sees too much to doubt but too little to believe. This summarizes the view that human nature makes us blind and thus limits how far natural theology can reach. However, natural theology is not useless. In Pascal's own words from around 1660, it goes like this: "All appearance indicates neither a total exclusion nor a manifest presence of divinity, but the presence of a God who hides Himself. Everything bears this character."[22]

---

21. Einstein, *Ideas and Opinions*, 45.
22. Pascal, *Pascal's Pensées*, no. 555.

Figure 6. Blaise Pascal (1623–1662), mathematician, physicist, philosopher, and author. Some only know Pascal as a natural philosopher and as the first to measure how air pressure changes with height above sea level. The unit for measuring pressure is therefore named after him. He also made important contributions to the calculus of probabilities and was one of the first to create a mechanical calculator. Others know Pascal only as an author. He is most famous for his book *Pensées*. It is a work on theology and philosophy and is considered one of the most elegantly expressed works in the French language. Pascal had several religious periods from 1646 on, but on November 23, 1654, he had a vision that was especially important to him. He sympathized with the Jansenists, a Catholic group that followed Augustine (354–430).[23]

Pascal always carried with him a note that read "God of Abraham, God of Isaac, God of Jacob, not of the philosophers and the scholars."[24] The note highlights the contrast between the vibrant faith of the living and the theoretical insight that scholars can draw from nature. The note was sewn into his jacket and found after his death. Pascal was inspired

23. "Blaise Pascal," image courtesy of the National Museum of the Palaces of Versailles and Trianon, CC BY 3.0, Wikimedia Commons.

24. Bishop, *Pascal*, 173.

by thoughts such as the biblical "no one knows the Father except the Son and those to whom the Son chooses to reveal him" (Matt 11:27) and thus was convinced that we are dependent on revelation to see God. His statement about the hidden God is from the Old Testament (Isa 45:15). Both Pascal himself and this verse have guided many researchers in the relationship between natural science and faith.

SEVEN DIFFERENT PERSPECTIVES

Earlier in this chapter, I mentioned the belief that many have that science conflicts with faith in God and has replaced it. At the same time, I have argued that there is coherence and harmony between them. These are two opposing perspectives, and it is possible to identify as many as seven different perspectives.[25] There are those who say that the world does not need a creator because the big bang and evolution are good enough explanations, and those who claim that the Earth is six thousand years old, and Noah's flood explains all the fossils. At first glance, these positions may seem to be opposites, but despite their differences, they share the assumption that Gen 1 must be read as a scientific textbook which conflicts with current science.

Some people set up science as the opposite of faith. They see science as something certain and tangible, and faith as something uncertain and abstract. The philosophically schooled Albert Einstein saw it differently, saying that "the belief in an external world independent of the perceiving subject is the basis of all natural science." Further he asserts that "it is a matter of faith that nature—as it is visible to our five senses—is such a well-formulated puzzle. The success of science certainly gives some encouragement to this belief."[26] Einstein sees faith in the lawfulness of nature as an assumption or prerequisite, and without such faith it is meaningless to engage in science. This is not so different from the theological assumption that God truly exists, which underlies all Christian thought. Since faith is a natural foundation both for science and theology, to avoid confusion going forward I will use the term *theology* to mean interpretation and understanding of the Bible—just as *science* is interpretation and understanding of nature. For the same reason, the word *faith* is not used in opposition to science in the subtitle of this book, but instead science vs. God.

---

25. I build in particular on Bube, *Putting It All Together*, with a slight modernization.
26. Einstein, *Ideas and Opinions*, 266, 94.

Conflict

There are two views that assume conflict and which lead to confrontation. The first is that *science is always right* and has removed the need for theology. Science is the only path to knowledge, and God can only be used as an explanation for things that are not yet understood. God fills the gap in our knowledge and is described as the God-of-the-gaps. Such a God will shrink more and more as time goes by, and most people conclude that they can do without God.

Paleontologist George Gaylord Simpson states in his book *The Meaning of Evolution* (1967) that "man is the product of a purposeless and natural process that did not have him in mind."[27] Here, he has made a scientific theory into a worldview, because science cannot answer the big questions of life, such as the question of meaning. In chapters 6 and 7, we will take a closer look at this again. The view that nature is all that exists is called naturalism. It entails a reduction of reality, so that man merely appears as a collection of atoms or as a complicated machine.

The other view of the relationship between theology and science can be seen as a reaction to the idea that science is always right. It claims on the contrary that it is *theology which is always right.* Theology here is a specific way of interpreting the Bible, where often statements about creation and nature are asserted to be "literal." The positive desire to take everything God says seriously underlies this view. But this does not consider the fact that the Bible is given to us in a cultural context and that it is written in many different genres. Being a textbook in natural science is probably not one of them. If one nevertheless chooses to read biblical texts as scientific descriptions, conflict quickly arises. One is then faced with the choice of either ignoring what established science says or creating one's own "science" tailored to one's theological views. Unfortunately, this perspective is often accompanied by a perception that established science is misguided and blind, almost a kind of conspiracy.[28]

Integration and Adaptation

There is also potential for conflict when theology and science must be adapted to each other—that is, theology is adapted to science or vice

---

27. Simpson, *Meaning of Evolution*, 344.
28. The best known book is Morris, *Scientific Creationism*.

versa. This can be done in several ways, and in the third view natural theology is pushed so far that *science is used as an argument for theology*. Such an argument can be seen as a reaction to naturalism and also to the irrationality and anti-intellectualism that arises when theology is always considered to be right. The argument can be that there is knowledge in the Bible that has been revealed thousands of years before science finally discovered it. It may concern coded messages about the future that only those who understand number and letter codes can grasp.[29] Similar thinking prevails among those who claim to find statements in the Bible both about the rotation of the Earth and the Sun's journey through the Milky Way.[30] Reality in this model is seen as a puzzle where science and theology each have their part of the pieces. The problem can be that when new science is discovered, the pieces of theology have to be reshuffled.

The image of the puzzle also fits when it is *science that redefines theology*, which is the fourth view. Many may feel the need to bring theology more in harmony with modern science and believe that two thousand years of development necessarily must influence theology. This clearly has some value. The Bible was shaped by the worldview of the people when it was written. For example, we no longer use an image of the Earth at the center of the universe to make theological points. It is far more problematic when science is used to assert that central stories in the Bible are myths. When the stories are redefined like this, the focus easily shifts from salvation theology to creation theology. Thus, God's first book, the theology of nature, dominates over the second book, the revelation in the Bible.

A fifth view tries to avoid conflict. The starting point is that science and theology should be in harmony, but because they are not, there is a need for a *new synthesis of science and theology* where both must change. The pieces of both science and theology must be rebuilt for the puzzle to fit together. This is a reaction to scientific rationalism and naturalism. Its adherents often seem visionary and use words from relativity theory and quantum physics to describe their ideas, but usually in such a way that it is incomprehensible to physicists. An example is the attempt to unite New Age pantheism with quantum physics.[31] Behind such attempts there is often a hope that theology and science will develop into a holistic discipline. Usually both must change so much that the result becomes both quasi-theology and quasi-science in conflict with real theology and real science.

29. An example is Drosnin, *Bible Code*.
30. These examples are from Comfort, *Scientific Facts in the Bible*.
31. Capra, *Tao of Physics*.

Independence

To avoid conflict, a sixth view can be asserted, where the starting point is that *science and theology are unrelated* and exist in different compartments. Paleontologist and evolutionary biologist Stephen Gould launched such a view in 1997 and called it nonoverlapping magisteria (NOMA). He believed that the two deal with separate areas of life that do not overlap each other. The consequence can be that humans have to live life in two different worlds, a secular and scientific one dealing with observable facts, and a religious one that deals with faith and values that are brought out on certain occasions. Francis Collins, who led the Human Genome Project and directed the National Institutes of Health in the USA, goes against such a view saying, "I'm a serious Christian. I take my faith seriously. I try to practice it every day of the week, not just on Sunday."[32] In the independence view, faith can easily be perceived as irrelevant because it does not deal with the real world, and either science or theology may take over and the other will suffer.

Coherence and Dialogue

The seventh and final view is based on the idea of God's two books. Here, *science and theology are descriptions that are coherent and in dialogue with each other*, they are neither in conflict nor independent.[33] This is about bringing the relationships under the line in figure 4 into harmony with what is above the line. This view is central to this book, and the existence of the six previous views shows that this is not an obvious perspective. Professor John Houghton (1931–2020), who was central in the UN's climate panel from 1988 to 2002, said this about integrating the two: "Think for a moment about the appreciation of depth which is contained in a scene viewed with both eyes rather than with one eye. . . . Putting the two revelations of God together is like having binocular vision. A new depth

---

32. Abernethy, "Dr. Francis S. Collins Interview," Q&A 1.

33. The word *complementarity* is sometimes used for this view as in Bube, *Putting It All Together*. This agrees with common use in science. If the academic background leans more toward theology, it seems that complementarity means that the two fields exist in different compartments, are independent, and do not interact as in Moreland, "Philosophical Apologetics," and Brooke, *Science and Religion*. Therefore, I have chosen instead to use the words *coherence* and *dialogue*, the latter taken from Barbour, *Religion and Science*, 90–97.

and reality are created in our appreciation of the world around us and of God himself."[34]

Two perspectives that are coherent are different from a synthesis, as the uniqueness of both perspectives are respected. It is also different from the view that science and theology have nothing to do with each other, as a continuous dialogue between them must take place. Science influences the understanding of the Bible, for example, in terms of the Earth's place in the universe, its age, and the age of man. Indirectly, science also tells us that God works in all natural phenomena, not just the special supernatural ones. At the same time, biblical revelation influences science. It provides the insight that man is widely controlled by egoism, and this makes the Bible's talk of sin and the need for rebirth credible. The Bible provides insight into human nature and thus a corrective to science's so-called objectivity; it also provides the basis for human dignity, priorities, and the handling of ethical problems.

The idea that science and theology are coherent with each other is not an acceptance of contradictions. Both in science and in theology, models that build on duality are common. In physics, both a particle model and a wave model are used to describe the electron, as each model on its own cannot describe all properties satisfactorily. The same is seen in theology—for example, in the idea that God is omnipotent while at the same time man is responsible for his life. Something similar comes to light in that Jesus Christ was both God and man simultaneously. The two descriptions each give a partial picture, and combined they say more than the sum.

Imagine Albert Einstein, Edvard Grieg, Vincent van Gogh, and King David standing on a hill, looking at a beautiful landscape soaked in the morning Sun. They agree to meet again with a description of what they have seen, each in the medium they master best. Einstein comes with pages full of formulas that describe the movement of the Sun and the Earth, the colors of light, and its refraction in the atmosphere. Grieg distributes the notes to his composition *Morning Mood* and asks us to listen to the orchestra playing. The artist Van Gogh shows his painting *Enclosed Field with Sunrise* with its strong colors. Finally, the psalmist David sings, "The heavens declare the glory of God, the skies proclaim the work of his hands" (Ps 19:1).[35] Can one say that only one of them has

---

34. Quote in Berry, *Real Science, Real Faith*, 53.
35. This story has been inspired by Hummel, *Galileo Connection*, 262.

the correct description? No, these descriptions do not contradict each other, and there is no conflict between them. Nor is it the case that only one of them describes the sunrise, while the others are irrelevant. Even though only one of the descriptions is scientific, they are coherent with each other.

The seven perspectives on the coordination of science and theology are summarized in the table. The second column is simplified to only four perspectives based on the four headings used in this section. It is also possible to reduce to only three different perspectives: in perspectives 3–5, where either theology or science—or both—must change, it also means there is a conflict—although at first glance it is not as prominent as in perspectives 1 and 2.

Seven perspectives	*Four perspectives*	*Three perspectives*
1. Science is always right	Conflict	Clash
2. Theology is always right		
3. Theology is proven by science	Integration and adaptation	
4. Science redefines theology		
5. A new synthesis of science and theology		
6. Science and theology are unrelated	Independence	Autonomy
7. Science and theology are in dialogue	Coherence	Dialogue

2

The Amazing Creation

> That the consideration of the vastness, beauty, and regular motions, of the heavenly bodies; the excellent structure of animals and plants; besides a multitude of other phenomena of nature, and the subservience of most of these to man; may justly induce him, as a rational creature, to conclude, that this vast, beautiful, orderly, and in many ways admirable system of things, that we call the world, was framed by an author supremely powerful, wise, and good, can scarce be denied by an intelligent and unprejudiced considerer.
>
> ROBERT BOYLE, *THE CHRISTIAN VIRTUOSO*

ALONG WITH ROBERT BOYLE, many feel awe and wonder when encountering creation. Even God, when looking at everything he had made, exclaimed that "it was very good!" (Gen 1:31). In fact, the word *good* is used seven times just in this chapter of the creation story. We tend to associate wonder with children, and as someone who has grandchildren of preschool age, I see how curious they are, especially if I tell them that there is a hidden world beside the visible one. Perhaps that is why Jesus encourages us to become like children to enter the kingdom of heaven? For children, nature and the unseen are not as separate as we adults often portray them. In this chapter, we will look at some aspects of creation that show how amazing it is. We will also use the model of the two books of the previous chapter and explore how God's revelation in the Scriptures can complement what we see in nature.

CONSCIOUSNESS AND LANGUAGE

The fact that we can exchange thoughts through speaking and listening is something that truly sets humans apart from other creatures. For this, we need muscles to control the speech organs, especially the vocal cords, tongue, and lips. We also need hearing and, most importantly, a brain and consciousness that can think the thoughts and control the muscles to express them, as well as create meaning from the sounds we hear.

I obtained my doctorate by analyzing sound. This is important in mobile phones, as sound needs to be encoded so that the complex sound signal can be sent over the limited radio link that constitutes the backbone of the mobile system. All languages have a certain number of meaningful sound units, *phonemes*, which are the smallest units needed to distinguish two words from each other. An example is *nice* and *rice*, which only differ in the first phoneme (*n* and *r*). The mouth position is different for each of these (see figure 7). A part of my project was to examine how much more difficult it became to distinguish such nearly identical words after coding.

English has about forty-four phonemes, while Norwegian with its many dialects has between twenty-six and thirty-nine phonemes. The language of Hawaii has only thirteen phonemes, while some languages in Africa have over a hundred. When considering all languages collectively, it is evident that humans are equipped to form and distinguish between hundreds of different phonemes. When we speak, the sound changes twenty to thirty times per second. It seems that this is some kind of measure of how quickly the combined system of the brain, speech organs, and hearing operates. But where does this unique language ability come from?

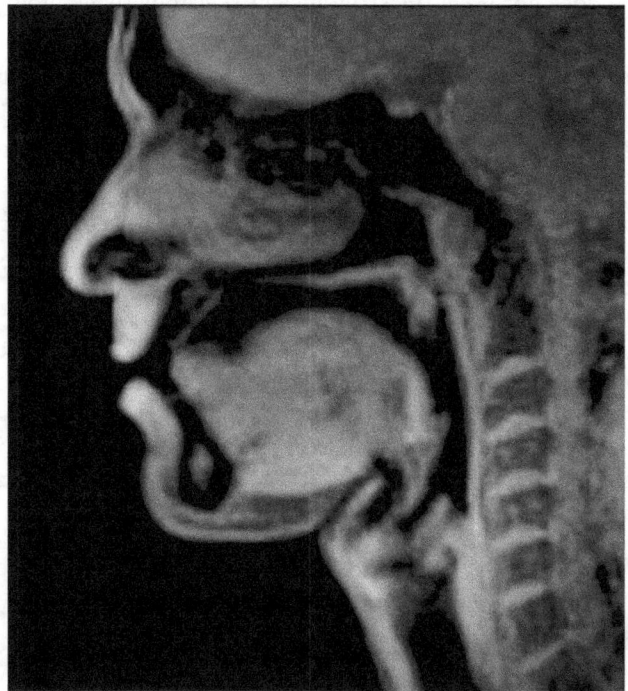

Figure 7. Magnetic resonance image (MRI) of the head and speech organ during the pronunciation of *s*.[1]

Modern humans are believed to have migrated out of Africa around sixty to seventy thousand years ago.[2] Today, all humans are considered to have a common origin, as also stated in the Bible,[3] and therefore we assume that language was already present at that time. A piece of evidence that seems to support this is the complexity of a language, measured in terms of the number of phonemes, decreases the farther geographically it is from Africa. The Pacific and South America, being the farthest away, is where the original languages have the fewest phonemes.[4] However, since

---

1. "Real-time MRI—Speaking (English)," image courtesy of Biomedizinische NMR Forschungs GmbH, CC BY-SA 3.0, Wikimedia Commons.

2. My source for the history of humanity is Tattersall, *Masters of the Planet*.

3. The alternative to common origin, or monogenesis, is polygenesis. It has been used as a justification for racism.

4. See Atkinson, "Phonemic Diversity."

language does not leave traces in ancient skeletons (paleontology), the estimates of the timeline are necessarily uncertain.[5]

An indirect sign of language is archaeological findings of art, with the oldest discoveries being around forty thousand years old. Inscriptions can also be an indication of language, and there are findings that date back approximately seventy-five thousand years. Nevertheless, it is remarkable that it seems not to be possible to accurately date and understand the origin of such a unique and special ability like language.

This is how a linguist expresses wonder:

> A hallmark of humans is that everyone learns a language while they are still children. . . . Considering how complex this system is, it's remarkable that it's possible to acquire it at such a young age. A five-year-old may not necessarily be able to tie their own shoes, but learning a complex set of grammatical structures is evidently without issue.[6]

We know a lot about how language works, and how different languages relate to each other. We also know much about which parts of the brain are active during speaking and listening, and how language has evolved since it became written six to eight thousand years ago. What we know little about is how we acquired this amazing language ability, the very outward sign of our special consciousness.

A Gene for Language?

The genome may also shed light on language. Since the completion of the mapping of the human genome in 2003, there have been high hopes of finding specific genes for all kinds of conditions. However, these hopes have only been partially fulfilled. In a highly cited article from 2009, with contributions from over twenty authors, a person's height is used as an example. There are at least forty locations in the genome that influence height. Yet, it is far more reliable to use the height of parents or a twin as a basis for estimating a person's height than to rely on genetic analysis. This is just one example of what some have dubbed the "dark matter" of the genome. Just as we assume there must be unknown matter in galaxies, there must be "something" in genes that we have yet to discover.[7]

---

5. See Fitch, "Empirical Approaches."
6. Busterud, "Natural Born Speaker," 62.
7. See Manolio et al., "Finding the Missing Heritability."

The same is true for a gene for language. One candidate has been the FOXP2 gene, shown in figure 8. A mutation in this gene is found in a family in London. Around half of the family members pronounce *spoon* as "boon," *table* as "able," and *blue* as "boo." This trait has persisted across three generations. They struggle with the rapid mouth movements required to pronounce complicated words. This speech defect and the FOXP2 gene mutation were discovered in the 1990s and the gene FOXP2 now even has its own Wikipedia page.

Figure 8. The FOXP2 gene is located on the long arm of chromosome 7 at position 31.[8]

It has also been discovered that if the same FOXP2 gene is "knocked out" in zebra finches, which live in Central Australia and Indonesia, their songs also become simplified. Such songbirds, like humans, must learn to sing from their parents. When the same gene is knocked out in mice, their "songs" also become simplified. These are ultrasonic sounds, meaning they are at higher frequencies than what humans can hear. We do not believe that mice learn to sing through imitation, so they differ from humans and songbirds in this regard. However, it is remarkable that the ability for rapid muscle control of the sound-producing organ is related to the FOXP2 gene in humans, birds, and mice.[9]

Even though FOXP2 was once considered a prime candidate for the "language gene," we now realize that many other factors are involved as well. However, FOXP2 still demonstrates the kinship humans share with both songbirds and mice when it comes to control and muscle coordination for producing complex sounds.

---

8. "FOXP2 Location," US National Library of Medicine, Wikimedia Commons.

9. FOXP2 in humans, songbirds, and mice is also discussed in Hauser et al., "Mystery of Language Evolution."

We Hear Better Than Most Animals

We are used to being told that animals have better senses than humans. Dogs can smell much better than us, bats can hear ultrasonic sounds, elephants are better at detecting infrasonic or low-frequency sounds, and lions can hunt at night because of their excellent night vision. In many areas, animals outperform humans. But there is one area where we excel, and that is in our ability to locate the exact direction of a sound source.

When the sound source is directly in front of us, we can pinpoint its location with an accuracy of 1–2 degrees, a skill that only owls, dolphins, and elephants share with us. It may not be so surprising that elephants have this ability, considering their large heads. One way we determine direction is by detecting the time difference between the sounds reaching each ear. Fortunately, our amazing brains automatically perform this analysis for us. With a larger head, the distance between the ears is greater, resulting in a larger time difference. However, there must be other factors at play, as cows and horses have larger heads than us but can only determine direction with an accuracy of 25–30 degrees. Even when the sound comes from directly behind us, humans perform better than that (around 20 degrees).

I have worked for many years in medical ultrasound imaging, where an accuracy of 1–2 degrees is also common. However, this requires activating nearly one hundred "ears" or sensors, whereas humans accomplish the same task with just two ears. Ultrasonic systems can only measure time differences between sensors, as previously described. Humans, on the other hand, can also utilize the shadow effect from the head. When someone speaks to us from the side, the sound is slightly weaker in the ear farthest away, and our brain interprets this as well. This was first understood by Rayleigh in 1907, and the combination of time difference and shadowing is known as the duplex theory of hearing.

However, the duplex theory fails to explain how humans can determine if a sound is coming from the front or back, and above or below. We are so adept at sound localization that we can differentiate with an accuracy of about 3.5 degrees vertically as well.[10] In addition to time and level differences, we have also learned that the shape of the outer ear, and in particular the tragus, the small, pointed part in front of the ear canal "color" the sound. For example, treble sounds become stronger when coming from above the head, while sounds from behind the head have

---

10. Data from Heffner and Heffner, "Evolution of Mammalian Sound Localization."

stronger mid-range tones.[11] This coloring of the sound can be used in video games to trick you into hearing things behind or above you when you are wearing headphones.

In summary, there are three factors that contribute to our remarkable ability to determine sound direction: (1) our ears analyze time differences, (2) they perceive level differences, and (3) they interpret sound coloring from the outer ear. This is known as the triplex theory of hearing. The combination of our two ears and the brain's processing of their signals allows us to outperform nearly all animals in sound localization.

By studying nature, one of God's two books, we can learn things like this about language and hearing. The other book, the Bible, complements and enhances our understanding. Here God poses the rhetorical question, "Who gave human beings their mouths? . . . Is it not I, the Lord?" (Exod 4:11). From this, we see that our ability to speak and hear seems to be connected to being created in God's image.

THE FINELY TUNED WATER MOLECULE

On Earth, water is essential for life. That is why water is one of the first substances we look for when searching for life on other planets. It is the connection between the two hydrogen atoms and the oxygen atom in the water molecule that makes water so special. A special bond called a hydrogen bond is formed between the water molecules (see figure 9). A characteristic of liquid water is that the molecules are constantly binding together and breaking apart. This creates a delicate balance between order and chaos, giving water a structure that is not as random as other liquids.

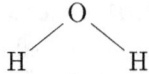

Figure 9. A water molecule consists of two hydrogen atoms (H) and one oxygen atom (O). In other similar molecules, the atoms are typically arranged at right angles to each other. The unique angle in water of 105 degrees allows the molecules to easily assemble into crystals (regular tetrahedrons), such as in ice.

The hydrogen bond seems to be finely tuned for life, as it is responsible for many important properties of water:

11. Hartmann, "How We Localize Sound."

- Water exists in all three phases—ice, liquid, and vapor—under near normal conditions on Earth. This is unusual, as neither hydrogen nor oxygen alone can do this, nor can other similar substances of the periodic table. These substances all have a boiling point below zero degrees Celsius and mainly exist as gases in their natural state. This is the basis for the life-giving water cycle, where water evaporates from the ocean, forms clouds, then falls as rain, and eventually returns to the ocean. All of this happens at temperatures that are compatible with life.

- Unlike almost all other substances, frozen water, or ice, floats. This is because frozen water forms hexagonal structures that take up more space than the more chaotic liquid water. Imagine how impossible it would be for life in lakes if the water froze from the bottom up, instead of from the surface down.

- The hydrogen bond creates the high surface tension of water. This is what allows insects to walk on water without sinking and prevents water from evaporating easily. The hydrogen bond also manifests in the capillary effect, where water can overcome gravity and be sucked up, carrying nutrients to everything from the smallest plants and to the tallest trees.

- The hydrogen bond also gives water one of the highest heat capacities of all liquids. This helps to stabilize the temperature in the human body, which is made up of 50–70 percent water. At the same time, it helps to stabilize the Earth's climate, since 71 percent of the Earth's surface is covered by water.

Here, too, the Bible complements the picture that nature gives us. The water cycle has been understood for a long time, and in the book of Job, one of the oldest writings in the Old Testament, it is said that God "draws up the drops of water, which distill as rain to the streams, the clouds pour down their moisture and abundant showers fall on mankind" (Job 36:27–28). This demonstrates that God is not only found in the extraordinary and miraculous but is behind everything. There is no contradiction between what can be described by natural laws and God, the lawgiver.

The Scottish physicist James Clerk Maxwell may have been thinking of this when he had a verse from one of the Psalms of the Bible inscribed at the University of Cambridge in England. The verse reads, "Magna opera

Domini exquisite: in omnes voluntates ejus," which is Latin for "Great are the works of the Lord; they are pondered by all who delight in them" (Ps 111:2). The inscription is found on a woodcut above the entrance to the old Cavendish Laboratory and is somewhat difficult to notice, but even after 140 years, it was still visible when I was there a few years ago and took the photo shown in figure 10. Maxwell viewed exploring nature and describing it with equations as to ponder the Lord's works.

Figure 10. James Clerk Maxwell (1831–1879), Scottish physicist best known for Maxwell's equations from 1865. Maxwell is a physicist not many have heard of, but he is considered the greatest physicist between Newton and Einstein. He laid the groundwork for the wireless revolution of cell phones, wireless networks, GPS, and broadcasting. Maxwell was the first director of the Cavendish Laboratory at the University of Cambridge. This laboratory has produced twenty-nine Nobel Prizes. The inscription in the picture can be found at the entrance to the old Cavendish Laboratory and is the first part of Ps 111:2 in Latin.

CREATED FROM STARDUST

I am not the only one fascinated by space. I remember very well the first time I saw the moons of Jupiter and the rings of Saturn in my own telescope. In my lifetime, we have also seen images of our own planet from the outside. In *Earthrise*, the famous picture taken from Apollo 8 as it orbited the Moon, the Earth is a globe with continents and oceans, with a clear distinction between night and day (figure 11). It probably surprised many when the three astronauts participating in the Moon mission read the Genesis creation story on Christmas Eve 1968 to a whole world watching them. In doing so, they demonstrated that a technological triumph, as represented by this journey, was not in opposition to the belief that God had created everything.

Figure 11. *Earthrise,* photo taken from Apollo 8 on December 24, 1968.[12]

I had the pleasure of participating in a preparatory study for the European Space Agency for the Cassini-Huygens voyage to Saturn. Our work was completed in 1989 and concerned the communication between the mother ship Cassini and the probe Huygens. Eight years later, they were launched from Cape Canaveral in Florida. In a beautiful picture taken from Cassini in 2013, the Earth and the Moon can barely be seen beneath Saturn's ring (figure 12). The distance to Earth is thousands of times greater than when Apollo 8 took its picture from the Moon. Such images give us a different perspective on ourselves.

12. *Earthrise,* by Bill Anders, NASA, Wikimedia Commons.

Figure 12. Image of Earth alongside Saturn's rings, taken July 19, 2013, by the Cassini spacecraft.[13]

Many people believe that it is only in our time that we have reason to feel small compared to the vastness of space. We are merely "stardust," as it is so poetically stated. Undoubtedly, humans are made up of oxygen, carbon, hydrogen, nitrogen, and calcium, each of them elements of which there are more than one kilogram each in an adult human. These are also elements that are abundant in space. But does the recognition that we are stardust naturally lead us to conclude that we are small and insignificant? Many modern scientists think so, but I find it strange that the elements should define who we are.

Blaise Pascal must also have thought about humanity's smallness in relation to the universe, but he still sees a difference, for he says that

> Man is but a reed, the most feeble thing in nature; but he is a thinking reed. The entire universe need not arm itself to crush him. A vapor, a drop of water suffices to kill him. But, if the universe were to crush him, man would still be more noble than that which killed him, because he knows that he dies and the advantage which the universe has over him; the universe knows nothing of this.[14]

---

13. *The Day the Earth Smiled*, by NASA/JPL/SSI/CICLOPS, Wikimedia Commons.
14. Pascal, *Pascal's Pensées*, no. 347.

The universe, in all its grandeur, lacks the consciousness that humans have, and this gives us a very special position. Although we will eventually return to dust, we also have a spirit and a connection to God as Eccl 12:7 says: "The dust returns to the ground it came from, and the spirit returns to God who gave it."

Another poet also understood that God knows our origins: "He knows how we are formed, he remembers that we are dust" (Ps 103:14). The image is complemented by the statement that "when I consider your heavens, the work of your fingers, the moon and the stars, which you have set in place, what is mankind that you are mindful of them, human beings that you care for them?" (Ps 8:3–4). Nature tells us only that we are dust. The picture is not complete until we also listen to God's other book, for it tells us about God's thoughts, which nature cannot say anything about. These verses provide a reason for awe of the Creator and gratitude that he cares even about a small human being.

Similarly, in late antiquity the philosopher Anicius Boethius (480–525) wrote a book which was widely read for the next millennium. He said,

> As you have learnt from astronomers' shewing, the whole circumference of the Earth is but as a point compared with the size of the heavens. That is, if you compare the Earth with the circle of the universe, it must be reckoned as of no size at all.[15]

He said this to emphasize how unimportant it really is to seek fame in such a small place as the Earth. Boethius had probably gained such a perspective on life on Earth because he was in prison awaiting execution. Nevertheless, here he expresses the prevailing view of the Middle Ages, namely that the Earth is just like a point, a dot, in the vast universe. This is not just a modern view, as Boethius also says that even the Earth itself is so large that the place that matters to a human being is also just like a small point on the Earth.

This view prevailed into the early modern period. In the preface to Copernicus's work *De revolutionibus* (*On the Revolution*), Nicholas Schönberg, the Catholic cardinal who had encouraged Copernicus to publish the book, described how the theory turned concepts upside down so that "the Sun occupies the lowest, and thus the central, place in the universe."[16] Galileo states it even more strongly when he writes about the new place we humans have been given, for the Earth is movable and "it is not the sump

---

15. Boethius, *Consolation of Philosophy*, bk. 2, sec. 7.
16. Danielson, "Great Copernican Cliché," 1032.

where the universe's filth and ephemera collect."[17] Copernicus and Galileo both say that Earth's former place at the center represented the lowest place at the bottom, and that the new heliocentric worldview elevated Earth.

It is not uncommon to hear the exact opposite—namely, the idea that Copernicus, contrary to what he himself said, displaced us from our exalted place at the center of the universe when he put the Sun at the center.[18] This great Copernican cliché appears to have started with the French playwright Cyrano de Bergerac as a protest against "the insufferable pride of humans."[19] This sentiment is even more strongly expressed by Bernard Le Bouyer de Fontenelle, who, in a dramatic piece from 1686, has a character who says that she is so happy that Copernicus had "humbled the vanity of mankind, who had usurped the first and best situation in the universe."[20]

Thus, we deceive ourselves into believing that the new science altered how we perceive our own position. The Copernican cliché can be compared with the equally illogical conclusion that many draw from Einstein's theory of relativity, that "everything is relative," whether it pertains to morals, psychology, or whatever it may be. But both Copernicus's and Einstein's theories are primarily descriptions of nature, and we must be careful not to extend them beyond this.

COSMIC EVOLUTION AND INTELLIGENT LIFE

Science has achieved impressive success and can provide explanations for many phenomena that were mysterious to the generations before us. When we take one step back to see the bigger picture, we observe the perspective known as cosmic evolution, which is illustrated in figure 13.[21] It encompasses the entire history of the universe, and these stages become apparent:

---

17. Danielson, "Great Copernican Cliché," 1032.
18. This paragraph builds on Danielson, "Great Copernican Cliché," and Singham, "Copernican Myths."
19. Danielson, "Great Copernican Cliché," 1033.
20. Danielson, "Great Copernican Cliché," 1033.
21. This perspective on history comes from physicist Eric Chaisson, who for several decades has upheld a cosmic evolution perspective; see, for example, Chaisson, "Synthesis of Matter and Life," and Chaisson, "More Than Big History." It has much in common with Big History, which is a project promoted by historian David Christian; see Christian, "Case for 'Big History,'" and Christian, *Maps of Time*. Both have a rather one-sided materialistic perspective, and, for example, Chaisson is content with a belief that, given enough time, life will arise on its own.

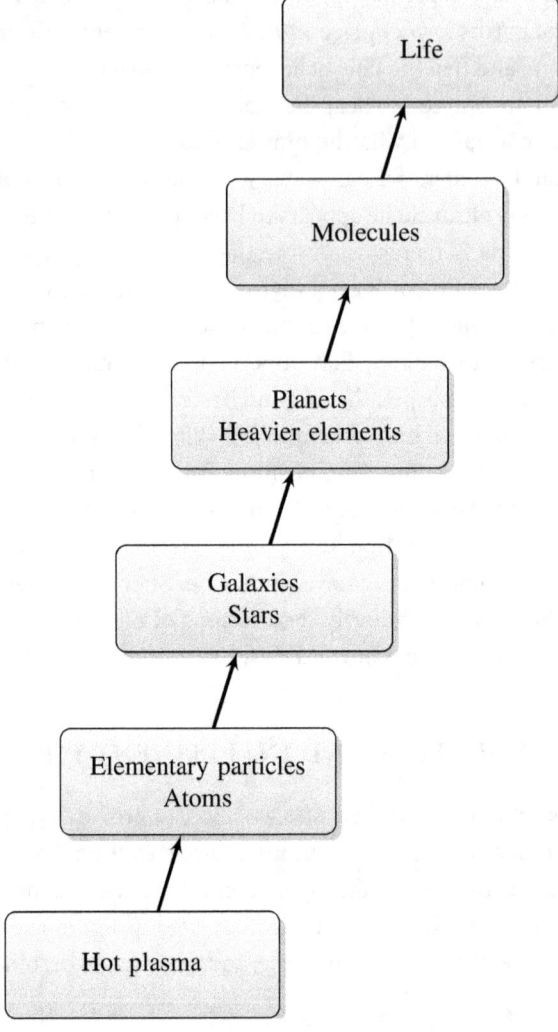

Figure 13. Cosmic evolution.

1. A hot plasma due to the big bang about 14 billion years ago (current best estimate for its age).
2. Elementary particles turn into atoms.
3. These atoms form galaxies and stars.
4. Planets—such as Earth around 4.5 billion years ago—are formed, including heavier chemical elements.

5. These elements form into molecules.
6. Life starts with these molecules approximately 3.5–4 billion years ago.
7. Biological evolution leads to humans.

Here we have evolution on a grand scale, and there appears to be a clear trend toward increasing complexity. It is also worth noting that it is only the last point that we usually associate with evolution. This is discussed in more detail in chapter 6.

There is a profound consistency between the different phases of cosmic evolution. We can draw an example from the latter half of the nineteenth century when the British physicist Lord Kelvin (see figure 14) estimated the Earth's age to be only between 20 and 400 million years. This was not consistent with the time thought necessary for life to develop to its current state. Today's estimate of the Earth's age at 4.5 billion years fits much better with what we now know about biological evolution.[22] Moreover, it agrees with the independent measurement of the universe's age at 14 billion years (see chapter 4). Here, I am using a slightly different benchmark than Karl Popper's criterion that science can only be disproven or falsified and not proven. It is not uncommon for critics of science within a field to search for a striking counterargument in an attempt to shake established science, whether it concerns climate research or geology and the age of the Earth. Seemingly, Kelvin's argument that the Earth was 400 million years old or younger could have served as such an argument against the idea of a slow evolution of life. As there was so much else that seemed to point to such a slow evolution, it was assumed instead that something was amiss with Kelvin's argument. This was based on the belief that, since nature is one, the sciences within different fields are interlinked. Even though science cannot be proven in a mathematical sense, consistency or coherence is a better argument than that provided by striking counterexamples. In hindsight, it turned out that the reason Kelvin's estimate was so off was because he did not factor in radioactive processes in the Earth's interior, which had yet to be discovered.

---

22. Barrow and Tipler, *Cosmological Anthropic Principle*, 159–79.

Figure 14. William Thomson, first Baron Kelvin (1824–1907), was a Scottish Irish physics professor. The industrial environment of Glasgow influenced his interests, and as a result, he worked on both the steam engine and the telegraph. He was knighted for his work on the transatlantic telegraph in 1866 and ennobled in 1892 for his contributions to thermodynamics. One of the seven base units in the International System of Units (SI) is named after him: Kelvin (K), the unit for absolute temperature.[23]

This almost purposeful trend toward complexity and the more advanced, whether it concerns the whole cosmos or just the evolution of life, some would say is luck. In other words, we humans were fortunate to win the lottery since the universe happened to order itself in such a way that we came into existence. I would rather argue that it seems so implausible it suggests nature does not follow a directionless process but rather that there is purpose behind it.

---

23. "Lord Kelvin," Smithsonian Libraries, Wikimedia Commons.

Increased Disorder

We expect that a glass falling onto the floor will shatter and become fragmented. However, the idea that these fragments would suddenly find each other and reassemble into a whole glass would seem utterly impossible without some intervention. There is an infinite number of ways the shards can be scattered across the floor, but only one or a few arrangements where they can form a glass.

This is an illustration of the second law of thermodynamics, which states that the degree of disorder (entropy) either increases or, at best, remains constant. The law was first formulated in the 1850s by the German physicist Rudolf Clausius and by Lord Kelvin. It is interesting how Kelvin's faith provided inspiration for his science, as a verse from the Bible stating that "the earth will wear out like a garment" (Isa 51:6 and Ps 102:26) was a significant influence leading him toward the second law of thermodynamics.[24] Clausius introduced the term *entropy* after combining the Greek words for *capability* and *transformation*. The term deliberately resembles the word *energy*, which means the capability for work. The higher the degree of disorder, the higher the capability or potential for transformation.

This law is one of the few physical laws that corresponds with the almost self-evident notion that time moves forward and not backward. We also have a fairly good intuition for it, as the example with the glass illustrates. If the law applies to the universe as well, as many believe, the development of the cosmos would seem as improbable as a pile of shards suddenly deciding to organize themselves into a complete glass. There is something paradoxical in both the properties of the universe and the development of life in light of the second law of thermodynamics. This is something that many have pondered over.

Is the Universe Headed Toward Dissolution?

If thermodynamics applies to the entire universe, we might think that the universe started in a highly unlikely state that it is still in. This began with the big bang (see chapter 4). The universe was given an improbable state that has led to cosmic development. Slowly, our solar system may now be heading toward the heat death that the German physicist Hermann

---

24. Stanley, "Why Study History."

Helmholtz already realized in 1854 would be a consequence of the entropy law. All energy will be used up, and the solar system will reach an equilibrium where the Sun has stopped giving heat and all life dies out.

An objection might be that the second law of thermodynamics was discovered in connection with the improvement of steam engines and applies to closed systems such as a fridge. We perhaps do not know enough to say that the law should apply to the entire universe as we do not really know if the universe is closed when it continuously expands. And what about entropy in a universe that contains black holes, and which we know so little about that we call the unknown dark energy and dark matter?

Whether thermodynamics can describe the universe as a whole or not, I am wholly convinced that an imagined observer, present at the big bang, would not have been able to predict that it would lead to intelligent life. Intelligent life is highly unexpected, surprising, unlikely, and paradoxical.

The Evolution of Life

The connection between the evolution of life and thermodynamics (point 7 in the list on page 45) is also such a paradox. Some use it to question whether evolution could have occurred at all and conclude that we must choose between evolution and a recent instantaneous creation of each species. But I have little sympathy for such a special science which is in conflict with everything else we know in standard science. It runs counter to the principle of two paths to truth we touched upon in chapter 1, and it creates far more problems than it appears to solve. I am thinking, for instance, of all the findings that hint at life having a long history on Earth, as chapter 4 will discuss. I would rather highlight the incredible process which evolution is in itself and that there are good reasons to study it with awe and reverence.

In 1944, physicist Erwin Schrödinger articulated the paradox that "living matter evades the decay to equilibrium" where life is not possible, and further said,

> Thus the device by which an organism maintains itself stationary at a fairly high level of orderliness (= fairly low level of entropy) really consists in continually sucking orderliness from its environment.[25]

---

25. Schrödinger, *What Is Life*, 79.

An organism can do this because it is not a closed system. The second law of thermodynamics only applies in closed systems. But life on Earth unfolds in an open system where the Sun provides life-giving energy. Why do islands of higher degree of order form in this system? Schrödinger's observation is that

> an organism's astonishing gift of concentrating a "stream of order" on itself and thus escaping the decay into atomic chaos—of "drinking orderliness" from a suitable environment—seems to be connected with the presence of . . . the chromosome molecules.[26]

This was written before the DNA molecule was discovered, and today we would rather say DNA than the chromosome. A complication is that life is much more challenging to define than it may seem at first glance. Some characteristics of life are the ability to take in nutrition, to adapt to environmental conditions, to reproduce, and to go through a life cycle from birth to death. Schrödinger's observation is only a problem if his statement is interpreted as an explanation. But that is not the case; it is an observation that calls for an explanation. Schrödinger, in many ways, was predicting the central role of DNA for life here.

Cosmic Evolution and Aquinas's Teleology

Why would energy in the universe form particles, which then become elements? And why would these elements form molecules that could become the building blocks of life? Why should life arise and evolve at all? And why should this lead to intelligent life capable of asking questions like the ones I have asked here?

Thomas Aquinas (1225–1274) is known for outlining five ways or arguments for the existence of God. Some people call them proofs, but Aquinas himself seems to present them merely as expressions of God's nature. The fifth way deals with purpose in nature. It is also called the teleological way, and we will look at it more closely in chapter 5. Aquinas says,

> Now whatever lacks knowledge cannot move towards an end, unless it be directed by some being endowed with knowledge and intelligence as the arrow is directed by the archer. Therefore,

---

26. Schrödinger, *What Is Life*, 82.

some intelligent being exists by whom all natural things are directed to their end; and this being we call God.[27]

Aquinas observes how everything in creation behaves regularly or nearly regularly. How can it be that all things seem to be heading toward a goal without someone directing it?

Aquinas had a completely different view of nature than we do today and, understandably, knew much less about cosmic evolution. Nevertheless, I think we can apply his thoughts on this grand perspective as well. How can it be that the universe seems to be moving toward something ever more advanced, and why does it seem like the universe has a goal?

A CREATION THAT POINTS TO A CREATOR

Following up on Aquinas's way of reasoning, one explanation is that it is the Creator who makes life in all its diversity possible. Our amazing abilities to speak, hear, and share complex thoughts with each other—what we perceive as unique to human consciousness—amaze and surprise us. The grandeur of space and the fine-tuning of the properties of water testify that creation is good for life and for us. When combined with God's second book, that of revelation, it is evident that the evolution from the big bang to intelligent life also points to purpose in creation.

At the same time, and as discussed in the previous chapter, the evidence found in nature gives us limited insight into God's properties. It is much easier to see the evidence based on a belief in God than without it, as Cardinal John Henry Newman wrote in a letter in 1870: "I believe in design because I believe in God, not in God because I see design."[28]

The biochemical and cosmic properties I have just touched on here are part of what is often called the anthropic principle.[29] The principle is based on the observation that the universe has properties that allow life to evolve and observers to exist. This may sound obvious, for how else could we exist? But the anthropic principle is not an explanation or cause. As John Lennox says, "The anthropic principle, far from giving an explanation of the origin of life, is an observation that gives rise to the need

---

27. Aquinas, *Summa Theologica*, pt. 2, question 2, art. 3, in Kreeft, *Shorter* Summa, 63.

28. Quoted in context in Roberts, "Newman on the Argument," 58.

29. From the Greek *anthropos*, which means "human."

for such an explanation."[30] Barrow and Tipler also say that the anthropic principle is "in no way either speculative or controversial."[31] Nor is it a useless circular argument.

Arguments based on fine-tuning can also be used for detailed calculations of the ratio between natural constants showing that slight variations can lead to the universe's collapse at different stages of cosmic evolution. I have deliberately not touched on this here, as I think the big picture can easily get lost in the details. To me, it is more important to highlight how amazing it is that absolutely all stages in cosmic evolution must have occurred for us to be created, suggesting that there is truth in one of the most radical statements of the Old Testament: "God created man in his own image, in the image of God he created him" (Gen 1:27).

The type of argument that I use here is based on what we know about nature. It contrasts with another type of argument for God that builds on what we do not know. I am thinking of properties of nature that are supposed to be so complex that some believe they could not possibly have resulted from a natural process and therefore must have been created by direct intervention. Such arguments are fragile since they do not handle well the arrival of new scientific discoveries. Arguments based on what we know, on the other hand, work in such a way that the more we learn, the better the argument becomes.

---

30. Lennox, *God's Undertaker*, 74.
31. Barrow and Tipler, introduction to *Cosmological Anthropic Principle*, 16.

3

Serious Science in the Middle Ages and the Unwavering Galileo

> When I lately stood with a friend in front of the cathedral in Amiens, and he beheld with awe and pity that monument of giant strength in towering stone, and of dwarfish patience in minute sculpture, he asked me how it happens that we can no longer build such buildings? I replied, "Dear Alphonse, the people in those old days had convictions. We moderns have only opinions, and it takes more than a mere opinion to build a Gothic cathedral like that."
>
> Heinrich Heine, "Neunter Brief"

In this chapter, we shall examine two common misconceptions. The first is that the Middle Ages at best contributed nothing to science, and at worst suppressed it. The second misconception is that the conflict between Galileo and the Catholic Church was primarily about science. These two examples show the importance of understanding historical events in the context of their own time and not ours.

It is not unusual to portray Galileo as a forward-looking genius who fought against prejudice. The result is that other outstanding astronomers like Tycho Brahe, who placed the Earth at the center, are dismissed as losers who must be explained away due to outdated thinking. Books with this perspective are still being published—for example, by astrophysicist Mario Livio, who sets up Galileo as a positive example contrary to those who deny science today.[1] Livio's book has received positive reviews, not least because the denial of science is on the rise today. At the same time, science historians are frustrated because the book so one-sidedly judges a situation from the 1600s in light of today's knowledge and understanding. Paradoxically, such books fall for their own trap when they deny science—both that of the 1600s and modern historical research—in an attempt to combat science denial in our time.[2]

With some effort, we can understand the science of the past based on its own premises. Then a different picture emerges. A common mistake will be revealed—namely, that many think if they can just show that the geocentric model of antiquity is wrong on one point, then the heliocentric model of Copernicus is automatically proved correct. We also become aware that Tycho's geoheliocentric model was taken seriously for several generations after his death—even though we no longer do so today. In fact, without an understanding of the high regard for Tycho's system in the seventeenth century, it is not possible to comprehend the science of the Galileo affair. A contemporary of Tycho had labeled a diagram that explained the model with "the spheres of revolution accommodated to an immovable Earth from the hypotheses of Copernicus."[3] Tycho's model produces the same planetary movements as Copernicus's model. The only difference is that there is no seasonal variation in the position of the stars in Tycho's model. Therefore, the difference between the two models is only apparent when we observe stars, while the observations of the planets remain the same.

The most important scientific question turns out to be that of the distance to the stars, where for a long time we believed space was much smaller than it really is. We have gained more knowledge about the consequences of this in the past decade, notably through the research of Christopher Graney.

1. Livio, *Galileo and the Science Deniers*.
2. Christie, "Create Your Own Galileo."
3. Gingerich, *Book Nobody Read*, 68.

EIGHTEEN DARK CENTURIES

"Between Archimedes and Galileo there were eighteen dark centuries for science."[4] This was asserted by the renowned Franco-Italian physicist Joseph Lagrange in the early nineteenth century, and most historians and philosophers agreed. The reason could only be that during this period Christianity truly took hold in Europe, and this evidently must have put a stop to rational thinking and impeded the progress of science.

The French physicist and historian of science Pierre Duhem (1861–1916) was in this tradition when, in the journal *La Revue des Questions Scientifiques* in October 1903, he wrote that the commentaries of the Middle Ages contributed nothing substantial to Aristotle's *Mechanical Problems* and to see these ideas bear fruit we had to wait until the beginning of the sixteenth century. Duhem had promised the journal a new article every three months. This was his first contribution in a series on mechanics, starting with statics.[5] The series of articles would overturn our view of science in the Middle Ages.

Duhem's statement reveals that he likely had not read much medieval history at the time. The book he referred to in the article, *Mechanical Problems*, was not known until the end of the 1400s, around the time the Middle Ages were coming to a close. Moreover, the book was probably not written by Aristotle, but by his followers. It seems as if Duhem was just repeating what everyone else said.

Lagrange and Duhem could indeed have sensed that something did not match up with the history they were perpetuating. The church's contributions to various areas during the Middle Ages were so visible that it should almost be unnecessary to recall them:

- The bold Gothic cathedrals that stretched the boundaries of the understanding of mechanics and statics at the time are among the most distinctive monuments of the Middle Ages. The northernmost of them, Nidaros Cathedral in Trondheim, Norway, where construction began in the mid-twelfth century, is one of them.

- The establishment of cathedral schools, in particular during the reign of Charlemagne in the eighth century. In Norway, this happened at

---

4. The time from about 500 to 1500 has traditionally been called the Dark Ages, but historians today are more nuanced.

5. Statics is the branch of mechanics that has to do with equilibrium. An example is the construction of bridges.

the cathedrals in Trondheim, Bergen, Oslo, and Hamar, which were all established shortly after 1152, when Norway became its own archbishopric.

- The establishment of the first universities in Europe in the eleventh and twelfth centuries arising from the monastic and cathedral schools. Many of them, such as the universities of Bologna, Paris, Oxford, and Cambridge, remain among the world's most prestigious even today.

- The idea of primary and secondary causation made it possible to study nature rationally without conflicting with God's sovereignty and omnipotence. This is explained in more detail in chapter 5.

Pierre Duhem and His Life's Discovery

Duhem encountered a problem as he prepared to send the next installment of his series on the history of mechanics. Before the January 1904 issue, he had to write a letter to the editors apologizing that he was not ready yet because he needed to read more. By the April issue of the same year, he came up with an entirely new story. By then, he had made the discovery of his lifetime.[6] He had found some references to the University of Paris in Leonardo da Vinci's notebooks from the early sixteenth century. This had led Duhem, who could read Latin, to delve into old manuscripts in the National Library of Paris. Here, he discovered medieval statics and, in particular, the work of the thirteenth-century German mathematician Jordanus Nemorarius (1225–1260). In Nemorarius's extensive writings, there was an analysis of levers and how objects behave on inclined planes—an idea for which Galileo was credited three centuries later. Leonardo da Vinci, who until then was thought to have worked in isolation, turned out to be building on the works of both Jordanus and the fourteenth century's Albert of Saxony, who later became a bishop. This was surprising, not least of all to Duhem himself. It turned out that this period in the Middle Ages contributed a great deal. After this, Duhem wrote an article for the journal every quarter for several years. In the twelve years from 1906 until he died at just fifty-five years old, medieval physics was his priority.

6. This section builds on Martin, "Genesis of a Mediaeval Historian," and Patapievici, "Pierre Duhem Thesis."

Duhem is now acknowledged as a pioneer of the history of medieval science, and the one who made this science into a respectable research field.[7] For it was not only the roots of statics that Duhem found. He also investigated the history of the other part of mechanics, what we call dynamics.[8] In 1905, he discovered that the Middle Ages had also made many important contributions to this field. This was an even more significant discovery than the one from the previous year. Duhem himself puts it this way:

> When we see the science of Galileo triumph over the stubborn Peripatetism of Cremonini,[9] we believe, since we are ill-informed about the history of human thought, that we are witness to the victory of modern, young science over medieval philosophy, so stubborn in its mechanical repetition. In truth, we are contemplating the well-paved triumph of the science born at Paris during the fourteenth century over the doctrines of Aristotle and Averroes, restored into repute by the Italian Renaissance.[10]

Duhem thus argued that the Middle Ages had progressed further than thinkers such as Aristotle and Averroes, even though it was these old-fashioned thinkers who were elevated during the Renaissance. One of the problems in dynamics, pointed out by Aristotle, involved explaining motion when no one was pushing or pulling. His solution was that when a stone is thrown, it pushes the air aside in such a way that the air flows back into the space behind the stone and continues to push on it even after it has left the throwing hand. Simultaneously, the same air is also the source of friction that ultimately stops the stone. This seems illogical and almost self-contradictory. Moreover, it would require a very powerful wind to be able to push something as heavy as a stone or a cannonball. Duhem found something resembling the modern explanation in writings from the first half of the fourteenth century. The idea was that the stone is imparted with a property that increases with both speed and mass, and this was called impetus. This impetus is in the stone itself, not in

---

7. See preface of Grant, *Foundations of Modern Science*.

8. Dynamics is the study of forces and movements. An example is the prediction of the trajectory of a cannonball.

9. Cesare Cremonini was a professor of natural philosophy and a contemporary of Galileo. Cremonini taught the philosophy of Aristotle, who founded the Peripatetic school as interpreted by, for example, Averroes, or Ibn Rushd as he is known in Arabic (1126–1198).

10. From Duhem's summary of his work when he was elected to the Académie des Sciences in 1913. See Duhem, "History of Physical Theories," 193.

the surrounding air, and allows the stone to continue moving. Impetus is what we today call momentum.

Duhem discovered the idea of impetus in the works of Jean Buridan (ca. 1301–ca. 1361), rector of the University of Paris. Buridan is considered the most important natural philosopher of the fourteenth century, and the University of Paris was where the science of the Middle Ages reached its pinnacle. The impetus theory allowed Buridan to offer a fairly accurate explanation for the trajectory of a projectile. However, Buridan was not the originator of the idea; it came from the often-forgotten John Philoponus who lived in the sixth century in Alexandria. Philoponus is regarded as one of the last natural philosophers of antiquity but, more importantly, as one of the first Christian natural philosophers. Buridan also applied the concept of impetus to the planets, which he thereby understood would move in their orbits indefinitely since there is no air resistance in space. This is the first explanation of planetary orbits that resembles the modern understanding, and it eliminated the need for something to continuously "push" the planets to keep them moving.

Buridan also thought it was more elegant to explain the "rotation of the heavens" throughout the day as due to the rotation of Earth, not the starry sky. The objection to this idea was that a rotating Earth would generate tremendous winds, especially since the Earth rotates incredibly fast at the equator. Buridan dismissed this objection with a theory that the entire atmosphere follows the rotation. The final explanation that the atmosphere rotates with the Earth came with Pascal's measurement of air pressure in the seventeenth century after the time of Galileo. This measurement established that air has weight, and thus gravity holds the air in place. This piece of the puzzle was crucial for the theory of Earth's rotation to be credible.

Similar ideas to those conceived in Paris were developed by The Oxford Calculators, associated with Merton College, and still part of the University of Oxford today. Among the most central figures were Thomas Bradwardine (ca. 1290–1349), one of the first to express physics in mathematical terms; Richard Swineshead, active in the period 1340–1355; and William Heytesbury (ca. 1313–1373).[11] Further development took place later in Paris by the successor to Jean Buridan, grand master of the university and later bishop Nicole Oresme (ca. 1325–1383). He argued that an arrow shot straight up would fall straight back down and not to

---

11. This is well explained in Hannam, *Genesis of Science*, who also gives Duhem credit for being the first to give medieval science its rightful place.

the side, even if the Earth rotated, a belief held by Jean Buridan as well. This would become an important argument for Copernicus a couple of centuries later.

Much of this science ended abruptly around 1350–1360 when the Black Death swept across Europe. Thomas Bradwardine fell victim to the plague, and possibly Jean Buridan as well. Although I have not seen any historians comment on this, the Hundred Years' War between England and France (1337–1453) cannot have been particularly favorable to the development of science, given that Paris and Oxford were so central.

Duhem's discovery led him to regard the science of the sixteenth and seventeenth centuries as a continuation of the Middle Ages, and not as a break and a revolution. His work has, after a long time, gained such acceptance among historians that today books are published with titles like *The Light Ages* to counter the image of the Dark Ages.[12] Duhem also argued that the real starting points for modern science were the condemnation of certain aspects of Aristotle's ideas by the bishop of Paris in 1277, and the ideas of Jean Buridan and the fourteenth century. This is more contentious and has been debated by historians since.

Long Time for Acceptance

Not many have heard of Pierre Duhem nowadays. He completed most of his work in the peripheral city of Bordeaux, where he was a professor of physics for the last twenty-two years of his life. One reason he never got a position in his native Paris could be his doctoral thesis from 1884. There he criticized the twenty-year-old thermodynamics theory of Marcellin Berthelot. Berthelot, who became France's minister of education a few years later, is said to have reacted with, "This young man shall never teach in Paris!" And his thesis was rejected. But Duhem was confident enough to publish his thesis as a book shortly thereafter, and, in retrospect, it has turned out his theories were correct. Although he delivered a new thesis on magnetism and earned a doctorate in 1888, that initial rejection was undoubtedly negative for his career. Many years later, after several of his academic opponents had passed away, he got a kind of vindication, to his great satisfaction: in 1913 he was elected as an external member of the French Academy of Sciences in Paris.

---

12. For example, Seb Falk's *Light Ages*.

Duhem's philosophy of science holds that results from experiments, what we call facts, do not have much value without a theoretical framework for interpretation. Facts in themselves are not sufficient to give direction to science.[13] Duhem was also a proponent of decoupling physics from underlying models or metaphysics. Here he is influenced by Pascal's view of science and the idea of the hidden God as mentioned in chapter 1. Duhem believed that natural science had its limitations and, for example, could neither be used to prove nor disprove God. Duhem was a big fan of Pascal, he knew large parts of Pascal's *Pensées* by heart and quoted from the book in almost every lecture. Another book he always kept at hand was Thomas à Kempis's popular *The Imitation of Christ* from 1419.

Duhem was against the mainstream in several ways; he was conservative, a royalist, and a Catholic. He was also quite a stubborn and sometimes controversial personality.[14] He made his most important work in thermodynamics but published books in several branches of physics. I have used the Clausius-Duhem theorem in thermodynamics in my own research in acoustics.[15] In the mid-1890s, Duhem began writing about the history of science and in total he wrote about twenty books.

It would take a long time for Duhem's ideas about medieval science to gain acceptance. One of the reasons even his discovery of the University of Paris's important role wasn't accepted is accusations that he was too strongly colored by his Catholic faith. Duhem himself was careful to distinguish his science from his faith, but in his historical writing it shines through that he believed he could see the work of Providence in history.[16]

In 1913 he wrote something that many since have used against him, and which may be the source of the accusation that he was a Catholic apologist. As a Parisian and Frenchman, Duhem expressed pride in the medieval French scholars at the University of Paris, wondering how he as a Christian could not thank God for this university that stood foremost in the battle to defend orthodox Catholic faith. It's not too difficult to understand this pride against the backdrop of a time with strong anti-Catholic currents. Catholic schools had just been closed, and separation of church and state had occurred in 1905, not at the time of the French

---

13. This is called the Duhem thesis or the Duhem-Quine thesis in the philosophy of science.

14. Biographical information is from Ariew, "Pierre Duhem."

15. Our study was on the impact of thermodynamics on ultrasound propagation: Holm and Holm, "Restrictions on Wave Equations."

16. Kragh, "Pierre Duhem."

Revolution as many believe. In the early twentieth century it had also become common not only to use science against the church but to assert that the church had been resisting science for a long time. Catholics reacted to this anti-church polemic by using science to defend Catholic doctrine. Duhem tried to take the middle ground.

The most important argument against the accusation is that Duhem's discovery was made many years before he wrote the words expressing his pride in being French, a Parisian, and a Catholic. Moreover, Duhem himself was as surprised as everyone else by the discovery of medieval science, hence his Catholic faith could not have played a significant role. And even if it had, historians ought to be objective and professional enough to let the facts speak for themselves. One cannot get away from the fact that the manuscripts of Jordanus de Nemore, Albert of Saxony, and Jean Buridan actually exist, completely independently of the motivations of the one who discovered them. They are available and show that such science existed from the thirteenth century onward.

Even today, more than a hundred years later, popular culture is still colored by a view of the Middle Ages as a period when the church weakened and suppressed science. This is clearly reflected in presentations by popular physics communicators like Neil deGrasse Tyson, who just a few years ago stated that without religion we would be a thousand years more advanced.[17] Stephen Hawking and Carl Sagan have made similar statements. Sadly, it's common for such celebrity scientists to be granted authority that leads to them being listened to even in areas where their expertise is lacking. But we should be highly skeptical when physicists and other scientists speak about the history of science without having delved into the field. Nevertheless, I remain optimistic; fortunately, even atheists and humanists have seriously begun to engage with the history of science in the Middle Ages, and thus also recognize the church's positive role.[18]

TYCHO BRAHE AND HIS RATIONAL ARGUMENTS

What does it say about a person that he possesses a tame elk? Danish Tyge Ottesen Brahe (1546–1601), residing on the island of Hven in the

---

17. Said at the launch of the documentary series *Cosmos: A Spacetime Odyssey* in 2014. It took its inspiration from Carl Sagan's *Cosmos: A Personal Voyage* from the 1980s.

18. See historyforatheists.com; Tim O'Neill is a historian and an atheist and has grown tired of other atheists' distortion of history.

Øresund (the sound between present-day Sweden and Denmark), was such a person. That is, the elk never actually arrived there; it met an unfortunate end in Landskrona on the present-day Swedish side, while Tycho and his friends awaited a boat transfer. As they were waiting, the elk accompanied Tycho to a party where it consumed too much beer. Regrettably, the outcome was tragic, as the elk stumbled on the steps and broke its leg. Despite receiving good care, it did not survive this incident.[19]

The eccentric Tycho Brahe, as he named himself in Latin, has fascinated many. There has been much speculation about his cause of death and if he could have been poisoned. In 2010, his grave in Prague was reopened. It turned out that Tycho suffered from a skeletal disease that could have been the result of a lifestyle with an ample supply of meat, fish, and alcohol, and that he was overweight. However, there wasn't enough mercury in the samples to assert that he was poisoned.[20]

It's also easy to think of Tycho as a superficial person, but his motto suggests a different image: "Rather to be than to be perceived to be."[21]

Tycho is best known for his accurate astronomical observations, but he also proposed a model of the solar system where the Earth was at the center. Today, Tycho Brahe's model is mostly forgotten. Those who recall it tend to use it as an example of someone who conformed to the church. They believe Tycho represented an ideologically colored worldview that has little to do with science.

Paradoxically, Tycho Brahe's model is depicted as victorious on the cover of a book by the astronomer and Jesuit Giovanni Battista Riccioli (1598–1671) (see figure 15). The book was published in 1651, fifty years after Tycho's death, and was so well-written and scientifically robust that it was used as a textbook for the next hundred years. Here, Copernicus's model, to the left, is compared with Tycho's to the right, while the old Greek model lies defeated on the ground. Surprisingly, Riccioli gives Tycho's system the greatest academic credibility—with Copernicus following as a close second.

---

19. Story confirmed by personal communications from Poul Grinder-Hansen, National Museum of Denmark, June 2020.
20. Kacki et al., "Rich Table but Short Life."
21. "Esse potius qvam haberi"—text on Tycho's tombstone.

Figure 15. The cover of Riccioli's *Almagestum Novum*, 1651. Copernicus's model is on the left and Tycho's model on the right. The Earth-centered model of Ptolemy lies defeated on the ground. Note that the scale tips in favor of Tycho.[22]

The Italian Riccioli, a professor in Bologna in 1636, included in his book a description of the Moon with place names we still use today. He honored, amongst others, Copernicus, Kepler, Galileo, and Tycho by naming craters after them. The book was significant for promoting Copernicus's model, even as it argued against it. The University of Oslo possesses an original copy of this book, and I have myself leafed through it with the reverence that a near four-hundred-year-old tome evokes.

22. "Almagestum Novum Frontispiece," by Franciscus Curtus, Wikimedia Commons.

Riccioli was the teacher of Giovanni Cassini (1625–1712), and the two were central in advancing Italian astronomy post-Galileo. Cassini was the founder of modern telescope-based astronomy, although Galileo is often credited with this. Cassini discovered Jupiter's Great Red Spot and measured the rotational speeds of both Jupiter and Mars. He also discovered the moons of Saturn, and he has been honored by having his name given to the aforementioned spacecraft that went to Saturn (chapter 2).

It wasn't just Riccioli who spoke positively about Tycho's model. Even a hundred years later another book spent many pages explaining it, though now the roles were reversed with the heliocentric system emerging as the winner.[23]

Riccioli lists a total of 126 arguments for and against Earth's motion—in other words, Copernicus versus Tycho. He has forty-nine arguments for Earth's motion and seventy-seven against. Only two of the counterarguments are religious in nature, but they are quickly dismissed. There are two scientific arguments that cause the balance to tip in Tycho's favor for Riccioli. The first concerns Earth's rotation and the second, and most important one, concerns the size of the stars. Let's take a closer look at these arguments, as they are central for understanding Galileo.

A timeline for the development of the various models at the time is presented in figure 16. It may be helpful to refer to this timeline as you read on. Note particularly that the Thirty Years' War, which started as a conflict between Protestants and Catholics, unfolds simultaneously with the key events related to Galileo. We will come back to this later.

---

23. *Atlas Coelestis* by Dopplmayer and Homann from 1742, as described in Graney, "Teaching Galileo? Know Riccioli!"

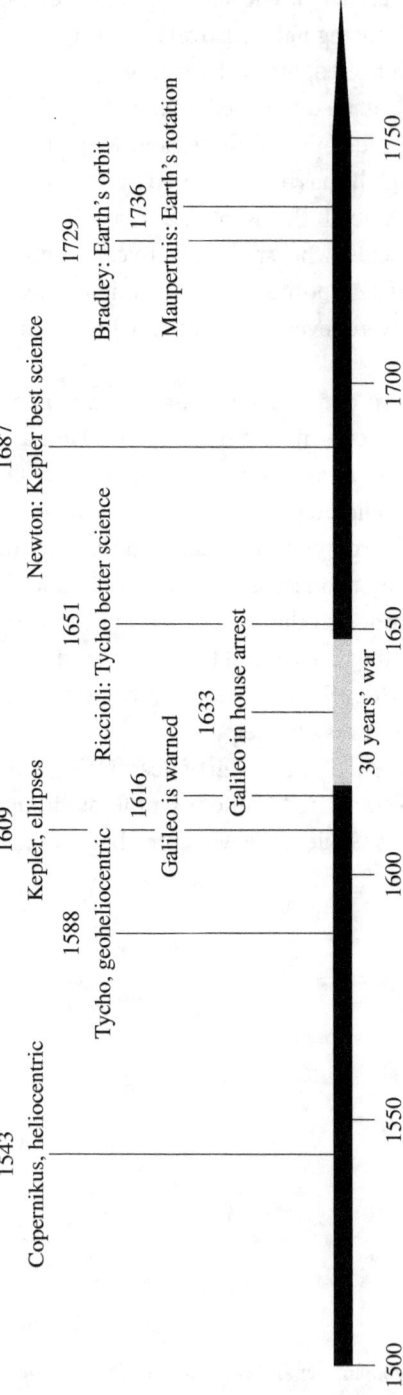

Figure 16. Timeline of important events in the development of the heliocentric model.

Let's start with Tycho Brahe himself. All portraits show him with a metal plate over his nose. Tycho was a multifaceted Dane with a fiery temperament. The metal plate covers the wound he got in a sword duel with a fellow student. He was twenty years old at the time and well into his astronomy studies. Already in his teens, Tycho was impressed by the accurate prediction of a solar eclipse to the very day, August 21, 1560. At the age of sixteen, he started a diary of astronomical observations. He quickly found out that not all predictions were precise, as Ptolemy's data from the second century were off by one month for a conjunction of Jupiter and Saturn. Improving these data became Tycho Brahe's life project. He conducted most of his measurements on the island of Hven, which is now Swedish. His underground observatory has been recreated at the museum I visited there a few years ago. The measurements Tycho and his assistants made here were distinguished by a much higher quality than all previous measurements, even though they had only their eyes aided by long sighting rods to observe with. The data collected here enabled Kepler to find the surprising fact that Mars moves in an elliptical orbit, not a circular one.

Today, it can be challenging to judge Tycho and his motives. Like most natural philosophers at the time, he was involved in astrology. There was a long tradition for this practice, even in monasteries. Astrology was usually placed within a medical context and wasn't primarily intended to predict the future, as today's astrology is best known for.[24] In a lecture in Copenhagen in 1574, Tycho justified astrology by pointing to the obvious influences of the Sun and Moon on Earth.[25] Everyone knows that the Sun determines both day and night and the seasons, and that tides follow the Moon. The latter, however, was something Galileo did not agree with, as we shall see later. Tycho continued by asking why the other five wandering celestial bodies shouldn't influence Earth as well, such as weather, accidents, and the plague?[26] The esteemed astronomical historian Pannekoek (1873–1960) surprisingly uses over two of thirteen pages in a chapter about Tycho to discuss the Copenhagen lecture. Pannekoek, who was also a Marxist theoretician, seems to have a wish to portray Tycho as irrational. He does not put much emphasis on the argument about star

24. Falk, *Light Ages*, 197–200, discusses astrology in English monasteries in the late fourteenth century.

25. Pannekoek, *History of Astronomy*, 204–16.

26. Some assert similar things today, such as the influence of Jupiter and Saturn on the climate. Arguments against this are in Holm, "On the Alleged Coherence" and "Prudence in Estimating Coherence."

size, which I will elaborate on here, but is very focused on the religious justification for Tycho's world system. This is typical for much history of astronomy, and therefore I will supplement it with more recent sources that are based on a better understanding of the science at the time.[27]

Tycho was born just three years after the Polish astronomer Nicolaus Copernicus (1473–1543) published his book *De revolutionibus orbium coelestium* (*On the Revolution of the Heavenly Spheres*). In this work, Copernicus presented a model where the Sun, not the Earth, is the center of our planetary system. Copernicus had been sharing his ideas about this for a long time but delayed publishing all the details until the end of his life. It is a myth that Copernicus waited so long due to fear of a reaction from the church. On the contrary, Cardinal Nikolaus von Schönberg encouraged him to get his theories published, and in a letter dated November 1, 1536, the cardinal offered to pay for it. Incredibly, the manuscript draft of Copernicus's book still exists. It clearly shows that he was improving and correcting tables until the very end, indicating that the main reason for delayed publication was fear of being ridiculed, or worse, being ignored.[28]

Strictly speaking, Copernicus couldn't prove his model. What spoke in its favor was that his new system provided a more elegant explanation than that of Claudius Ptolemy (100–168) for the retrograde motion of the outer planets. Both Tycho and Galileo would later also seek proof.

Ancient Astronomy

In the physics of antiquity, all things sought their natural place. For heavy stones, this meant that they fell back to Earth when thrown. The planets were exempt from such tendencies, so the physics of the heavens was therefore considered to be different from the physics on Earth. Circles were the most logical path for planets to take, also because they are one of the few types of motion that are stable, at least when one does not have a good theory for gravity and other forces.[29] The reason why the physics of the celestial realm beyond the Moon was different was because it was a "perfect" place where the gods were thought to reside. Since the circle was considered a perfect geometric figure, it was also natural to use circular motion in the models for their orbits. This corresponds to a notion

---

27. An important source is Graney, *Setting Aside All Authority*.
28. Gingerich, *Book Nobody Read*, 10–28.
29. Singham, "Copernican Myths."

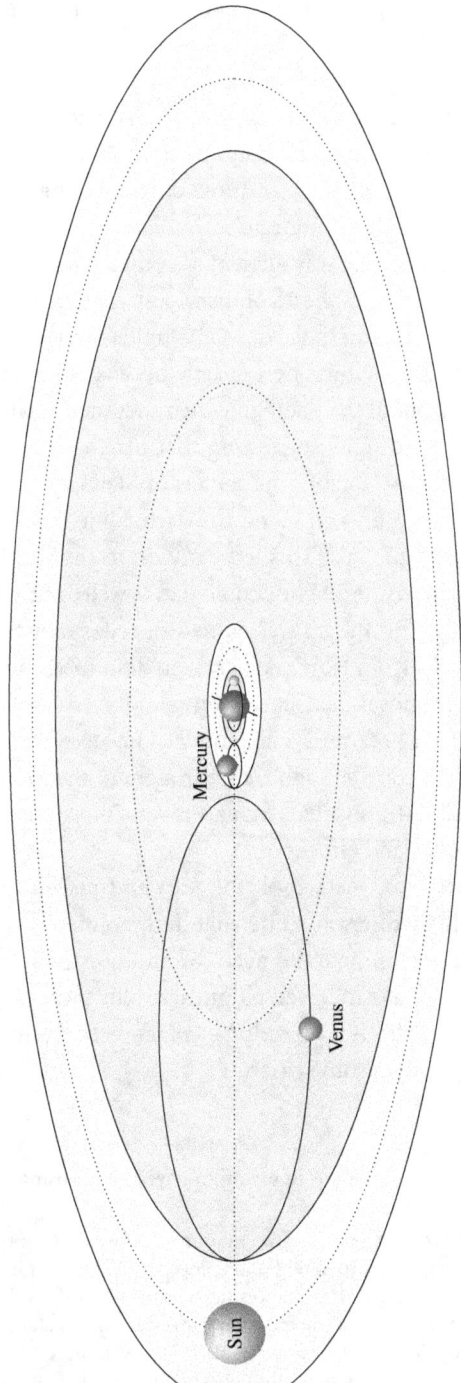

Figure 17. The view of antiquity with the earth in the center. Shown here are the spheres for the inner celestial bodies, the Moon, Mercury, Venus, and the Sun. Note that the secondary circles of Mercury and Venus always lie on the line between the Earth and the Sun. Mercury and Venus can only be seen in the morning or evening and the epicycles are determined from the fact that Venus is never farther away from the Sun than forty-eight degrees and Mercury is never farther away than twenty-eight degrees.

that many still have today, that a good physical theory should preferably be beautiful and simple.[30]

However, reality doesn't always follow our notions. To make the orbits match observations, ancient astronomers placed each planet on a second circle—called an epicycle—as shown in figures 17 and 18, for the inner and outer solar system, respectively.[31] In these diagrams, the emphasis is on showing the planetary spheres more clearly than the actual orbits, as the spheres were so central to the way ancient astronomers thought. In the inner solar system, these are the spheres of the Moon, Mercury, Venus, and the Sun, and in the outer system, those of Mars, Jupiter, and Saturn. There were even more circles than shown here, partly because the planets also move up and down (i.e., out of the plane in which they are drawn).

In hindsight, there are signs suggesting that placing the Sun at the center makes the most sense. Notably, the centers of Mercury's and Venus's epicycles always follow the Sun and lie on the dotted line from the Earth to the Sun, as shown in figure 17. This led early on to the realization by several thinkers that Mercury and Venus could just as well orbit around the Sun as around the Earth. This model was named Capella's model, after the Roman Martianus Capella from North Africa, who described it in his fifth-century book. Similar proposals also exist from antiquity. Capella's model is a precursor to what later became Tycho's model. However, the argument for celestial spheres was strong enough that, throughout the Middle Ages, it was Ptolemy's model that prevailed, though it was improved in certain aspects by Arabs, Persians, and Greeks.

Copernicus, as we have seen, took the leap and placed the Sun at the center. It is possible that he was somewhat disappointed with his new model because it did not eliminate the need for additional circles. Before it was understood that planets followed elliptical orbits, these circles were necessary. His model also did not provide better predictions than the old one, but rather the opposite in some cases.

---

30. A modern critic of similar notions in quantum physics and cosmology is Hossenfelder, *Lost in Math*.

31. The illustrations show a simplified representation of the model of antiquity with only the main and secondary circles (deferent and epicycle). First, a shift in the center of the Sun's main circle is also needed to make summer in the northern hemisphere seven days longer than winter. Second, the trajectory speed is not constant in relation to the center of the main circle, but a fictitious point. Third, even more epicycles must be added to make this accurate, among other things to include movement up and down from the orbital plane shown here (the ecliptic).

SERIOUS SCIENCE IN THE MIDDLE AGES AND THE UNWAVERING GALILEO 69

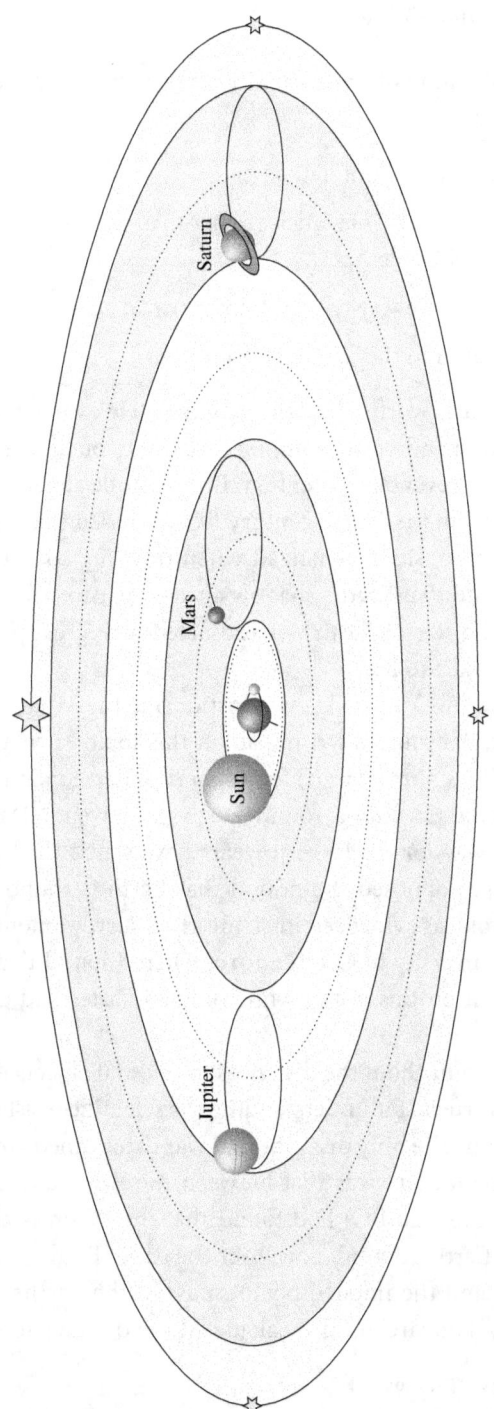

Figure 18. The outer planets Mars, Jupiter, and Saturn and their spheres in the ancient worldview. Note how the epicycles, the small secondary circles, for these planets are almost a mirror image of the Sun's orbit around the Earth.

The Path to a Modern View

A correct understanding of Earth's place in the cosmos includes the acknowledgment that:

1. Earth is spherical and not flat.
2. The distance to the stars is much greater than was assumed in antiquity and in the Middle Ages.
3. Earth rotates once every twenty-four hours.
4. Earth orbits around the Sun once a year.

The first point is worth clarifying immediately as many confuse it with Earth's rotation and orbit, thinking that clarity on all these matters was achieved in the seventeenth century. But Aristotle already knew that Earth was spherical in the fourth century BC. He based this on observations that the stars' positions changed when traveling southward from Greece to Egypt and that Earth's shadow always appeared round during a lunar eclipse. The size of Earth was estimated with great precision by Eratosthenes around 240 BC.

Some believe this knowledge was lost during the Middle Ages, but that's not correct. All sources writing about this topic, such as the thirteenth-century *King's Mirror*, argue for a spherical Earth,[32] and in Dante's (1265–1321) *Divine Comedy* a round Earth is a given.[33] Despite this, textbooks in Norway for the last 150 years have stated that the church in the Middle Ages opposed the notion that Earth is round. And this myth has taken hold, as evidenced in an informal survey among bachelor students at the University of Oslo in 2010, where I found that just over half were mistaken on this point, while only a quarter had the correct understanding.

The second point about the distances to celestial objects tends to be overlooked but is crucial for understanding the scientific resistance to the Copernican system. The only distance that was determined with reasonable accuracy in antiquity was that between the Earth and the Moon. Hipparchus (ca. 190–120 BC) had found that the Moon is about sixty Earth radii from Earth. As a sidenote, note the use of Earth radii as a unit of measurement and the implied obviousness of the Earth's roundness even in antiquity. Hipparchus also calculated the distance to the Sun as

---

32. Larson, *King's Mirror*, 95–99.
33. Cormack, "Flat Earth or Round Sphere," 366.

2,550 times the Earth's radius, but here he was greatly mistaken. The Sun is actually almost twenty times farther away. Ptolemy estimated that the distance to the stars was twenty thousand Earth radii. To put it another way, light from the Sun takes in reality eight and a half minutes to reach Earth. In antiquity, it was assumed that even the sphere of the stars was just seven minutes away. Today, we know that light from even the closest star takes more than four years to reach us. The universe of antiquity may seem tiny to us, but for people at the time it was so vast that Earth was just a mathematical point if they tried to draw it all, as Boethius said (chapter 2).

Before Copernicus, it was mostly assumed that Earth neither moved nor rotated; only the planets, the Sun, and the Moon did. The stars were thought to be immutable and were therefore called fixed stars. There was one sphere each for the Moon, Mercury, Venus, the Sun, Mars, Jupiter, and Saturn, and these seven wandering celestial bodies gave us the seven days of the week. The fixed stars lay in the eighth sphere. In Dante's *Divine Comedy* from 1320, the ninth sphere was the abode of angels. At the outermost, in the tenth sphere, was the Prime Mover, essentially God. Over time in the Middle Ages, the belief solidified that there was nearly impenetrable crystal between the spheres.

Tycho's first discovery challenged the view of the immutable starry sky. On the evening of November 11, 1572, as usual, he looked up at the sky. He knew all the visible stars well after years of observation and stated himself that it wasn't that difficult to learn them, it was just a matter of putting some effort into it. That evening, he saw something clearer than even Venus, and this "something" stayed there for a year. Eventually, he became quite certain that it was a star and not a planet, since it did not move. The book he wrote about this star was his first step toward fame. The title *De nova stella* (On the new star) gave the phenomenon the name "nova," which we still use today. The sphere of fixed stars was evidently not as unchanging as had been thought since antiquity.

Tycho's second discovery was made at the age of thirty-one and was even more epoch making. During the winter of 1577–1578, a comet appeared in the sky over Denmark. Farther south, in Germany, a six-year-old Johannes Kepler also caught sight of the comet, and he remembered the view for the rest of his life. The comet moved, and Tycho tried to measure its distance by observing how it moved over the course of the night. He concluded that the comet had to be six times farther from Earth than the Moon. This contradicted the ancient belief that comets were atmospheric phenomena and closer than the Moon. Michael Mästlin in Germany,[34] later Kepler's teacher, had calculated that the comet was even more distant. This could mean only one thing: it had pierced right through the "crystal sphere" of Venus (see figure 17). Perhaps these spheres weren't as fixed and immutable as had been believed after all.

A Test to Confirm Copernicus's Model

These two discoveries by Tycho Brahe made him more open to considering Copernicus's model. Eventually, he devised a test to differentiate between the old Ptolemaic system and the new Copernican model. According to Copernicus, the planet Mars, which is farther away from the Sun than Earth, sometimes gets closer to us than the Sun (see figure 19), but in the Ptolemaic model (figure 18), Mars is always farther away than the Sun.

Tycho aimed to determine the distance to Mars. He could do this by observing Mars at two different points in time, evening and morning, when it was closest, similar to his observations of the comet. This effect, called parallax, is like looking at a finger on an outstretched arm with your left and right eye alternately. You observe how the finger appears to move against the background. The closer the object, the more displacement there is. But if the object is too far away, the displacement is impossible to detect.

Tycho's measurements of Mars were made during the winter of 1582–1583, and the year after he reported that he had not found any displacement. This is consistent with what we know today, as Mars's parallax is too small to be observed with the naked eye, which was all Tycho had at his disposal since the telescope had not yet been invented. Both the Sun and Mars are much farther away than he had anticipated. Strangely, in 1587, Tycho changed his stance and claimed that he had detected that Mars was a third closer to Earth than the Sun. After Tycho's death, Kepler reviewed his notes to try to understand this and thought he had found an error possibly made by Tycho's assistants.[35] It's also possible that Tycho simply deceived himself. Many researchers can recognize that the desire to have an assumption confirmed can be so strong that it can make you somewhat blind to your actual findings.

34. Gingerich and Westman, "Conflict and Priority."
35. Gingerich and Westman, "Conflict and Priority."

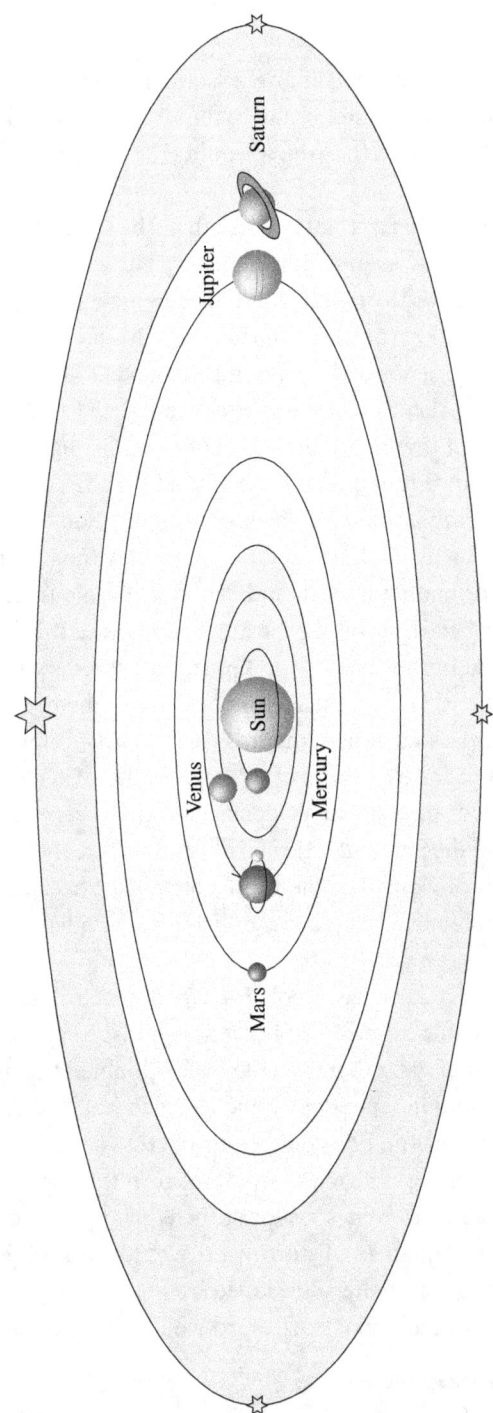

Figure 19. Copernicus's model with the Sun in the center. The distances between all the nearest planets up to and including Mars are to the correct scale, while Jupiter and Saturn are too close to Earth in this figure. The outermost circle of fixed stars is not part of today's model.

Earth's Rotation

The next element in Copernicus's model was the rotating Earth (item 3 on page 70). Although the rotation is not as important in the heliocentric model as Earth's orbit around the Sun, it would take almost two hundred years to confirm it.

At the equator, the Earth rotates faster than the speed of sound, so the gut reaction of many, even today, is that it will lead to unimaginably strong winds. There were important arguments against this wind in the fourteenth century from Jean Buridan and Nicole Oresme at the University of Paris, as mentioned earlier in the chapter. Their arguments contradicted in fact Aristotle's physics, which suggested that the Earth must be stationary, but these natural philosophers didn't have much of a problem with that. Since it had long been argued that the Earth rotates, it was easier to accept that than the Earth orbiting the Sun, even though no one could explain why the Earth rotates before Newton did in 1687.

In the model of mathematician and canon Copernicus from 1543, the idea of a rotating Earth orbiting the Sun was central. It is likely that Copernicus had read both Buridan and Oresme, as their arguments are found in *De revolutionibus*,[36] but he does not reference them. This sort of practice would not pass current standards for scientific publishing but was more common in the early days of science. Galileo also did this.

Galileo provided some strong evidence when he observed that sunspots rotated around the Sun and returned after about twenty-seven days. However, it was not obvious that the Earth rotates just because the Sun does. As long as Galileo lived, there was only indirect evidence of Earth's rotation.

Isaac Newton's (1642–1726) book *Principia*, which describes how gravity leads to the elliptical orbits of planets, was also very convincing. So convincing that after 1687 there were few who doubted that the Earth rotated. However, could independent evidence be found, and also an indisputable prediction that no one could contradict?

Surprisingly, Tycho was also an early thinker in this regard. He reasoned that since the Earth rotates fastest at the equator and slows down farther north, a cannonball fired northward would miss slightly. This argument would later be further developed by Riccioli.[37] In 1651, Riccioli wrote that cannonballs shot northward would bend to the right, as

---

36. Copernicus, *On the Revolution*, 22–25.
37. Graney, "Coriolis Effect."

shown in figure 20 taken from Riccioli's book. The problem was that no one had observed such a deviation. Both Tycho and Riccioli therefore concluded that there was no scientific basis for saying that the Earth rotated. In hindsight, we know that the effect of Earth's rotation is tiny, and in practice it is mostly weather systems that are affected. But surprisingly, even sharp shooters aiming at targets several kilometers away must take the effect into account.

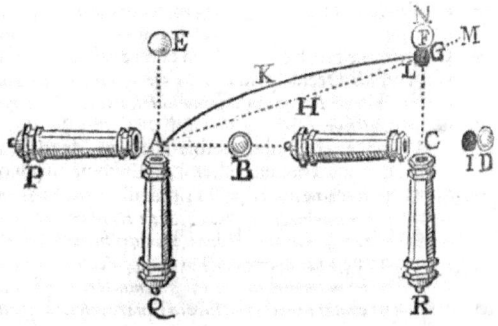

Figure 20. Illustration from Riccioli's book, 1651. When a cannon ball is fired toward the north (E), the earth's rotation causes it to go sideways and instead end up at point G. Such bending does not happen if the cannon is fired toward the east (B).[38]

In 1835, Gaspard-Gustave Coriolis was the first person to describe and quantify the effect of Earth's rotation, now known as the Coriolis effect. The Foucault pendulum, first exhibited at the Pantheon in Paris in 1851, is also a very visual demonstration of Earth's rotation. It has only recently been discovered that both Tycho Brahe and Giovanni Battista Riccioli had similar ideas long before Coriolis.[39] There is nothing about the Foucault pendulum that suggests it could not have been discovered by Kepler or Galileo, and we can only imagine how different the history of science would have been if that had happened.

Seasonal Variation in Star Positions

The most significant argument against Copernicus's model concerns Earth's orbit around the Sun (Item 4 on page 70). The Earth moves so

38. "Riccioli-Cannon," Almagest Novum/Astronomia Reformata of 1651/1665, Wikimedia Commons.

39. Graney, *Setting Aside All Authority*, ch. 3.

quickly around the Sun that it travels about one Earth diameter every seven minutes. Tycho reasoned that if the Earth orbits the Sun, it will be at two diametrically opposite positions relative to the stars at the vernal and autumnal equinoxes. See figure 19 and Earth's position to the left of the Sun. An astronomer on Earth would then see the upper star slightly from the left side. Six months later, Earth would be on the right side of the Sun, and it would appear as if the star had shifted slightly. The same logic was behind the ancient measurement of the distance to the Moon, so all astronomers of the sixteenth and seventeenth centuries knew that this was a good test. Despite diligent searching, no one had managed to observe such a displacement. Tycho assumed the stars were about the same size as the Sun, a reasonable starting point. If the stars he observed were that large, they must be just outside the planets—that is, a few tens of times farther out than the Sun. But if they were so near to Earth, they would have to move if the Earth orbits the Sun, and some of the stars should show seasonal variations (parallax).

Unable to observe this, Tycho instead suggested a slight twist on Copernicus's model. He kept Earth stationary relative to the stars, while the Sun moved. Otherwise, everything was as Copernicus had proposed. This is called the "geoheliocentric model."[40] In this model, Earth is still at the center and has only the Moon and Sun orbiting it, while other planets orbit the Sun. Mathematician and astronomer Nilakantha Somayaji (1444–1544) in Kerala, India, had proposed this model as early as 1501, unknown to Europeans. Tycho presented the model, shown in figure 21, in 1588. It was proposed by several others in Europe around the same time also. Although Tycho believed that Earth was stationary, the model could also be combined with a rotating Earth.

The geoheliocentric model is poorly understood today. Tycho has been accused of preferring it for aesthetic reasons or out of ideological motives, as it aligns more closely with the Bible's presumed assumption of a stationary Earth. However, the scientific arguments were more important. Those who see in Tycho's model nothing more than an attempt to "save" an old view have an insufficient understanding of the science of his time. Therefore, we will revisit the arguments for Tycho's model later.

---

40. *Geo* means earth and *helio* Sun, so the three main classes of models are geocentric, heliocentric, and geoheliocentric.

JOHANNES KEPLER THINKS "GOD'S THOUGHTS"

German Johannes Kepler (1571–1630) was a contemporary of Galileo and a bit younger than Tycho Brahe. He is most famous for his laws stating that planets move in slightly elongated, elliptical orbits with the Sun at one of the foci of a planet's orbit, as shown in figure 22. He also showed that planets move fastest in their orbits when they are closest to the Sun. Indirectly this indicates that the Sun plays a central role and must be the source of a force that governs the planets, in addition to providing light and heat. Here, Kepler saw a glimpse of the gravitational force acting at a distance, which Isaac Newton would later formally present. Kepler was inspired by magnetism, described by the English physician and physicist William Gilbert a few years earlier.

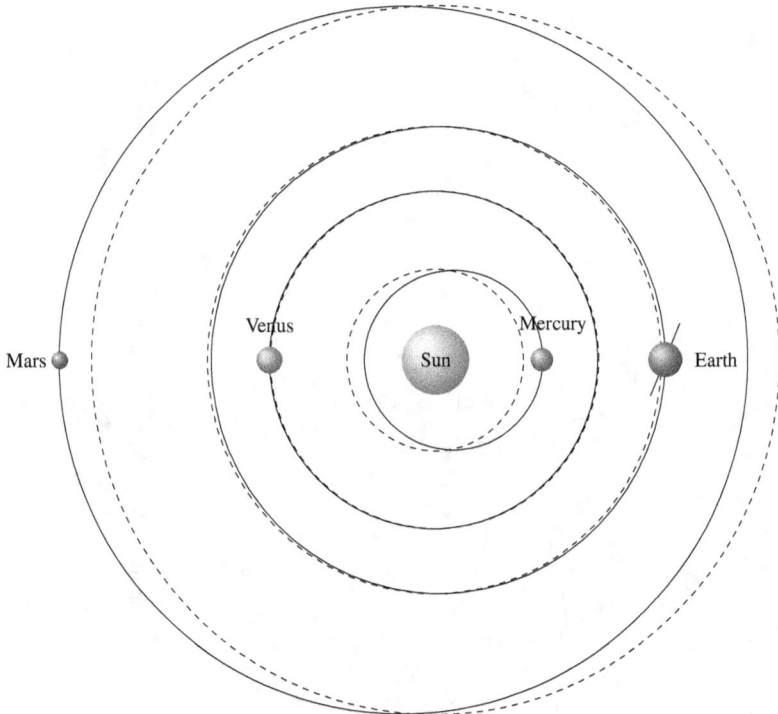

Figure 22. Kepler's elliptical orbits shown in correct scale. The corresponding circular paths are shown with dashed lines. The difference is greatest for Mercury and Mars. The most important effect is the displacement of the center of the path, not that the path is no longer round, because that would not have been visible here. The displacement of the center is also included in Ptolemy's model.

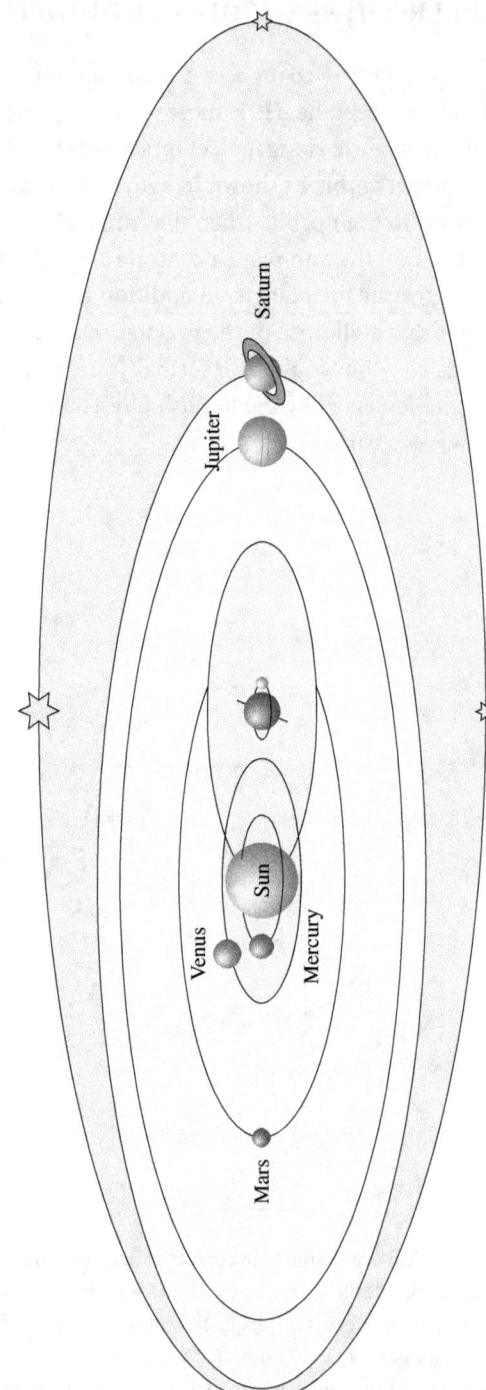

Figure 21. Tycho's geoheliocentric model. It is like Copernicus's model in all essential respects, except that the earth is stationary relative to the stars.

In Pannekoek's history of astronomy, mentioned earlier, Kepler is portrayed as the "first modern scientist." However, it seems that Pannekoek only believes that those researchers who found something still in use today are heroes. This would mean Kepler's achievements are celebrated, but Tycho's contributions will be undervalued. This approach creates a misleading picture of science, overlooking how knowledge is built, brick by brick.

Kepler's Science

Kepler was also a mystic—this is evident in his book *Mysterium Cosmographicum*, which appeared in several editions (1596, 1621). The title can be translated as "the secret of the universe," thereby being an early "theory of everything." This genre continues today with contributions from both Albert Einstein and Stephen Hawking, although Hawking eventually realized that such a theory might not be possible. Kepler tried to fit the five Platonic solids between the orbits of the six (then known) planets.[41] On the one hand, this was entirely new, as he considered Earth as a planet and the Sun at the center as self-evident. In this way, it was a defense of Copernicus's theory, which made Tycho Brahe aware of Kepler. On the other hand, it is very foreign to us today to think that nature is ordered after ideal geometric models.

When Kepler described the refraction of light in 1604, he was the first to use the word *focus* (Latin for "fireplace") for the point where light rays meet. He had a good understanding of optics but did not discover the law of refraction, which we call Snell's law (1621), important for understanding light refraction in optical instruments such as telescopes and microscopes.[42] As a sidenote, it has recently become clear that this law had previously been described by the Persian scholar Ibn Sahl as early as AD 984.[43] After learning about Galileo's discoveries due to the telescope, Kepler was the first to explain how the Dutch (or Galilean) telescope functioned. This became his second major contribution to astronomy, beyond his planetary laws. Kepler also proposed an improved telescope

---

41. The simplest of the five Platonic solids is a cube, where all six sides are equal and square. Tetrahedrons, octahedra, and icosahedrons have four, eight, and twenty triangular sides, respectively. The last of the five is the dodecahedron, with twelve pentagonal sides.

42. Named after Willebrord Snellius, a Dutch mathematician and physicist.

43. Kwan et al., "Who Really Discovered Snell's Law?"

design with a larger field of view. Although Galileo described Kepler's theory as unreadable, it is Kepler's design, not Galileo's, that has become the foundation for the telescopes still in use today.

The book *Astronomia nova* (*New Astronomy*, 1609) is based on Kepler's many years of analysis of Tycho Brahe's data for Mars. This is where his first and second laws are found. Kepler shows that he is much more up to date than Galileo, as we shall see, when he discusses the models of Ptolemy, Copernicus, and Tycho against his own. He also explains in detail that Tycho's and Copernicus's models, despite having different centers, predict exactly the same observations for the planets.

Kepler's vivid imagination is clearly expressed in his writing in support of Galileo's observations of moons around Jupiter. He writes with great conviction that there must be inhabitants on both the Moon and Jupiter. Soon, he believes we will be able to "sail" there, just as we have recently become able to sail across the great oceans. He was surely thinking of the first circumnavigation of the Earth ninety years earlier. Here he was 350 years ahead of his time.

In the book *Harmonices mundi* (*The Harmony of the World*, 1619), only one of the book's pages is devoted to what we today call Kepler's third law. Kepler's books are almost autobiographical, so we know that the discovery occurred on March 8, 1618, but due to a presumed calculation error, he did not believe in the result until May 15. The law states that the planets move slower the farther they are from the Sun, as shown in figure 23. The figure also shows that Earth is just one planet among many, and Kepler's third law states this even more clearly than the first two laws. It emphasizes again the important role of the Sun.

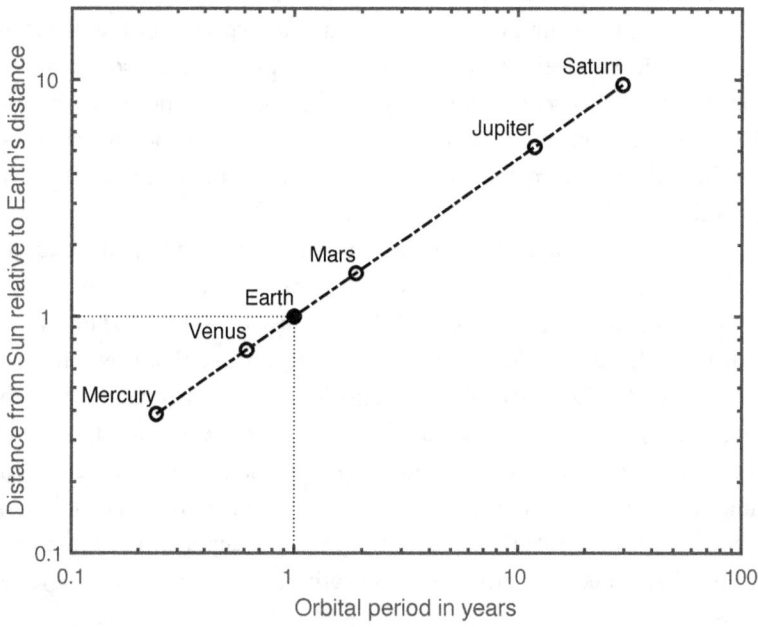

Figure 23. Kepler found the relationship between orbital period and distance from the Sun for the planets. Earth appears here as any other planet, and that is a strong indication that Copernicus's Sun-centered universe is correct.

However, a recent book on science and religion goes too far in interpreting this result when it says that "the final acceptance of the model [i.e., the Copernican model] would have to wait for the detailed work by Kepler in the first two decades of the seventeenth century."[44] If this were true, it would mean that during the Galileo affair, the church opposed an accepted scientific theory. However, this is not right, and Galileo knew this well, as will be evident later.

It would take the theory of gravitation seventy to eighty years later, where Newton showed that Kepler's third law is a consequence of this theory, for Kepler's model to be fully accepted.

The main theme in Kepler's book is otherwise how planetary orbits correspond with musical harmonies in "a music of the spheres." Kepler indicates here that he wanted to make physics beautiful and simple, like in antiquity, but it was the Christian God who was the source of his belief in such harmonic relationships.

44. McGrath, *Science & Religion*, 32.

Kepler's three-volume work *Epitome of Copernican Astronomy* from 1617 to 1621 is the first to provide a complete overview of the heliocentric worldview with elliptical orbits for all the planets. He also discovered that the four moons of Jupiter obey his third law. It is not so surprising that he is proud when he concludes that we now have gained more insight into how the world really is and that we know more of the truth about the universe.

It took time for Kepler's work to be understood by others, and this may be due to the complicated way in which he wrote. Over time, it turned out that Kepler's planetary tables from 1627, dedicated to Emperor Rudolf II (*Tabulae Rudolphinae*), were so precise that they provided good estimates for when Mercury and Venus would transit across the Sun. Such transits were important for calculating the distance to the Sun. They are used even today to find planets in distant solar systems. The tables inspired others to show that even the Moon moves in an elliptical orbit.[45] These tables also contributed to greater acceptance of his theories, but this happened only after Kepler's death.

Kepler and the Church

Kepler might well have felt alienated as a natural philosopher,[46] and this sense of alienation likely applied to the church as well. He was born into a Protestant family in Swabia, in southern Germany, but obtained his first job in Austria. He initially studied the seven liberal arts before taking a degree that prepared him for a career either as a teacher or as a pastor.[47] During his studies, he learned about Copernicus from his teacher Michael Mästlin, and, because he held some unorthodox views on Lutheranism, which we will discuss later, his first job in Graz was that of a mathematics teacher. This was a time when tensions between Catholics and Protestants were escalating, culminating in the Thirty Years' War, which began in 1618. Eventually, Kepler was forced to leave Graz, and later also Linz, when the emperor banned Protestants in Austria.

---

45. Thorvaldsen, "From Keplerian Orbits."

46. Connor, *Kepler's Witch*, which emphasizes Kepler's personal life, describes his alienation.

47. The seven arts were the trivium (three ways), which consisted of grammar, rhetoric, and dialectic; and the quadrivium (four ways), which dealt with astronomy, geometry, arithmetic, and music.

During this chaotic period, science may have been the only place where Kepler found tranquility. His work titled *The Harmony of the World* illustrates how he sought harmony in astronomy. Pascal seems to have felt similarly on the night in 1658 when he reportedly had a severe toothache. Seeking distraction, he turned to a mathematical problem, and the tooth pain was forgotten. Over the course of eight frantic days, he had written down the solution.

Kepler's best time as a natural philosopher may have been when he worked for the Catholic Emperor Rudolf II in Prague, using Tycho's data. His situation would have been much simpler had he converted to the Catholic Church, but his conscience held him back. Kepler himself wished for a reunification of the different denominations, but he wasn't well received by any of them. He was excommunicated from the Lutheran Church in 1619 due to his views on the presence of Jesus in the Eucharist. Here, he believed the other Protestant tradition, Calvinism, was closer to the truth. This was at the start of the Thirty Years' War, so religious statements could be interpreted politically. In the same year, the Catholic Church placed the first volume of his book on the Copernican model on the index, the list of dubious works. The book, however, was quickly reissued in a corrected edition with assurances that it was only a mathematical model.

Kepler's Faith was Deeply Personal

Despite a somewhat strained relationship with the church, Kepler was comfortable quoting the Bible in his writings. Other astronomers did something similar, like Tycho Brahe, who wrote, "The wondrous and perpetual laws of the celestial motions, so diverse and yet so harmonious, prove the existence of God."[48] Galileo also said similar things. Pascal distinguished between the God of the philosophers and the God of Abraham and Isaac (i.e., a personal God), and there is little of the latter in the writings of Tycho and Galileo. It is only Kepler who clearly expresses that his belief in God meant something to him personally. In a letter from 1599, he wrote,

> In the whole material world, God has enacted laws, numbers, and proportions of sublime order and arrangement. . . . These

---

48. From *De disciplinis mathematicis* in 1574 cited in Ruby, "Origins of Scientific 'Law.'"

laws fall within the reach of the human spirit. God intended for us to recognize them when he created us in his image so that we might share in his own thoughts.[49]

This inspires me also, more than four hundred years later, to view my own science as a form of worship. The reference to being "created in God's image" provides, better than anything else, an answer to Einstein's wonder that "the most incomprehensible thing about the world is that it is comprehensible," as mentioned in the introductory chapter. Moreover, Kepler articulates how natural laws are an expression of God's thoughts. Here there is no contradiction between the laws of nature and God, as some atheists depict it.

Kepler calls astronomers "priests of the highest God in regard to the Book of Nature"[50] and thus fully subscribes to the idea of the two books. Nevertheless, it is somewhat unsettling that he places such emphasis on the idea that not just anyone can read the book of nature. This has only been further reinforced in the centuries since, as natural scientists have become a sort of intermediaries between nature and ordinary people. Kepler, regardless, saw God's greatness in nature, specifically in space, and he refers to God in several places as "the divine artist."

Reflecting on his work near the end of *The Harmony of the World*, Kepler expressed satisfaction in gaining insights. He also demonstrates an understanding of his own limitations. Above all, it is a prayer that his work might honor God:

> O you who by the light of nature arouse in us a longing for the light of grace, so that by means of that You can transport us into the light of glory: I give thanks to You, Lord Creator, because You have lured me into the enjoyment of Your work, and I have exulted in the works of Your hands: behold, now I have consummated the work to which I pledged myself, using all the abilities You gave me.
>
> I have shown the glory of Your works to men, and those demonstrations to readers, so far as the meanness of my mind can capture the infinity of it, for my mind was prepared for the most perfect philosophizing.
>
> If anything unworthy of Your deliberations has been proposed by me, a worm, born and raised in a hog-wallow of sin, which You want mankind to know about, inspire me as well

---

49. Letter from 1599 in Baumgardt, *Johannes Kepler*, 50.
50. Baumgardt, *Johannes Kepler*, 44.

to change it. If I have been drawn by the admirable beauty of Your works into indiscretion, or if I have pursued my own glory among men while engaged in a work intended for Your glory, be merciful, be compassionate, and forgive.[51]

He adds this prayer at the very end of *The Harmony of the World*:

> Great is our Lord, and great is His excellence and there is no count of His wisdom. Praise Him heavens; praise Him, Sun, Moon, and Planets, with whatever sense you use to perceive, whatever tongue to speak of your Creator; praise Him, heavenly harmonies, praise Him, judges of the harmonies which have been disclosed; and you also, my soul, praise Him and in Him are all things, "both sensible and intellectual," both those of which we are entirely ignorant and those which we know, a very small part of them, as there is yet more beyond. To Him be praise, honor, and glory from age to age. Amen.[52]

The central role of the Sun in all of Kepler's laws was a strong indication that the heliocentric system had merit. Kepler was therefore on the right track, but he could not explain the role of the Sun within the framework of Aristotelian physics. Kepler's thoughts around cause and effect still make sense today and this makes it all the more tragic that the next natural philosopher we shall meet, Galileo Galilei, completely overlooked Kepler's insights. History might have been different if he had taken the time to understand Kepler's laws and used them, not to prove his case as that wasn't possible, but to substantiate it.

GALILEO GALILEI WAS RIGHT, AND SO WERE HIS CRITICS

Italian Galileo Galilei (1564–1642) was convinced that Copernicus's model, with the Sun at the center, was the correct one, just like Kepler also thought. Galileo was also well versed in the tradition of God's two books and is often quoted for his science-philosophical statement:

> Philosophy is written in this grand book, the universe, which stands continually open to our gaze. But the book cannot be understood unless one first learns to comprehend the language and read the letters in which it is composed. It is written in the language of mathematics, and its characters are triangles, circles

---

51. Stephenson, *Music of the Heavens*, 236.
52. Kepler, *Harmony of the World*, 498.

and other geometric figures without which it is humanly impossible to understand a single word of it; without these, one wanders about in a dark labyrinth.[53]

Perhaps it was the disagreement with the church that made Galileo, even more than Kepler, emphasize that only a few can read the book of nature? It is no longer generally accessible and can only be read by those who understand its language. It is also noteworthy that by the time Galileo entered the scene, several years had passed since Kepler had mathematically formulated his laws. Thus, Galileo's statement here about the "language of mathematics" was already well known. Despite this, it is usually Galileo who is quoted on the importance of mathematics in science. One reason is that Galileo probably was much better at elegant and quotable statements than Kepler. Another reason is that Galileo attempted to elevate the status of mathematicians who were not supposed to deal with physical aspects of nature. This was the domain of philosophers who were ranked higher than mathematicians.[54]

Galileo's conviction about the Copernican model was based on the four moons of Jupiter, which Galileo was among the first to observe. They were, indeed, a clear sign that not everything revolves around the Earth. Moreover, his observations of sunspots showed that the Sun rotates, and therefore the Earth could also rotate. Even clearer was the finding that Venus had phases, just as the Moon could be new, waxing, or full. Even today, I feel excitement and a connection to Galileo and other early astronomers when I see this through my own telescope. The phases of Venus, in particular, are impossible to explain with the traditional model with the Earth at the center.[55]

Desperate for Evidence

There was just one catch with Galileo's conclusion. He was right that the ancient model could not explain the new findings. However, it was not only Copernicus's model that agreed with them; Tycho Brahe's model also agreed with these observations. As mentioned, Tycho's model was a further development of Capella's model from the fifth century, which

---

53. Written in 1623; Tanzella-Nitti, "Two Books Prior," 243.

54. Biagioli, *Galileo, Courtier*, 6.

55. The title for this section has been taken from Olson, "Galileo Was Right—But So Were His Critics."

only had Mercury and Venus orbiting the Sun. Even the ancient Capella model agrees with Galileo's observation of the phases of Venus. All Galileo had shown was that the ancient geocentric model could no longer hold, and this was something most astronomers at the time already agreed on.[56] Therefore statements like this, as found in a recent paper on science and religion and believed by many, makes Galileo's observations more important than Galileo himself thought they were: "There is observational evidence (which Galileo obtained using his telescope) which indicates it is true that the Earth orbits around the Sun."[57]

Both Tycho's model and Capella's old model predict that Venus and Mercury should have phases. Mercury's phases are a bit harder to observe but were spotted by Giovanni Zupi in 1639. As a sidenote, the fact that Zupi was Italian is interesting here because science in Italy did not nearly come to an end after Galileo's trial, as some claim.[58] That is a myth. The research of both Cassini and Riccioli, as mentioned earlier, shows that astronomy actively continued in Italy.[59]

Based on the ambiguity in interpreting Galileo's results, it is understandable that Cardinal Bellarmine asked for clear scientific proof of Copernicus's model. In a letter to the theologian and astronomer Foscarini in 1615, Bellarmine wrote,

> Third, I say that if there were a true demonstration that the Sun is at the center of the world and the Earth in the third heaven,[60] and that the Sun does not circle the Earth but the Earth circles the Sun, then one would have to proceed with great care in explaining the Scriptures that appear contrary, and say rather that we do not understand them than that what is demonstrated is false.

Bellarmine's reference to Galileo "explaining the Scriptures" goes to the heart of what the dispute with the Catholic Church was all about. I shall return to that later.

---

56. This chapter has been inspired by the historian Thony Christie and blog articles of his like "Galileo's Reputation." Christie can hardly be called an apologist, as he is an outspoken atheist, but he is someone who first and foremost wants to get the story told correctly.

57. Loke, "New Fourfold Taxonomy."

58. Gribbin, *Fellowship*, xiv.

59. Brooke, *Science and Religion*, 108–9, says that "this did not prevent Italian scholars from making original contributions" in many fields of science.

60. The order of the planets is Mercury, Venus, and the Earth, so the Earth is in the third sphere or heaven.

It is also worth noting that Bellarmine was open to reinterpreting the Scriptures—for example, a verse like this: "He set the Earth on its foundations; it can never be moved" (Ps 104:5), regarding the Earth standing still, or "In the heavens God has pitched a tent for the Sun. It is like a bridegroom coming out of his chamber, like a champion rejoicing to run his course" (Ps 19:4–5), which seems to say that the Sun moves. Bellarmine thus asks for concrete proof and appears as someone willing to be convinced. Perhaps he was, but it could just as well be that he speaks as one who is convinced that such evidence is not possible to find.

Galileo's Tidal Evidence

Galileo believed he had found this evidence. First, the rotation of the Sun demonstrated that it was possible for celestial bodies to rotate. Galileo's second point, which he himself considered to be the real proof, was described in a letter from 1616 titled "Discourse on the Tides." The daily variation in the tides could only be explained if the Earth rotates and orbits the Sun, Galileo argued. However, this "proof" did not convince many, and that same year, the church decreed—without mentioning Galileo—that the heliocentric model could be discussed as a practical computational model, but not as the truth. Consequently, Copernicus's seventy-year-old book also ended up on the list of books that needed to be corrected. The ten necessary corrections came in 1620, but the implementation was probably somewhat half-hearted. In an examination of nearly all existing copies of Copernicus's book, it turned out that two-thirds of the Italian copies were corrected, but almost no others, not even in Catholic countries like Spain and France.[61]

Galileo's attempt at proof was based on the Earth's orbit around the Sun. Today we know that the Earth travels as fast as 110,000 km per hour, but Galileo probably thought it was less, because he, like everyone else, assumed the distance to the Sun to be much smaller than it actually is. The Earth's daily rotation was easier to calculate accurately—and the result is that the equator moves at 1675 km per hour. Depending on where one is on Earth and the time of day, the speed due to the Earth's rotation will either add to or subtract from the orbital speed. Therefore, Galileo concluded, the water in the ocean would slosh back and forth like water in a moving vessel. Surprisingly, Galileo's model did not initially

---

61. Gingerich, *Book Nobody Read*, 135–51.

involve the Moon, thus dismissing the well-known correlation between the Moon phase and tides.

Ever since antiquity, the correlation between the Moon and the tides had been understood. As previously mentioned, Tycho Brahe pointed this out in his lecture in Copenhagen in 1574. The connection had been analyzed by the Greeks as early as antiquity. The Venerable Bede (672–735) in England analyzed the connection in 725 in the work *De temporum ratione* (*The Reckoning of Time*), where he noted that the tide arrives four-fifths of an hour later each day, just as the Moon also sets four-fifths of an hour later each day. Several Muslim astronomers had described similar connections, including Abu Ma'shar in the ninth century. *The King's Mirror* also mentions the connection with the Moon, and that the difference between high and low tide is smallest at half-moon. Even Johannes Kepler, who lived in Prague in the middle of the European continent and far from the sea, wrote about the connection between the Moon and the tides in *Astronomia nova* in 1609. This book was known to Galileo, as Kepler had sent it to him as part of their correspondence.

Galileo Galilei was already established as a mathematician. He had argued against Aristotle's theory of the speed of falling masses and had made important contributions to mechanics.[62] In 1610, when he was forty-six years old, Galileo wrote the book *Sidereus nuncius* (*The Starry Messenger*). He had made a breakthrough because he was one of the first to use the telescope, an instrument he learned about from the Netherlands. In January 1610, he had a telescope made that could magnify twenty times, slightly more than a regular binocular, and two months later one that could magnify thirty times. These first telescopes were far from ideal and had a very narrow field of view. It required great patience to see planets and stars clearly in them, and the findings could be difficult to verify. Although several people had observed the same things, Galileo was the first to publish that the Moon was like Earth with mountains, craters, and valleys. It was not at all the perfect, smooth sphere Aristotle believed everything from the Moon and beyond was supposed to be. Galileo wrote about all the new stars he could see, particularly in our galaxy, the Milky Way. He described something entirely new he had spotted by Jupiter; the four largest moons. The moons were named after the rich Medici family in Florence. The book made him a celebrity almost

---

62. Aristotle's theory for falling objects is much better than many people think; see, for example, Rovelli, "Aristotle's Physics," for a defense of why this theory often agrees well with experience.

overnight, and he received the financial support from the Medici that he had hoped for and was even elevated to the rank of philosopher.[63] Later that same year, Galileo made the important observation of the phases of Venus, and eventually he also noticed dark spots rotating around the Sun. The heavens were thus not as unchangeable as Aristotle had thought. But Galileo was desperate for a truly convincing argument that everything revolved around the Sun.

Galileo's tidal model was meant to be this proof, and, on the surface, it was both elegant and innovative. Yet it did not provide the breakthrough for Copernicus's theory that he had hoped for, because the model did not predict very well how tides actually behave. It didn't seem to bother Galileo much that high tide in this model always occurred in the middle of the day, and low tide always at midnight. In reality, the tides do not follow the Sun, and they occur roughly twice as often as Galileo suggested. But he believed he had an explanation for that, too, because in the Mediterranean basin the tidal wave would hit land either in the east or in the west and then reflect back. Just like water sloshing back and forth in a vessel, it would create a secondary wave that could explain why there were two and not just one peak per day. Roughly in the middle between east and west, the tide would almost disappear completely, which is actually the case in parts of the Adriatic Sea. The Mediterranean, in general, has very small tidal differences, and they are strongly influenced by the fact that it is a closed sea. Thus, understanding tides there is more complicated than in the Atlantic, and this could explain why Galileo could be so wrong. He probably was also not sufficiently familiar with conditions outside the Mediterranean. To begin with, for example, he claimed that there was only one tide per day in Lisbon, Portugal. This is something we, who live in countries bordering a large open sea, know very well is not true. Later, when he wrote more about this in 1632, he had received so many objections to his Lisbon argument that he dropped it.

In his refined model from 1632, Galileo also considered the tilt of the Earth, and in his model, the difference between high and low tide was greatest at midsummer and midwinter. When he also accounted for the Moon in his model, he concluded that spring tides would occur once a month. However, the fact is that the difference in tides is smallest, not greatest, at midsummer and midwinter. Moreover, spring tides occur

---

63. Biagioli, *Galileo, Courtier*, 134.

twice as often as Galileo's calculations suggested.[64] This probably says something about Galileo's stubbornness, as he continued to cling to his model despite its poor accuracy. I have been in research long enough to have met scientists who are so singularly focused on one thing that they almost become blind to anything outside of it. Some of them are so "infatuated" with their own theory that they become quite uncritical as well, just like it seems that Galileo was.

Galileo and the Church

The story of Galileo Galilei is often the first that comes to mind when the topic of the relation between faith and science is discussed. Galileo was indeed sentenced to life in prison by the Catholic Church in 1633 for defying the 1616 prohibition against treating the heliocentric model as truth rather than just a computational model. The sentence was immediately changed to house arrest under comfortable conditions and probably did not restrict the nearly blind seventy-one-year-old Galileo all that much. He served his sentence in a villa near Florence until his death nine years later. During this time, he wrote *Discourses and Mathematical Demonstrations Relating to Two New Sciences* (1638), which deals with the strength of materials (statics) and motion (dynamics). The book builds on work done before Galileo turned to astronomy around 1610, and here he is among the first to use mathematics to describe motion. It is this book that has had the greatest impact on posterity. In the preface, Galileo mentioned that he had originally not intended to write any more books, due to the disappointment and despondency he had felt after the misfortune that befell his earlier books (i.e., the resistance from the church). It's easy to understand this sentiment.

The Galileo affair is certainly an egregious example of the Catholic Church interfering in matters that it should have left alone. And it's important not to forget that the church stayed out of the way of other contemporaries of Galileo who expressed views similar to his. Much can be understood from Galileo's personality, as we will see in due course. The fact that it was Aristotle's theories that Galileo turned upside down should also mean that the church did not really need to concern itself. At least, that's how it might look to us four hundred years later.

---

64. Naylor, "Galileo's Tidal Theory."

It is worth remembering that the freedom we take for granted today was not at all obvious a few hundred years ago. That was the case in many states of Europe. This example from 1804 in Denmark-Norway is typical. The state's governance was described as follows:

> A totalitarian absolutism, with strict censorship of all printed expressions, with bans on assembly, organization, and travel for the common people, with prohibitions against non-clerical preaching, with systematic cultural and religious standardization by the state.[65]

This is a description of conditions almost two hundred years after Galileo. In Galileo's time, the church was one among many state powers, and it also acted accordingly. It is appropriate also to recall that the leaders of the French Revolution imprisoned one of the most important chemists at the time, Antoine Lavoisier, in 1793. Contrary to Galileo, he was not given house arrest but was executed by guillotine the following year. Rehabilitation did not come until 1889.[66]

The Galileo story continues in 1712, when the prohibition against books stating that the Earth moves was no longer enforced.[67] Until then, Italian natural philosophers like Riccioli and Cassini had avoided trouble by describing Copernicus's system as a computational model that was not in accordance with reality. The final lifting of the prohibition against books stating that the Earth moves came in 1757, and in 1820 the church ensured that a textbook was printed which confirmed the Earth's orbit around the Sun. The ban against Galileo's book was formally removed in 1837. It was not around 1981–1992 as some claim. What happened then was that the case was reviewed anew, and Pope John Paul II apologized by saying,

> The problem posed by theologians of that age was, therefore, that of the compatibility between heliocentrism and Scripture. Thus the new science, with its methods and the freedom of research which they implied, obliged theologians to examine their

---

65. Address at the tomb of the Norwegian lay minister, spiritual leader, business entrepreneur, social reformer, and author Hans Nielsen Hauge on Norway's national day, May 17, 2018. Gundersen, "Forandringens fellesskap" [Community of change], para. 17.

66. See Smeaton, "French Scientists," for the account of Lavoisier. Another with a similar fate was the mathematician Condorcet, who was driven to suicide in 1794. Just as with Galileo, their fates can be explained by many other factors than science alone.

67. Heilbron, *Galileo*, 207.

own criteria of scriptural interpretation. Most of them did not know how to do so.

Paradoxically, Galileo, a sincere believer, showed himself to be more perceptive in this regard than the theologians who opposed him. "If Scripture cannot err," he wrote to Benedetto Castelli, "certain of its interpreters and commentators can and do so in many ways."[68]

Pope John Paul II continued by saying,

> From the beginning of the Age of Enlightenment down to our own day, the Galileo case has been a sort of "myth," in which the image fabricated out of the events was quite far removed from reality.... The clarifications furnished by recent historical studies enable us to state that this sad misunderstanding now belongs to the past.[69]

Surprisingly, history has shown that the Catholic Church has, for the most part, been positively disposed toward science. Science historian Heilbron says it—with a small reservation—like this:

> The Roman Catholic Church gave more financial and social support to the study of astronomy for over six centuries, from the recovery of ancient learning during the late Middle Ages into the Enlightenment, than any other, and probably all, institutions. Those who infer the Church's attitude from its persecution of Galileo may be reassured to know that the basis of its generosity to astronomy was not a love of science but a problem of administration. The problem was establishing and promulgating the date of Easter.[70]

Heilbron's comment on Easter relates to its timing on "the first Sunday after the first full Moon following the vernal equinox," which requires accurate astronomy for calendars to be made many years in advance.

The Galileo affair, like the French Revolution's treatment of Lavoisier, was a rather isolated case.[71] Four reasons stand out as potential explanations for the unfortunate outcome and will be discussed in detail below:

1. Galileo engaged in private interpretation of the Bible

---

68. Pontifical Academy of Sciences, *Papal Addresses*, 339.
69. Pontifical Academy of Sciences, *Papal Addresses*, 341.
70. Heilbron, *Sun in the Church*, 3.
71. See Hannam, *Genesis of Science*, chs. 19–21, for a more complete story of Galileo.

2. His personality
3. He completely ignored other related works
4. He took a rather light view of "proofs" as long as they supported his own opinion

First, Galileo's relationship with the Bible must be understood in light of a century of conflicts between Catholics and Protestants. Protestants, after all, emphasized that individuals could interpret the Bible independently of the church. Galileo shared his thoughts on how the Bible should be read in a letter to a former student in December 1613. This letter was published, and a little over a year later, it was reported to the church authorities. Here Galileo was quoted as saying, "In the Scripture one finds many propositions which are false if one goes by the literal meaning of the words."[72] Galileo continued by asserting that this was so in order to be understood by common people. The undiplomatic expression "false propositions" was a direct challenge to the Catholic Church's monopoly on interpretation.

A week after the report, Galileo defended himself and wrote that the person who had copied the letter had deliberately altered it to put him in a worse light. He explained that what he actually had written was that "in the Scripture one finds many propositions which look different from the truth if one goes by the literal meaning of the words."[73]

In 2018, a manuscript was discovered that changed the entire picture. The letter was archived under the wrong year in London, which may have been the reason it has not been known until now. The letter showed revisions from the letter's critical version to a milder one, not the opposite. The remarkable thing is that the revisions were made in Galileo's own handwriting.[74] The discovery shows that it was Galileo himself who edited it to deceive the Inquisition. He toned down the claims and then lied about his edits. Here was a man who successfully had moved from being a mere mathematician to being a philosopher at the Medici court. Now he was trying to obtain the patronage of the most powerful court

---

72. Camerota et al., "Reappearance of Galileo's Original Letter," 15.
73. Camerota et al., "Reappearance of Galileo's Original Letter," 15.
74. The twelve most important corrections can be found in Camerota et al., "Reappearance of Galileo's Original Letter." The find is also reported in the more popular Abbott, "Discovery of Galileo's Long-Lost Letter."

of them all, but his undiplomatic ways made sure that he would never obtain this favor from the pope.[75]

About a year later, Galileo wrote a forty-page letter to the Grand Duchess Christina of the Medici court (1615). The often quoted "The intention of the Holy Ghost is to teach us how one goes to heaven, not how heaven goes" comes from here.[76] It's important to note that although Galileo was in conflict with the church, he did not perceive this as a conflict between the new science and the Bible. The quote is used in our time to show how sensible Galileo was to separate the essential from the nonessential. He had learned this from cardinal and church historian Caesar Baronius a few years earlier.

Not everything Galileo wrote about the Bible has held up to scrutiny. In the mentioned letter, he tried to make his new worldview align with the account of the Sun standing still in the sky during one of Israel's battles.[77] He believed that the Sun's rotation, which he himself had discovered, gave rotation to the other planets as well. Therefore, he explained the whole event by the Sun ceasing its rotation for a few hours. This is a rather unscientific argument and appears as an attempt to force the Bible to align with science (concordism).

When interpretations of the Bible came from a mathematician or astronomer during one of the tensest periods in European history, during the Counter-Reformation just before the Thirty Years' War, they sounded like Protestant undermining of the church's authority. Such statements about Scripture were the background for Cardinal Bellarmine's warning in 1616, and for the requirement to correct Copernicus's book. However, Galileo himself wasn't tried until 1633. The Thirty Years' War (1618–1648) was now raging in Europe, ostensibly as a conflict between Protestants and Catholics, but just as much as a showdown between the great powers. The Swedish King Gustavus Adolphus invaded Germany in the summer of 1630, and over the course of the following year, the Protestant Swedes constantly won victories over the Catholics, with support from France, which paradoxically was itself Catholic. In the spring of 1632, Swedish troops invaded Bavaria in the south of Germany, and even though the Swedish king himself was killed in November that year, the progress continued. The following year there was fear that the Swedes

---

75. Biagioli, *Galileo, Courtier*, 248 and 313.

76. Drake, *Discoveries*, 186.

77. Josh 10:12, 14. A possible explanation is in Humphreys and Waddington, "Solar Eclipse of 1207 BC."

could even enter Italy itself, and in June 1633, the verdict against Galileo fell. It thus came at a time when the church and the pope were under perhaps the greatest pressure in their entire history.[78]

John Milton, the English Puritan who visited Galileo in Florence five years after his trial, must also be interpreted in the context of these conflicts. He wrote that he found the famous Galileo in old age, essentially a prisoner of the Inquisition for thinking differently about astronomy than the Franciscans and Dominicans. This encounter and perspective provided long-lasting ammunition against Catholics at a time when skepticism toward anything associated with Catholicism ran deep, especially in England following the wars against Spain and the Gunpowder Plot of 1605 which aimed to blow up the English Parliament. As the years passed, such arguments against the Catholics, unfortunately, came to be used as arguments against any form of faith, Protestant as well as Catholic.

Second, Galileo was a rather arrogant and assertive individual. Both his suppression of observations that did not confirm his own hypothesis (see next section) and the white lie about the diplomatic letter being corrected by others emphasize this. Pope Urban VIII was also not the easiest person to deal with. His birth name was Maffeo Barberini, and he was originally a friend of Galileo, becoming a cardinal in 1606. Galileo had reason to believe that his friend's elevation to pope in 1623 would make things easier for him, but he himself contributed a great deal to the eventual difficulties. In Galileo's book *Dialogue Concerning the Two Chief World Systems* from 1632, he recounts a discussion between three people: Salviati, who supported Copernicus; Sagredo, who is intelligent and initially neutral; and Simplicio, who defends the old geocentric system. Both the name and the nature of his arguments show how foolish Simplicio's reasoning is. The similarity to Pope Urban VIII's arguments is striking, and so may the alleged insult have been.[79]

Third, Galileo in his science only considered the models of antiquity and Copernicus. He disregarded everything Johannes Kepler had proposed and neither did he engage Tycho Brahe's model. His relationship with Kepler is interesting and well-documented through their correspondence. Galileo had mentioned Kepler's work in optics when he wrote a book about his discoveries with the telescope in 1610 and he had sent the book to Kepler. Kepler responded by publishing an enthusiastic

---

78. Miller, "Thirty Years War."
79. Biagioli, *Galileo, Courtier*, 339.

paper, which he titled *Conversation with the Starry Messenger*, endorsing Galileo's observations. Nevertheless, Kepler must have been disappointed when he sent Galileo his significant observation of elliptical orbits in his *Astronomia nova* in 1609, and Galileo did not respond. In *Dialogue Concerning the Two Chief World Systems*, Galileo even went so far as to write that we do not know the orbits that the planets follow. He had little interest in the advanced astronomy of Tycho and Kepler and always began with the works of the ancient Greeks.

Fourth, Galileo believed he could prove Copernicus's model. Unfortunately for him, here his neglect of Kepler's work really proved decisive as Kepler's third law about the relationship between orbital period and distance from the Sun points much more clearly to the Sun being at the center than Galileo's erroneous tidal argument. It is Galileo's lack of evidence for his claims that I am highlighting here. This is the most mythologized and least known aspect of the conflict between Galileo and the church, and the astronomer Christopher Graney has recently brought to light new material that sheds fresh insight on it; this chapter builds on his work.

One person who exploited Galileo to the fullest was the Enlightenment philosopher François-Marie Arouet, better known as Voltaire. As mentioned, Galileo was neither imprisoned nor had he proven Earth's motion. Yet Voltaire referred to him in 1734 as "the great Galileo, at the age of fourscore, groaned away his days in the dungeons of the Inquisition, because he had demonstrated by irrefragable proofs the motion of the Earth."[80] Similar statements are still heard today.

What surprises me most in writing this chapter is that Galileo actually had a rather weak case scientifically. Since the heliocentric model ultimately emerged as the victor, this may sound strange. It is far too easy to interpret the past in light of the present and focus solely on the end result, as Voltaire does, and not on the status of proofs at the time of Galileo. Therefore, we will once more delve into the astronomical science of the time.

The Double Star Test

Like other astronomers, Galileo was keen to find the seasonal variation in a star's position, parallax, to finally confirm Copernicus's model. Very accurate angle measurements are needed to register a star's movement

---

80. Voltaire, "Lettre XIV," 129.

from summer to winter, and Galileo's measuring methods did not have the required precision. However, there is a better test, and Galileo himself had described it in 1632. Instead of using measurements of absolute angle, it would be much simpler to record how two nearby stars move relative to each other. Although such a binary star appears as a pair, the fainter one is usually farther away from us than the brighter one.

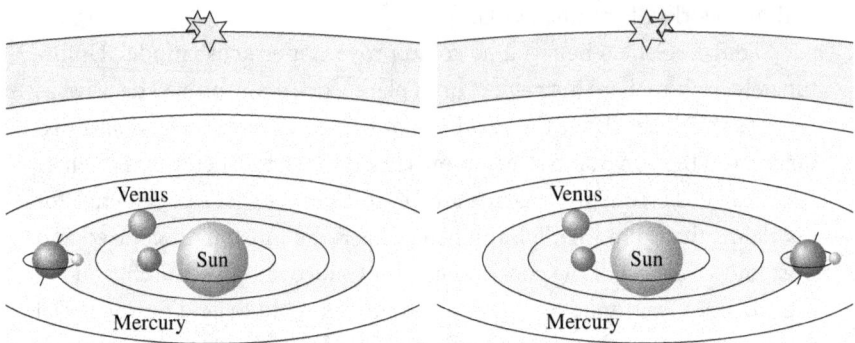

Figure 24. *Left*, Copernicus's model with the Earth in summer position. The farthest star appears to be to the left of the nearest star when viewed from Earth. *Right*, in winter, the farthest star appears to be to the right of the nearest star when viewed from Earth.

Galileo had correctly written that in such a case, it should be possible to register the stars moving in relation to each other over the course of the year (see figure 24). He referred to it as a hypothetical case, as if he had presumably not himself discovered such a pair. It has recently become clear from Galileo's notes that he in fact had found several of these binary stars.[81] One of them is Mizar, which is located in the middle of the "handle" of the Big Dipper. He had observed Mizar as early as 1617. At that time, he estimated that one star should be 300 times farther away than the Sun and the other 450 times farther away. Seen from Earth, therefore, these stars should switch positions relative to each other over the course of the year, as the figure shows. However, Galileo had not registered any such change, a result he chose not to report. Presumably, he may have been so convinced that the elegant Copernican system was correct, that he was willing to overlook evidence to the contrary.

81. Graney, "But Still, It Moves."

Optical Effects Made Space Too Small

We know today that Galileo's estimates, like those of Tycho Brahe, for the distances from Earth to the two stars in Mizar were far too small. This stemmed from a poor understanding of the relationship between the size of a star and the size seen by the naked eye or through a telescope. Astronomers thought the relationship was simple and that the larger the spot of light, the larger the star. This holds true for objects that are large enough, but when it comes to small objects like stars, the relationship is far more complex. For such objects, the measured size will depend both on the star's brightness and on the aperture of the telescope or the size of the eye observing it. This complication was not understood in the seventeenth century. As a result:

- The size of the Moon and the Sun appear correctly to the naked eye.
- Planets appear too large when seen with the naked eye but are the right size through seventeenth-century telescopes. Hence, the phases of Venus can be seen with even the simplest telescopes, but not with the naked eye.
- The apparent size of stars will vary with brightness, but they will seem to be about one thirtieth of the size of the Sun with the naked eye and a few hundredths of the size of the Sun with early telescopes. In both cases, they appear far too large.[82]

The fact that small objects appear too large is due to a phenomenon known as diffraction, which can be explained by the fact that light behaves like waves. It wasn't until 1835 before the full explanation of this limitation was given.[83] It's the size of the aperture, whether it's the pupil of the eye or the lens of the telescope, which ultimately determines the apparent size of small objects. This applies to all wave phenomena, from light to medical ultrasound and radio waves. This insight, however, was unknown to both Tycho and Galileo, and even after it was explained it

---

82. The large ten-meter telescopes that exist now are approaching what is needed to give a true image, but then there are other effects that complicate matters, such as disturbances in the atmosphere.

83. The size of the eye means that no point in the sky can appear smaller than approximately one minute of arc. This does not affect the Moon and Sun, which are both about 0.5 degrees or 30 arc minutes. The five visible planets, on the other hand, cover much less than a minute of arc, and their true sizes can only be assessed by telescope. George Airy came up with the correct description of diffraction in 1835.

took a long time for astronomers to fully understand the implications of this insight.[84]

A convenient way to save the Copernican system was to think that the stars are so far away that seasonal movement is imperceptible with simple instruments. That is indeed how we understand it today, but based on the knowledge of the seventeenth century, the stars would then need to be correspondingly larger. They would have to be hundreds of times bigger than a typical star like the Sun, meaning they would actually have to be larger than even Earth's orbit around the Sun which has a diameter of 215 suns. Surprisingly enough, proponents of Copernicus could say that such large stars were no problem since God is so great! Copernicus had also used this argument, but neither Tycho nor Riccioli, despite being a Jesuit priest, were willing to incorporate such arguments into a scientific theory.[85] Interestingly, it was the "new" Copernican theory that required this supernatural addition, not the geocentric theory.

Copernicus's Model After Galileo

In the seventeenth century, there were three main classes of models of the planetary system: (a) the *geocentric* picture from antiquity, (b) the *geoheliocentric* models of Tycho Brahe and others, and (c) the *heliocentric* models of Copernicus and Kepler.[86] Today, we of course know the answer. It was neither Tycho's model nor Copernicus's model that lasted, but rather Kepler's version of Copernicus's model with elliptical orbits. This is the second of the models that Galileo did not bother with. In hindsight, even Kepler's model has been improved, as not everything follows simple elliptical orbits; these actually only apply when a single planet is alone with the Sun.

---

84. This presentation is based on Danielson and Graney, "Case Against Copernicus," and the more detailed account in Graney, "Objects in Telescope"; Graney, "Telescope Against Copernicus"; and Graney and Grayson, "On the Telescopic Disks of Stars."

85. This is discussed in detail in Graney, *Setting Aside All Authority*, ch. 5.

86. This ends up being at least nine different models: (A) *Geocentric*—1. Ptolemy; 2. Ptolemy with rotating earth. (B) *Geoheliocentric*—3. Capella with Mercury and Venus around the Sun; 4. Somayaji and Tycho with all planets except Earth in orbit around the Sun; 5. Longomontanus's model which is Tycho's, only with a rotating Earth; 6. Riccioli with Mercury, Venus and Mars in orbit around the Sun as shown in figure 15 of this chapter; 7. Riccioli who later combines Tycho's model with elliptical orbits. (C) *Heliocentric*—8. Copernicus with circular orbits; 9. Kepler with elliptical orbits.

By the 1660s, twenty years after Galileo's death, the opinion among scholars was beginning to shift in Kepler's direction and away from Tycho's model. This was due to some comet observations and also a book by Nicolaus Mercator in 1664 that provided a better formulation of Kepler's second law.[87] Moreover, with Cassini's measurement of the distance to Mars in 1672, a new understanding of the size of the solar system began to take hold. Now that the relationship between planetary orbits was known, it was also possible to calculate the distance to the Sun and how much larger it was than previously thought. When Newton introduced his theory of gravity in 1687, the Sun—being so much larger than the planets—became the central "engine" of the planetary system, as Kepler had assumed, and consequently the natural center of our solar system.

The problem with seasonal shifting of stellar position (parallax) remained unsolved for a long time, until Friedrich Wilhelm Bessel managed to measure it in 1838 after twenty-eight years of work. The star he measured was eleven light-years away.[88] This is seven hundred thousand times farther away than the Sun, not a few hundred or thousand times, as was assumed based on simple telescope observations in the seventeenth century. Nevertheless, Earth's orbit around the Sun was confirmed before this, due to a phenomenon called aberration. It resembles the experience of rain falling more and more at an angle the faster one runs in the rain. This was discovered by astronomer and priest James Bradley in 1725–1727 and was the first demonstration that the Earth moves, close to a century after Galileo's time.

Newton also launched a way to measure Earth's rotation in *Principia* in 1687.[89] He postulated that the Earth would be slightly flattened at the poles. This was not measured until the French surveying expedition led by Maupertuis went to Lapland, Northern Sweden, in 1736.

The history of Tycho's model is a reminder that it's not only the victorious theories that teach us how science develops. There's just as much to learn from the process around theories that eventually had to give way. Galileo did not point his telescope at the sky and observed that Copernicus's theories were correct. Such a claim is actually false. When Galileo's research still stands as a valuable contribution in the history of science, it is due just as much to his contributions in mechanics. The Galileo affair

---

87. Christie, "Emergence of Modern Astronomy."
88. A light-year is the distance light travels in one year.
89. Newton, *Principia*, bk. 3, prop. 19, prob. 3.

is a result of projecting the Enlightenment image of conflict between faith and science back in time and distorting history in light of it. That is a very unfortunate way of dealing with the history of science.

4

The History of Life and the Universe

> The stars lost their divinity as astronomy developed.... But that is not the whole story. It is not the greatest of modern scientists who feel most sure that the object, stripped of its qualitative properties and reduced to mere quantity, is wholly real. Little scientists, and little unscientific followers of science, may think so. The great minds know very well that the object, so treated, is an artificial abstraction, that something of its reality has been lost.
>
> C. S. Lewis, *Abolition of Man*

HISTORIAN TOM HOLLAND RECOUNTS how his childhood faith began to show cracks when he was six years old. He had come across a children's Bible that depicted dinosaurs and humans living side by side. Already then, he was convinced that no human had ever seen a dinosaur, but no Sunday school teacher seemed to care about this contradiction. Such a reaction may be due to the uncertainty of some Christians about what to think regarding the age of the Earth and life and whether it is possible to take the Bible seriously while also accepting science that claims the Earth is billions of years old.

It also concerns two of the least intuitive aspects of modern natural science: determining the age of the Earth and determining the distance to stars. The latter was a topic, as we saw in the previous chapter, already during the time of Tycho and Galileo. It wasn't until the twentieth century that we could conclude regarding age and distances. Like other sciences from the last century, such as relativity theory and quantum physics, they have little to do with everyday life. They are based on complex theories concerning radioactivity and the life cycles of stars and are therefore inaccessible to most people.

The legacy from Aristotle was the belief that both the Earth and life had always been there and, in addition, a cyclical view of life. Life was not seen as so complicated because most believed that simpler forms of life could arise spontaneously. In contrast, the Bible said that both the world and life had a beginning. These were competing beliefs, and there was no scientific method to determine and prove whether the Earth was eternal or not.

In the nineteenth century, it finally became possible to say something about the history of life based on empirical data. The uncovering of this history and the rejection of spontaneous creation therefore weakened the Greek view. Similarly, the idea of the big bang, proposed in 1931 by the physicist and priest Georges Lemaître, challenged the Greek universe, which seemingly had neither a beginning nor an end. Today's knowledge about a finite age for the universe and for life, therefore, fits better with a creation perspective than with the eternal universe.

In this chapter, I will first delve into the legacy from the Greeks and then what science discovered about the history of life, about how life can arise, and about the history of the universe.

ETERNAL UNIVERSE OR A BEGINNING?

Eternal and Cyclical Universe

The ancient view was that the world and life had always existed and that there had been no beginning. Some of the earliest Greek philosophers, the Pythagoreans,[1] also believed that everything would return to what it once was, and that this process would continue indefinitely.[2] This belief

---

1. Followers of Pythagoras, 570–495 BC.
2. Much of the material on eternal cycles is based on Van der Waerden, "Great Year."

has much in common with reincarnation, as known from Indian thought. The Pythagoreans held this idea so concretely that Eudemus[3] could say that, in the future, he would stand exactly where he stands now, with the same staff in his hand and with the same listeners who would hear him speak. Stoic philosophers held the same view.[4] They predicted that the planets would give rise to a great destruction, after which the Earth would be recreated; Plato and Socrates would return, and everything would repeat both in the heavens and on Earth.

Thus, antiquity emphasized two characteristics of our universe: (1) it is eternal, and (2) all events repeat at regular intervals. The idea of the eternal universe has persisted up to our own time. So deeply ingrained was this belief that Einstein felt compelled to add an extra term to the equation of general relativity to keep the universe stable and eternal. He would later call this his greatest blunder.[5]

The second characteristic is the repetitions. It is quite natural to think that events repeat, as this is something we observe everywhere: day alternates with night, Moon phases come and go, and the seasons change. It shows how obvious it is for us to think in cycles. The orbits of the planets repeat with periods ranging from four months to just over two years from Earth's perspective. The Saros cycle, a little over eighteen years, which is the time between lunar eclipses, has been known since Babylonian times. An impressively long astronomical period of 25,800 years was already discovered in antiquity. This is the Earth's precession, which implies that the Earth's north-south axis wobbles slightly, just as a spinning top.[6] The Greeks understood that the North Star, which today stands at the northern celestial pole, did not do so when the Egyptians built the pyramids, nor will it do so in a few thousand years. This slight wobble is due to the influence of the Sun, the Moon, and especially Jupiter among the planets.

We can also think of a person who is born and dies, while the children continue to live and repeat the life cycle. Everything follows this pattern, from life to death and from summer to winter. Today, we do not

---

3. Eudemus of Rhodes, ca. 370–300 BC.

4. Stoicism was (and is) a popular Greek philosophy founded by Zeno of Cyprus (334–262 BC).

5. Some doubt that Einstein said this, but most likely it is true; O'Raifeartaigh and Mitton, "Interrogating the Legend."

6. Discovered by Hipparchus (190–120 BC).

think that the life cycle has anything to do with the planets, but this has been linked together in astrological traditions in many cultures.

Plato called the universe's cycle the Perfect Year, and Aristotle called it the Great Year. There are many different durations given for this cycle, including 10,800, 120,000, and 3,600,000 years. As in ordinary calendar years, the seasons alternate, and there are times of prosperity and periods of disaster and flood. Similar ideas can be found in nearly all ancient cultures: Greek, Babylonian, Persian, Indian, Chinese, and among the Mayans. This also plays a role with the Persian Al-Biruni (973–1048), who attempted to find the time of the great flood based on the positions of the planets and astrology. In his Muslim culture, this was Noah's flood, which is mentioned both in the Quran and the Bible.

Science historians often mention the idea of the Greeks' eternal universe.[7] They do not discuss as often the eternal cycles, but there are exceptions.[8] One who has particularly focused on the importance of the cycles is the American Hungarian Catholic priest, physicist, and philosopher of science Stanley Jaki (1924–2009). He points out that, in Greek thought, the heavens were divine while the Earth was chaotic. Norse mythology has similar beliefs, a pantheistic way of thinking that cannot separate between the divine and nature. The study of astrology is therefore in some sense the study of the divine. It is not dead matter that is being studied, but a world that is a living organism. Jaki thus describes the Greek mythological worldview as both pantheistic and animistic.[9]

Such a belief in repetition and predestination makes the astrological examination of stars and planets important. The purpose would be to find out where one is in the cycle and whether we are moving toward worse or better times, "winter" or "summer." This is diametrically opposite to how we think today. Contemporary science is instead about a nature that behaves in a regular way, without necessarily repeating itself, and where the laws of nature are understandable.

---

7. See, for example, Grant, *Foundations of Modern Science*, 54–69, and Lindberg, *Beginnings of Western Science*, 45–66. Lindberg also discusses Aristotle's determinism in ch. 10.

8. Notable exceptions are Kragh, *Entropic Creation*, ch. 1, and Badash, "Age-of-the-Earth Debate."

9. Stanley Jaki is considered a controversial historian by some due to his sometimes apologetic points of view, but he has some really good insights. His books, like *Science and Creation*, may be hard to read, but the summary in Trasancos, *Science Was Born of Christianity*, or the abridgment by Jeynes, "Science and Creation," are easier.

A Universe with a Beginning

The theory of an eternal universe was not without its critics. As early as ancient Greece, some pointed to the mountains that were continually worn down by weather and wind. Wouldn't all mountains have disappeared and all valleys have been filled in if the world had existed for eternity? Since this was not the case, the Earth could not always have been the same. Others, like the Roman poet and philosopher Lucretius (ca. 95–55 BC), argued that human history was known only for a few thousand years. If humans had always been here, where was their history?[10]

The creation narrative in the beginning of the Bible also contrasts with the idea of the eternal universe. It was understood that before the world was formed, God existed. God exists in himself, independently of nature. He is not a part of nature as in pantheism. Only God is eternal, not nature or the universe. There was also a time when neither the Earth, the planets, the Sun and Moon, sea creatures and birds, land animals, nor humans existed. The Sun, Moon, and stars are lights placed there by God; they are not divine and do not determine our fate. All this is entirely opposite to what Aristotle and the neighboring cultures around Israel stood for.

Thus, it is not surprising that the church fathers in the first centuries advocated for a created Earth. A typical opponent of this view was the Greek Proclus (412–485), who presented eighteen arguments for an eternal Earth. He used these to attack the Christian belief in creation. John Philoponus, whom we encountered in the previous chapter's discussion of impetus, defended creation in his discussion of Proclus's arguments. At the same time, he provided arguments for why the Greek idea of a great divide between a divine heaven and a chaotic Earth was wrong. However, no one could provide empirical data that indicated whether the Earth was eternal or not.

In the Middle Ages, this question was considered impossible to resolve, and it was taken as good science that the Earth was eternal. Thomas Aquinas argued convincingly that even an eternal world needs a creator. It needs something outside itself as a reason for its existence. In 1277, Archbishop Étienne Tempier in Paris, then Europe's intellectual center, issued 219 theses condemning some of Aristotle's doctrines. Twenty-seven of the theses asserted that the world is not eternal, others stated that it is possible for something to be created from nothing, that God can

---

10. Kragh, *Entropic Creation*, ch. 2.

create something entirely new independently of astrology, that history will not repeat itself every thirty-six thousand years, and that the world is not an organism.

Pierre Duhem believed that these condemnations were so important that 1277 can almost be regarded as a starting point for modern natural science, as mentioned in the previous chapter. Other historians strongly disagree, but the American historian Edward Grant (1926–2020), a specialist in the Middle Ages, takes a middle position. In his view, these condemnations broadened the horizons of natural philosophers and made medieval science more interesting than it otherwise would have been.[11]

The Bible opposes the idea that the world is eternal when it says, "In the beginning, God created the heavens and the Earth" (Gen 1:1).[12] Such a beginning is common to the three monotheistic religions: Judaism, Christianity, and Islam. But it is only in Christianity that not only a prophet, but God himself, came to Earth. The uniqueness of Jesus Christ coming into the world at a specific time made it even clearer that history does not proceed in eternal cycles. This has contributed to what seems obvious today—namely, the Western way of thinking where history has a start and an end and does not repeat itself.

Perhaps our ancestors did not reflect much on it when they set Jesus's birth as the start of our era, but it is nonetheless a reminder of our belief in a linear historical trajectory from a beginning to an end. The end is clearly present in the Bible as well, when Jesus says, "Heaven and Earth will pass away, but my words will never pass away" (Matt 24:35). The moments of creation, Jesus's birth, and God's judgment over the world are thus crucial events that tell us more than anything else that history does not repeat itself in a predetermined way.

Nonetheless, the cyclical worldview lived side by side with the biblical one in early science. Belief in astrology is a remnant of such a worldview. This was something natural philosophers we consider modern today—such as Tycho Brahe, Johannes Kepler, Galileo Galilei, and Isaac Newton—also were concerned with. Even in the 1856 discussion between the physicist Heinrich Helmholtz and the philosopher Karl Rosenkranz, the latter argued for an organic and cyclical worldview where things progressively become better and better.[13]

---

11. Grant, *Foundations of Modern Science*, 70–85.

12. For more on the meaning of "beginning," see Walton, *Lost World of Genesis One*, 38–53.

13. Kragh, *Entropic Creation*, 37.

I am sure Thomas Aquinas would have been surprised that it would eventually become possible to scientifically show that the Earth and life are not eternal. That was indeed what happened in the nineteenth century.

Six Thousand Years?

Two of the greatest authorities in the Middle Ages were the Bible and Aristotle. Even those who did not read the Bible as science could not avoid noticing that the two said completely different things. Either the Earth had a beginning, which according to a literal reading of the Bible was quite recent, or life was eternal and cyclical. In the absence of other knowledge, these were the only sources to turn to. Johannes Kepler, for example, concluded that creation occurred in 3992 BC. He likely had the majority of Christians with him in the belief that the Earth was about that old. There were also those who allowed for interpreting the six days of creation as something other than concrete twenty-four-hour days. The church fathers opened up for this, and Augustine (354–430) warned against placing too much emphasis on the apparent science in the Bible:

> Usually, even a non-Christian knows something about the Earth, the heavens, and the other elements of the world, about the motion and orbit of the stars and even their size and relative positions, about the predictable eclipses of the Sun and Moon, the cycles of the years and the seasons, about the kinds of animals, shrubs, stones, and so forth, and this knowledge he holds to as being certain from reason and experience.
>
> Now, it is a disgraceful and dangerous thing for an infidel to hear a Christian, presumably giving the meaning of Holy Scripture, talking nonsense on these topics; and we should take all means to prevent such an embarrassing situation, in which people show up vast ignorance in a Christian and laugh it to scorn.[14]

Behind Augustine's conviction lies a respect for natural science and the belief that reason and experience can provide certain knowledge. At the same time, he warns against setting natural science in opposition to a superficial reading of the Bible. Before him, one of the early church theologians, Origen (185–254), explicitly stated that the story of creation should not be read literally:

---

14. Augustine, *Literal Meaning of Genesis*, 42–43.

> What intelligent person would fancy, for instance, that a first, second, and third day, evening and morning, took place without Sun, Moon, and stars; and the first, as we call it, without even a heaven? Who would be so childish as to suppose that God after the manner of a human gardener planted a garden in Eden towards the east, and made therein a tree, visible and sensible, so that one could get the power of living by the bodily eating of its fruit with the teeth; or again, could partake of good and evil by feeding on what came from that other tree? If God is said to walk at eventide in the garden, and Adam to hide himself under the tree, I fancy that no one will question that these statements are figurative, declaring mysterious truths by the means of a seeming history, not one that took place in a bodily form.[15]

This can be read in his book *On the First Principles*, from sometime before AD 231. Origen came from Egypt and suffered several years of imprisonment and torture for his faith. What he says here might give the impression that he speaks derogatorily of the creation story. But Origen is considered one of antiquity's foremost theologians. He is honored by all church communities—although he was also controversial. Swedish theologian Peter Halldorf calls him one of the world's greatest thinkers and theologians. He also mentions that Origen may have gone a step too far in synthesizing Greek philosophy and Christian faith, but also that among the spiritual teachers of the early centuries, Origen stands in a class of his own.[16]

Both Augustine and Origen suggest that the story of creation can be read with a certain amount of freedom. The ancient church creeds, which nearly all church communities adhere to, seem to confirm this stance, as they affirm that God is the creator of heaven and Earth but remain silent on when or how this happened.

As mentioned earlier, people in the Middle Ages were likely more concerned with the meaning behind events than with precisely how or when something happened. This changed in the early modern period. The language of mathematics, measurement, and weighing became prominent. It was therefore natural to apply these new perspectives to the Bible as well. The most famous person to do this was the Irish Archbishop James Ussher (1581–1656). Many today like to ridicule his dating of creation, and it is easy to categorize him as a fundamentalist. But that is

---

15. Quoted in Gwatkin, *Selections*, 137–39.
16. See chapter on Origen in Halldorf, *21 kirkefedre* [21 church fathers].

interpreting him through the lens of our time. Here, we would rather try to understand a past that was quite different from our own.

When we mentally transport ourselves to 1650, the year Ussher's book on the chronology of the Old Testament was published, we see that the bishop's contribution was the best attempt of its time to apply new methods to history itself. The highly respected bishop was known far beyond Britain. He was said to have read and spoken thirteen languages, both living and dead, placing him in a unique position to connect the Old Testament with historical sources in Greek, Old Syriac, Aramaic, Hebrew, and Arabic. Some of these had recently become available to Europeans.[17]

There was also a great belief in numerology, the mysticism of numbers, at the time, alongside an expectation that the Earth would last six thousand years before Jesus's return. This calculation was based on the six days of creation and a literal reading of the statement that "A thousand years in your [God's] sight are like a day" (Ps 90:4; see also 2 Pet 3:8). With such thoughts in mind, it was naturally important to determine when the Earth was created. It was generally accepted that creation had to have occurred about four thousand years before Christ's birth. If it turned out that creation happened, for example, five hundred years earlier, the whole theory on the timing of Jesus's return would be wrong, for in 1650 this would mean that six thousand years had already passed. On the other hand, if creation turned out to have been in the year 4300 BC, there would only be fifty years left to prepare for Jesus's return.

Archbishop Ussher's chronology was in many ways at the forefront of contemporary historical research. His arguments were as follows:

- An accurate analysis of Old Testament chronology and other historical sources gave a date for creation four thousand years before Christ's birth, thus confirming the date suggested by numerology. It was already known that the monk Dionysius Exiguus misdated Jesus's birth when he established our current calendar system in the year 525. Thus, creation was adjusted to 4004 BC.[18]
- Based on the idea that God thought rationally and mathematically, Ussher concluded that creation occurred around the autumnal equinox, partly because that is when the Jewish year begins.

17. Ussher's story is based on Chapman, *Caves, Coprolites and Catastrophes*, 35–36; Barr, "Pre-Scientific Chronology"; Macdougall, *Nature's Clocks*, 6; and Christie, "In Defence of the Indefensible."

18. Barr, "Why the World."

- Sunday had to be the day of creation since the seventh day, the day of rest, was Saturday. The most modern astronomical calculations in 1650 showed that the Sunday before the autumnal equinox in 4004 BC was October 23. To us, this may seem a month late, for the autumnal equinox is on September 22 or 23 today. The explanation lies in the difference between the Julian and the Gregorian calendars. When the more accurate Gregorian calendar was introduced in Denmark-Norway in 1700, we jumped straight from February 18 to March 1.[19] When Ussher calculated back to the year 4004 BC, the difference amounted to thirty-two days.

- The time of creation was set at the beginning of the night, which could mean 6:00 p.m., as that is when the new day begins for the Jews.

Ussher therefore arrived at 6:00 p.m. on October 23, 4004 BC. This was different from that of the Byzantine calendar, which starts in 5509 BC, or the Jewish calendar, which sets creation to 3761 BC. Neither of them is based on as careful a survey of Persian history as Ussher's. Unfortunately, the year 4004 BC became nearly set in stone when Ussher's chronology was printed in the King James edition of the English Bible in 1701, and it remained there for two hundred years. Many thus considered it orthodox teaching, though it was really just an expression of historical research at the dawn of the Enlightenment.

Today, there are young Earth creationists who maintain that the Earth is about six thousand years old. Although the modern creationist movement has roots going further back, it was the book *The Genesis Flood* by John Whitcomb and Henry Morris from 1961 that gave it momentum.[20] The young Earth creationists differ on an important point from Ussher and his contemporaries. In the 1600s, there was little scientific understanding of the Earth's age, so Ussher represented a rational approach to dating based on the best knowledge of his time. Today's young Earth creationists, on the other hand, oppose large parts of modern science. Although six thousand years are common for both, they therefore represent two entirely different approaches to rationality and science. Put somewhat pointedly, we can paradoxically call Ussher's attitude "modern" and the other "anti-modern."

---

19. Britain waited until 1752 for the adoption of the Gregorian calendar.

20. Whitcomb and Morris, *Genesis Flood*. The history of this movement can be found in Numbers, *Creationists*.

In today's young Earth creationism, much science must be explained away. One way to do this is to say that observations back in time do not count as true science since the past cannot be repeated and tested. The rest of this chapter will discuss how true science, despite this objection, is actually possible.

Another way to explain away today's science is based on the book *Omphalos* by the Englishman Philip Gosse from 1857. The title is Greek for "navel," and its hypothesis was a reaction to science that ceased to assert that the Earth is young. For Philip Gosse, it was obvious that when God directly created Adam, Adam must have had a navel, otherwise, he wouldn't have been a real human being. Thus, God would have created Adam in such a way that he appeared to have been born naturally. But then God could just as well have created the rest of the world with mountains and valleys that look old, trees with growth rings, and all other signs used for dating. In this way, knowledge of nature no longer concerns rationality and objective truth; it implies that God, for some reason, tries to deceive us. It is hard to imagine that anyone could think that it is possible to investigate such a world rationally—that is, in the end science would hardly be possible.

Early on, an alternative to the young Earth model was proposed. This was the chaos-restitution interpretation of Genesis where a gap of unspecified length is inserted in Gen 1:1–2. The view held from about 1660 by educated Christians can be summarized in this way:

> They did not hold to a literal Six-Day Creation. The majority held that the Six Days work was a final re-ordering of a much older previously created Chaos. However, Man remained a recent creation.[21]

This interpretation was common through the eighteenth century and is, for instance, the interpretation implied in Haydn's oratorio *The Creation* from 1796.

Ussher's six thousand years met increasing resistance as the discovery of fossils and the understanding of geology grew near the end of the eighteenth century. This led even Christian researchers to follow Augustine and rely more on what they found than on what written sources said. They also did not feel that Ussher's dating was a significant limitation when it came

---

21. Roberts, "Genesis of John Ray," 150.

to forming hypotheses about the history of life.[22] Before I delve into this, let's first look at how we have thought about life from antiquity to our time.

LIFE HAS A BEGINNING

Life from Nothing

An ancient belief, dating back to antiquity, is the notion that life could arise spontaneously. Aristotle believed that frogs, insects, and other bloodless animals could be spontaneously generated in the earth if there was moisture, warmth, and some decaying matter present. The Roman philosopher Lucretius (ca. 95–55 BC) went even further and believed that this was how the first animals and humans also came into being. He claimed that conditions have changed, and now such spontaneous creation only applies to lower forms of life. Humans, on the other hand, have become subject to sexual reproduction, and the Earth has degenerated compared to how it once was. This was a teaching that followed the Greek philosopher Epicurus.[23]

Lucretius's argument that humans had emerged by themselves was used as a basis for atheism.[24] The spontaneous creation of life that seemingly was so easy to observe in a pile of manure seemed to support this. The invention of the microscope in the 1600s strengthened this perception, as it revealed many new microorganisms that were believed to arise in a similar way.

Nevertheless, the belief in such creation waned toward the end of the 1600s. Italian physician and scientist Francesco Redi had conducted experiments with rotting meat and discovered that meat covered with a thin fabric did not give rise to, nor harbor, new flies. This was further confirmed by priest and professor Lazzaro Spallanzani, who conducted many precise experiments and wrote about the phenomenon in 1765.[25] However, this did not stop the discussion. It wasn't until nearly a hundred years later, when Louis Pasteur in 1862 won a prize from the French Academy of Sciences for even more controlled experiments, firmly establishing the principle that "life only comes from life."

---

22. Brooke, *Science and Religion*, 238.

23. Epicurus lived from 341 to 270 BC. Epicureanism says that everything that happens is due to movements and mutual influence between atoms that are otherwise in a void, and that the gods do not reward or punish man.

24. Goodrum, "Atomism, Atheism, and Spontaneous Generation."

25. Capanna, "Lazzaro Spallanzani."

Paradoxically, this happened nearly at the same time as Charles Darwin's (1809–1882) important book *The Origin of Species* was published in 1859. Here he deliberately avoided saying anything about how life might have started, since his theory did not address that. However, in a letter from 1871, Darwin did speculate that spontaneous creation might have occurred. He mentioned that we might imagine "some warm little pond with all sorts of ammonia and phosphoric salts, light, heat, electricity etc., present, so that a protein compound was chemically formed ready to undergo more complex changes."[26] He made it clear, though, that this was only speculation on his part. The similarity to the ancient idea of spontaneous creation of life is unmistakable. It is also noticeable that, despite claims to the contrary, after 150 years of research, the origin of life remains an unsolved problem despite many sharp minds pondering over it.

The discussion about spontaneous life is part of a larger debate about what life really is and how life comes into being in an individual. Is life preformed and transferred from parents to offspring, or does it gradually come into being as different molecules come together, organize, and become life? The first view is *preformation*, and the second is called *epigenesis* (new formation).[27]

Aristotle supported epigenesis. He believed that some material acquired form as a fetus developed into a human being. Through Thomas Aquinas, this also became Catholic doctrine, with the idea that a fetus did not become human until about forty days. A challenge with such epigenesis was explaining how molecules could acquire life force, obtain a soul, and become life. This process was called *vitalism* and was set up in contrast to *materialism*. Vitalism is a school of thought with something mystic and inexplicable about it, and it has been abandoned today. The Catholic Church also changed its stance, and in 1859 Pope Pius IX declared that life begins at conception, when sperm and egg cells meet.

Preformation in the 1600s and 1700s stated that a miniature version of a human was transferred to the fetus. This couldn't originally be observed. Better understanding of genes, egg and sperm cells, and DNA over the last 150 years has given rise to a modern form of preformation. Now, it's the genes through the egg and sperm cells that transfer life from one generation to the next. This is central to neo-Darwinism, and in a pure materialistic form, it leads to a belief that an individual's characteristics are almost predetermined.

26. Darwin, "Letter to Hooker," para. 2.
27. The discussion follows mostly Maienschein, "Epigenesis and Preformationism."

In recent decades, epigenesis has played a new role in what is called the *extended evolutionary synthesis* (EES), where factors outside of genes also come into play. Today, the perspective on the development of new life tends more toward a mix of preformation and epigenesis. I will return to this in chapter 6.

We now understand that the origin of life is far more complicated than previously thought. We also understand more about the central role of genes in the transfer of traits from one generation to another. Still, the notion that first life arose spontaneously remains an unconfirmed assumption for a purely materialistic view of life. Although we know little about how life originated, we have a much better understanding of how long ago it happened.

Discovery of the History of Life

Augustus, who was the Roman emperor when Jesus was born, was known for decorating his villas with so-called bones of giants. These fossil remains of dinosaurs have always fascinated us, but it wasn't until the nineteenth century that we began to grasp something of their history.

In 1823, William Buckland (1784–1856) wrote a book titled *Reliquiae Diluvianae, or Observations on the Organic Remains Contained in Caves, Fissures, and Diluvial Gravel, and on Other Geological Phenomena, Attesting the Action of an Universal Deluge*. The point was to show that Noah's flood in the Bible could explain discoveries he had made in England—perhaps not directly, but at least in the form of a great tidal wave. Buckland, who started as a theologian and can be characterized as being on the fringe of Evangelicalism or an evangelical sympathizer,[28] had secured a position in geology at the University of Oxford a few years earlier. He had travelled across Britain, studying geological layers and the animal remains within them.

One of Buckland's most famous examples was from a cave in Yorkshire, where there were remains of hyenas (see figure 25). These were covered by a thin layer of sediment. Buckland believed that this and similar findings from other locations were traces of the flood. Even then, he was aware that the creation of the Earth could not have happened just a few thousand years ago, but he still held on to the flood narrative. Many believed that exotic animals like hyenas had been swept north from Africa

---

28. Expressions from Roberts, *Evangelicals and Science*, 86.

by the flood. The findings in this cave argued against that, as fossil excrement from the hyenas was also found. Buckland named them coprolites, initiating a new field of study: the analysis of fossil excrement. Could it be that hyenas actually lived in England once, alongside elephants and rhinoceroses? If so, the climate must have been completely different at one time, and the hyenas might have been surprised by the flood in the cave.

Figure 25. Caricature drawing of William Buckland in the hyena cave drawn by geologist, paleontologist, and priest William Conybeare in 1822.[29]

Buckland must have been an interesting person whom I would have liked to get to know. He was curious enough to obtain a live hyena from South Africa to confirm that it gnawed on bones in a way that left the same marks as those found in the cave. It turned out that the feces were identical in both appearance and chemical analysis. He and his family had an army of pets—rats, mice, hedgehogs, frogs, snakes, a donkey, and even a small crocodile. He had a habit of "eating his way through" most of the animals he found as fossils, and guests might find themselves served

29. "William Buckland sticking his head into a hyena den," by William Conybeare, Wikimedia Commons.

these animals, as well as squirrels, dogs, cats, badgers, tigers, and moles. Incidentally, he wasn't driven solely by scientific curiosity. He was also looking for alternative food sources for England's population, especially during the crisis period after the Napoleonic Wars in 1815.

Interestingly, thirteen years after the book on the flood, Buckland had abandoned the idea of such a global flood. He had been invited by the Earl of Bridgewater to contribute to a book series meant to demonstrate the power, wisdom, and goodness of God as manifested in creation. Buckland contributed with *Geology and Mineralogy Considered with Reference to Natural Theology*. Here, gradual processes played the key role, not catastrophes like a flood.[30]

Eventually, Buckland became convinced of the central role of the ice age. Knowledge of how glaciers shape the landscape came from countries in Europe that still had glaciers. Danish Norwegian Jens Esmark, a professor at the University of Christiania,[31] wrote an article as early as 1824 stating that Norway had been covered by ice, which had created valleys and fjords. He observed that the landscape in Norway resembled that shaped by ice at the outlets of contemporary glaciers.[32] Esmark published in Danish, but his paper was translated into English already in 1826. Swiss scientist Louis Agassiz presented similar ideas in 1837, and it was Agassiz that eventually convinced Buckland, although he also mentioned Esmark's contribution in a lecture in 1840.[33] Buckland was humble enough to recognize that the ice age was a much better explanation for landscape formation than a great flood, and so he changed his mind.

I use Buckland as an example here because he started with a desire to reconcile a literal reading of the Bible with geology and was flexible enough to see that many things then didn't match up. His story demonstrates how the view that life was of recent origin was abandoned for scientific reasons. This story parallels the Galileo debate in the 1600s. Galileo's opponents in the Catholic Church insisted that the Bible says the Earth stands still but were nevertheless open to reconsidering their view if it were demonstrated that it moved. Since no such proof existed in Galileo's time, the church saw no reason to change its stance. Once it was eventually proven, the church concluded that the Bible does not intend

---

30. Buckland is described in Armstrong, "William Buckland in Retrospect," and Chapman, *Caves, Coprolites and Catastrophes*.

31. Now University of Oslo.

32. Hestmark, "Esmark's Mountain Glacier Traverse."

33. Worsley, "Jens Esmark."

to teach us about the solar system, it merely describes how it appears to us from Earth. Similarly, Buckland realized that the Bible's account of Earth's creation does not aim to teach us geology and biology, but rather to convey something about God as the creator and sustainer of nature, about humanity's unique position, and that history does not go in cycles.

Figure 26. Nicolas Steno (1638–1686) or Niels Steensen, which was his Danish name. As an anatomist, he found the outlet duct of the parotid gland, which used to be called ductus stenonis. He also laid the foundations for geology. This also led him to study crystals, and he formulated Steno's law, which states that the angles are the same in all crystals from the same mineral.

During his inaugural lecture at the University of Copenhagen in 1673 (which the statue is supposed to represent) he said,

Beautiful is what we see
More beautiful is what we know
Most beautiful by far is what we don't know

The last sentence is a bit ambiguous. It can be about the quest for new scientific knowledge, or about "Now I know in part; then I shall know fully, even as I am fully known [by God]" (1 Cor 13:12)—or both. The quote is the epigraph in my book on acoustics.

> Steno converted to Catholicism in 1667 and in 1677 he became a bishop in Northern Germany with responsibilities including Scandinavia. He was beatified in 1988, which is the last step before becoming a saint.[34]

His change of stance is part of a larger debate on what is known as the principle of *uniformitarianism*, and whether this offers a better explanation than so-called *catastrophism*. In other words, are gradual changes more important than catastrophes such as volcanoes and floods? As early as 1785, James Hutton had put forward arguments suggesting that it was not catastrophes, such as a biblical flood, that shaped the Earth, but rather gradual processes.

To understand the development of geology, we must go back to 1669, when Danish scientist and later bishop Nicolas Steno (see figure 26) established four principles for understanding stratification in line with the principle of uniformitarianism. These principles are: (1) younger sediments are deposited on top of older sediments, (2) layers originally lie horizontally, (3) layers extend horizontally unless interrupted by something else (such as a valley), and (4) if something cuts through a layer, it must be younger than the original layer. Steno, who was originally an anatomist, had dissected a shark that had washed ashore in Livorno, Italy. He noticed that the teeth looked exactly like certain stones found on hills in Tuscany. From antiquity, there had been a belief that these "tongue stones" had fallen from the sky, or that they grew out of rocks. Steno, however, argued that the explanation was much simpler: when the stones looked like shark teeth, it was precisely because they were remains of shark teeth.

Another important principle was established by English surveyor and geologist William Smith. During the Industrial Revolution, the number of mines in England increased, and large cuts were made in the terrain to form canals for transporting coal. In 1796, Smith observed that rocks could be identified by the fossils contained within them, and he became known for his ability to "read" the terrain to determine the presence of coal. Smith could trace layers of rock over large distances across the landscape, even if they had been folded or thrust under other layers. This became a key to understanding rock formations. He also created the first geological map of Great Britain.

---

34. Photo courtesy of Virginia Gregorio, CC BY-SA 3.0, Himetop.

Catastrophes or Continuity?

In the late 1700s, attempts to classify Earth's geological epochs began to resemble the system we have today. One of the pioneers was Giovanni Arduino, who in 1769 classified rocks into four time periods based on the fossils they contained: Primary, Secondary, Tertiary, and Quaternary. This classification system has since been developed into a formal and scientific division into various levels, which are continually refined and updated. Interestingly, the original demarcations between Arduino's four levels have been retained. The term Quaternary is still used, while Tertiary is used informally. The three most important boundaries remain:

- When life truly proliferated 541 million years ago during the Cambrian explosion. This event marked the boundary between the Primary (Precambrian) and Secondary periods.
- When the dinosaurs disappeared 66 million years ago, marking the beginning of the Tertiary period.
- The beginning of the Quaternary period 2.58 million years ago, which is the start of an era with alternating ice ages and warmer periods that we are still in today.

Since it was still considered reasonable in those times that Noah's flood had impacted the entire Earth, it was dated to the transition between the Tertiary and Quaternary periods.

The first half of the nineteenth century was a period of transition in the understanding of what had shaped the Earth. It was then that we began to understand ancient bone remnants and fossils. The French zoologist and paleontologist Georges Cuvier (1769–1832) discovered in 1800 that elephants and mammoths were not the same species, and therefore, that mammoths were extinct. He was therefore the first to establish that species had gone extinct, and that life had a history. Eventually, he found many examples of extinct species, ranging from the giant Irish elk to much older species like flying reptiles.[35] Cuvier believed that extinctions could be explained by the Earth having undergone many catastrophes. Cuvier, who came from the formerly German region of Alsace and was a Protestant and an active supporter of the French Bible Society, saw his catastrophism theory as potentially reminiscent of Biblical catastrophes.

---

35. Kolbert, *Sixth Extinction*, 23–45.

However, it was likely more the fact that extinctions had occurred that inspired him to this theory of catastrophism.

Around 1810, Mary Anning (see figure 27), and her brother Joseph, found and assembled one of the first ichthyosaurs, a five-meter-long prehistoric crocodile-like skeleton, which was excavated from the cliff at Lyme Regis on the English Channel. In 1824, Buckland was the first to describe "Megalosaurus"—the first dinosaur. This gave a new understanding that life had a history.

Figure 27. Mary Anning grew up in a Dissenter congregation. Even without an education, she became an outstanding fossil hunter and paleontologist, and she was known for her ability to assemble bone remains into complete skeletons. She handed them over to other researchers, such as Buckland, without initially getting much credit for it. In 2010, she was on the list of the ten most important female researchers in Great Britain.

> She left behind a notebook of poems and prayers that give a clear impression of a living faith. After a landslide in 1830, in which she escaped while her dog in the picture, Tray, did not, "the word of the Lord . . . became precious to her," a friend wrote.
>
> The Geological Society of London did not admit women as members until 1904, yet in 1850 they contributed to a stained-glass window in the church at Lyme Regis with the six services of mercy from Matthew 25 in memory of her goodness and integrity.[36]

Charles Lyell, who had been Buckland's student, built on the work of Hutton and Smith and published the multi-volume work *Principles of Geology* between 1830 and 1833. The subtitle was *An Attempt to Explain the Former Changes of the Earth's Surface, by Reference to Causes Now in Operation*. Lyell argued against Cuvier's catastrophism and believed that the key to studying the past lies in understanding present processes, in line with the principle of uniformitarianism. Lyell's work had a significant influence on Darwin, who referred to it in his 1859 book on evolution.

Lyell's uniformitarianism was central to the perspective on development for the next 120 years. When Americans Walter and Luis Alvarez, father and son, in 1980 proposed a catastrophe in the form of something as exotic as an "Extraterrestrial Cause for the Cretaceous-Tertiary Extinction" they were therefore not believed.[37] They had found a one-centimeter-thick clay layer with iridium in Italy, Denmark, and New Zealand. Iridium is hard and metallic and almost three times as heavy as steel. It is rarer than gold and platinum. In the clay layer, the Alvarez duo found thirty times more iridium than usual. Meteorites contain a lot of iridium, so they proposed that a large meteorite caused the extinction of the dinosaurs 66 million years ago. The story of this is almost as thrilling as a detective story, and the way the Alvarez duo worked resembles a police investigation. Eventually, they found that the impact must have been on the Yucatán Peninsula in Mexico, and their explanation was accepted. Today, the principle of uniformitarianism remains important, but catastrophes such as meteorite impacts and volcanic eruptions also play a crucial role.

It is therefore not surprising that Buckland in the first half of the nineteenth century revised his views in light of the theories of catastrophism,

---

36. "Mary Anning Painting," Natural History Museum of London, Wikimedia Commons.

37. This is the title of their paper in *Science* in 1980. The exciting story about their find is in Kolbert, *Sixth Extinction*, 70–90.

uniformitarianism, and ice ages. In his book *Geology and Mineralogy Considered with Reference to Natural Theology* from 1836, he discussed alternative interpretations of the Bible to reconcile these views. The interpretation he preferred was that of the Scottish theologian Thomas Chalmers. This was the gap theory, which is a development of the chaos-restitution interpretation, and where the period between the first and second verses of Gen 1 is set equal to geologic time. In this old Earth model, God created the world a long time ago, then life was created over six distinct days six thousand years ago (see appendix). Buckland explained that the Bible does not provide a detailed historical description of geology, just as it does not mention that Jupiter has moons and Saturn has rings. These belong in scientific works, not in the Bible, which is primarily about "religious faith and moral behavior," as he put it. Buckland concluded:

> Geology has shared the fate of other infant sciences, in being for a while considered hostile to revealed religion; so like them, when fully understood, it will be found a potent and consistent auxiliary to it, exalting our conviction of the Power, and Wisdom, and Goodness of the Creator.[38]

As understanding of different layers and fossils increased, researchers also realized that it was impossible to think that life could have emerged quite recently. Scottish science popularizer, geologist, and apologist Hugh Miller reasoned this in a fascinating book in 1859. It was then clear that many animals in England had been present thousands of years before humans arrived, including extinct mammoths, hippos, tigers, and cave bears. There were also shells found on the British Isles that are now only found in Iceland and Svalbard, indicating that the climate had changed. Geologists could also point to clear evidence that sea levels had been up to ten meters higher in the past. However, it was clear that when Hadrian's Wall was built in AD 140 to separate what we now call Scotland and England, the sea level was the same as today. All this indicated that England was much older than six thousand years and that the flood in the Bible was a local flood that had such a strong impact that it was remembered.[39]

These findings and arguments also convinced Buckland that one day in the creation story represents an age. In this day-age view, each day is considered a time epoch instead of a literal twenty-four-hour day. This is a progressive creationist interpretation, which similarly to the

---

38. Buckland, *Geology and Mineralogy*, 18.
39. Miller, *Testimony of the Rocks*, 115–56.

gap theory maintains that there is a correspondence between the days of creation and scientific epochs.[40] Buckland showed a rare flexibility by being willing to revise his stance multiple times. In this, he acted entirely in line with Augustine's advice to adopt certain knowledge and avoid "presumably giving the meaning of Holy Scripture, talking nonsense on these topics."

Even though Buckland accepted an old Earth, I'm sure it would surprise him that the hyena cave is now dated to be 120,000 years old. This is part of the fascinating story of how we found different methods for dating and ultimately discovered the age of the Earth.

The Age of the Earth

As noted in the beginning of this chapter, the determination of the age of the Earth is part of a scientific field that is not easily understood intuitively. Therefore, it is not surprising that it took a long time to achieve reliable results in this discipline. The lack of good alternatives is also one of the reasons why Aristotle and the Bible remained authoritative for so long. It wasn't really until the early twentieth century that different and independent disciplines of science began to agree on dating the Earth.[41]

Newton assumed that the Earth had originally been hot and was now cooling, and in 1687 he calculated that this process could have been ongoing for fifty thousand years. No one came up with a better alternative for the next hundred years, and when Comte de Buffon conducted experiments in 1779 with small models of the Earth that he heated and measured, he only increased the estimate to 96,670 years.

Thermodynamics eventually became an established discipline, and in 1862, one of its pioneers, Lord Kelvin—originally William Thomson before he was ennobled thirty years later—made a similar calculation. Kelvin's idea of a cooling Earth was partly based on the fact that the deeper you go into a mine, the warmer it gets. He thus estimated the Earth's age to be considerably higher than previously thought, proposing that it could be somewhere between 20 and 400 million years. The theory of a continuously cooling Earth was not in accordance with Lyell's assumption of uniformitarianism. According to Newton's and Kelvin's model, if

---

40. This view is called *concordism* and is explained more in the appendix.
41. The next paragraphs are based on Badash, "Age-of-the-Earth Debate" and Stinner, "Calculating Age of Earth and Sun."

carried to its logical conclusion, the Earth would eventually become so cold that all life would die out. Kelvin was likely inspired by his work on the second law of thermodynamics, which states that everything moves toward equilibrium, as mentioned in chapter 2. By the late 1890s, he had reduced his estimate to 20–40 million years. He represented the best science of his day, but today we know that several of Kelvin's assumptions were incorrect, especially his lack of knowledge about radioactivity in the Earth's interior which continuously produces energy. The Earth is in thermal equilibrium and essentially maintains its temperature, it does not continually fall.

An entirely different method is to look at the annual rate of erosion from weathering and in 1868 this was used to give an estimate of 100 million years.[42] A similar estimate was provided in 1899 by calculating how much salt was carried into the sea by rivers. The result was that the current salinity of the oceans must have been built up over 80–90 million years.[43] However, this method also proved unsustainable since ocean salinity is in equilibrium and does not increase over time.

By the turn of the century, it was accepted that the Earth was very old but not eternal. It might be as much as 100 million years old, but it was impossible to say anything definitive. However, this age was still young enough to be used as an argument against the theory of gradual evolution. Kelvin's calculations were also used to try to disprove evolution. The new understanding of radioactivity and isotopes, which emerged in the early twentieth century, radically changed this scenario. Radioactive elements spontaneously transform into new elements, emitting high energy that is unaffected by external factors such as weather and climate. This makes the radioactive process a highly accurate clock.[44] Based on radiometric dating, estimates of the Earth's age increased significantly, and between 1907 and 1911, estimates ranged from 1.6 to 2.2 billion years. The current estimate of the Earth's age is based on meteorites that contain elements dating back to the formation of the solar system and the Earth. In 1955, meteorite fragments were dated and found to be around 4.5 billion years old. The oldest terrestrial rocks are estimated to be a few hundred million years younger.

Today's date estimates are based on the uranium-lead method. Both uranium 238 and uranium 235 are radioactive and slowly transform into

42. Work done by Archibald Geikie, head of Scotland's geological surveys.
43. Done by Irish geologist John Joly.
44. Macdougall, *Nature's Clocks*, 43.

lead. The half-life, the time it takes for half of uranium 238 and uranium 235 to decay, is 4.47 billion years and 710 million years, respectively. The uranium-lead method is unique because uranium is found in zircon, a mineral that is so durable it can withstand nearly nine hundred degrees before melting and is not broken down by weather or low temperatures. Therefore, zircon remains intact in the oldest rocks. Zircon can be clear and is then considered a gemstone.[45] There are several other processes that can be used for dating in addition to uranium-lead, such as calcium, which decays into argon with a half-life of 1.3 billion years.

To understand our own history, the time span of particular interest is a few hundred thousand years. Radiometric dating using the carbon 14 method, which works up to about fifty thousand years ago, plays a central role. There are also other methods to cross-check these findings. Both the counting of layers in ice cores and tree-ring counting are much simpler methods to understand. It is possible to count layers in ice cores up to about fifty-five thousand years, though some uncertainty in dating must be considered. The oldest known trees are bristlecone pines, which grow in California, and the oldest known living tree is just over five thousand years old. By comparing the rings in dead and living trees, it has been possible to count back eight thousand to nine thousand years. This has been used to confirm the carbon 14 method.[46]

The carbon 14 method is based on cosmic radiation creating a rare variant of carbon, the isotope carbon 14, with six protons and eight neutrons in the nucleus. This is two more neutrons than in common carbon (carbon 12). Carbon 14 is absorbed by plants through photosynthesis, and all living beings that eat plants will take in this isotope. Carbon 14 is not stable and spontaneously transforms into nitrogen with a half-life of 5,730 years. Accurate measurement of carbon 14 content therefore indicates when a piece of wood was cut down or when an animal or human last ate plants. The cave with hyenas that Buckland examined was dated to 120,000 years using another isotope method, which is based on uranium 234 decaying into thorium with a half-life of 245,000 years.

Even though the Earth is dated to be billions of years old using radiometric dating, it was already clear to science by the mid-nineteenth century that it was hundreds of thousands, perhaps millions of years old.

---

45. The red-yellow variant of zircon is called jacinth and is interestingly mentioned as part of the decoration in the new Jerusalem in Rev 21:20.

46. Walter Libby received the Nobel Prize for the development of the carbon 14 method in 1960.

It is interesting to examine what Hugh Miller draws from this knowledge in his apologetic work titled *The Testimony of the Rocks: Or, Geology in Its Bearings on the Two Theologies, Natural and Revealed*. The book was published just before Darwin's work *The Origin of Species*. A conclusion reached by Miller is that Scripture is given to us to discover what we cannot find out on our own. Examples are God as the creator, that nothing exists without him, and that humanity can only be understood in light of having separated ourselves from God. Scripture is not given to tell us about what we are competent enough to find out for ourselves. Miller also points out that geology confirms that all forms of life, both plants and animals, had a beginning. There was a time when they did not exist on Earth. Science, Miller claims, can therefore be used against atheists who, in line with Greek thought, argue that life has always existed. In fact, geology has become a better argument than theology for the necessity of a creator, he argues. The story of how we discovered that the universe has a beginning provides even more reason to believe this.

THE BEGINNING OF THE UNIVERSE

At the start of the twentieth century, one of Aristotle's assertions remained unshaken. Even after the Earth's age was estimated to be several billion years, it was still believed that the universe itself had existed eternally. The twentieth century would change this view. Central to this shift is Albert Einstein's general theory of relativity, and one of the few who truly understood it was the remarkable physicist and priest Georges Lemaître, who practically calculated the time of the big bang.

The Pope and Georges Lemaître

In November 1951, science enthusiast Pope Pius XII declared that contemporary science seemed to have succeeded in uncovering the moment of the event "fiat lux" ("Let there be light" from Gen 1:3). He described this moment as "when, along with matter, there burst forth from nothing a sea of light and radiation, while the particles of chemical elements split and formed into millions of galaxies."[47] As expected, the statement made headlines around the world. However, the person who contributed the science

---

47. Pius XII, "Proofs," para. 44.

behind this, Belgian Georges Lemaître (1894–1968), cringed upon hearing the pope's words.

Lemaître had become a member of the Pontifical Academy of Sciences when it was established in 1936 and knew Pope Pius well. Nine years earlier, he had discovered that the universe is expanding. Time and space expand in the same way as a balloon being inflated, which means that the farther away something is from us, the faster it is moving away. Russian Alexander Friedmann had suggested this a few years earlier as one among many mathematical solutions to Einstein's equations of relativity, but Lemaître was unaware of this. Lemaître saw that the mathematics agreed with data on the speed and distance of stars, turning the concept of an expanding universe from a mathematical theory into a physical theory consistent with observations. It had been known since 1912 that there are objects in space moving away from us, but no one before Lemaître had interpreted this as the expansion of space.[48]

Lemaître also made the crucial suggestion that the expansion must have started at some point in time. He called this beginning a "primeval atom," which would later become known as the big bang.[49] Lemaître was largely forgotten when, in 2018, the International Astronomical Union (IAU) decided that the law of the universe's expansion should be called the Hubble-Lemaître law. Until then, it had only been named after Edwin Hubble, who had measured and found that the farther away from Earth a star is, the faster it is receding. Now the theorist Lemaître, who had first derived the law, was also recognized, and historians today say that no one else has had a greater influence on modern cosmology than he.[50]

---

48. Kragh, "Origin and Earliest Reception."

49. This was in 1931. Interestingly, Lemaître published this in the same journal that Pierre Duhem, in chapter 4, had published his findings in about the Middle Ages, *La Revue des Questions Scientifiques*, a Belgian Catholic journal.

50. Kragh, "Georges Lemaître."

Figure 28. Georges Lemaître in priestly garb in the early 1930s.[51]

Interestingly, Georges Lemaître was also a priest, as figure 28 shows. He had decided on this path as early as the age of nine. Simultaneously, he was determined to become a scientist. He said that he was interested in truth both from a salvific perspective and in science. It was the idea of God's two books that formed Lemaître's two paths to truth. Truth was so central to him that he began a speech in 1936 by saying that the pursuit of truth is the highest form of activity and something unique to being human.[52]

Lemaître first studied to become a civil engineer but eventually switched to physics and mathematics. At the same time, he continued his classical Jesuit education, although without becoming a Jesuit himself. In 1923, he was ordained a Catholic secular priest. It was his time at Cambridge University in England as a student of Arthur Eddington, along with studies at Harvard and MIT in the USA, which steered Lemaître toward cosmology and astronomy, and he earned a PhD from MIT in 1927. Eddington was no ordinary figure. During a solar eclipse in 1919, he had confirmed that gravity affects light just as Einstein's theory had

---

51. "Portrait of Abbé Georges Lemaître," Wikimedia Commons.

52. The story about Lemaître is largely based on Farrell, *Day Without Yesterday*, and Felipe et al., "Georges Lemaître's 1936 Lecture."

predicted, and his confirmation quickly elevated Einstein from an ordinary researcher to a global star.

Lemaître's 1927 paper on an expanding universe was published in a local French-language journal, and after some years, Eddington had it translated into English. The idea of an expanding universe did not seem to go well with the prevailing notions of the time. Even an authority like Einstein is said to have told Lemaître that his calculations were correct, but the physics was "abominable." When Lemaître further developed the theory to include the primeval atom, Eddington found the idea "repugnant." So well entrenched was the ancient notion that the universe is infinitely old and infinitely large. Although Einstein changed his mind, Eddington held on to this view until his death in 1944.[53]

However, after Lemaître's ideas were published to a broader audience in 1932, he gained more recognition and, like Einstein, frequently appeared on the front pages of newspapers. His generally good mood certainly played a role too. Additionally, journalists were intrigued by how he combined cosmology with being a priest—at that time, the conflict thesis had become widely accepted.

But what exactly did Lemaître react to in the pope's 1951 statement? It was the connection between creation and the primeval atom. The big bang is a point where both time and space begin, and we can only know about what has happened after this moment. Strictly speaking, we cannot even know everything that has happened since then because there is a boundary, right after the big bang, where all current theories break down.[54] Whether this was a beginning from something or nothing is not something a scientific theory can address.

God as the Reason for All Things

Creation is about more than something that might have happened 14 billion years ago. It involves a much deeper question, that which Leibniz, who we encountered in the introductory chapter, posed: "Why is

---

53. An interesting comparison of the views of Lemaître and Eddington that includes the influence from their theologies, Roman Catholic and Quaker respectively, is in Appolloni, "'Repugnant,' 'Not Repugnant at All.'"

54. Our theories are not validated for time before about 10^{-14}–10^{-12} seconds after the big bang when temperature and pressure exceeded anything ever measured, and especially not before the Planck time, which is the unbelievably small 5.4×10^{-44} seconds. Rees, *Just Six Numbers*, 112–27.

there something rather than nothing?"[55] It concerns God as the origin of everything and the source of all existence. You may use Shakespeare and the play *Hamlet* as a comparison. Shakespeare is the author of the play, but you don't find him acting in it. If your world is limited to what happens within the play, then Shakespeare is not a visible explanation for what and why. Yet he is the origin and creator of the entire play and influences everything. Similarly, God influences all of creation without being directly seen. He is the underlying reason for existence.

Lemaître enjoyed quoting "Truly you are a God who has been hiding himself" (Isa 45:15), inspired by Pascal (chapter 1). God is present everywhere but is hidden within creation, and natural science cannot really reveal him. He cannot be discovered within creation, as he lies behind and beyond it. It requires a metaphysical vision to see the invisible, as indicated by Heb 11:3: "By faith we understand that the universe was formed at God's command, so that what is seen was not made out of what was visible."

Lemaître was of the opinion that there is no need to reconcile religion and science, simply because there is no conflict. It is imagined—as I argue in this book. But it's also the case that one cannot really find science in the Bible. As Hugh Miller, referenced earlier in this chapter, said, divine revelation does not teach us anything we could find out for ourselves, at least not when these scientific truths are unnecessary for understanding supernatural truth. Lemaître also emphasized that the Bible is adapted to use language that people could understand at the time it was written—in other words, the principle of accommodation, as discussed in the appendix.

The more I study Lemaître, the more my respect for him grows. We can only imagine how the creation account would have been received by its first listeners if the theory of relativity had been described in it. Or what we would think of the Bible if it were updated with Newton's theories but stopped there. Wouldn't we consider it outdated since it hadn't included Einstein's refinements?

Thus, Lemaître distanced himself from those who reject the Bible because they think its "science" is wrong. Interestingly, he called such opponents of the Bible "second- and third-rate popularizers" and who are actually "provocateurs."[56] For him, extracting natural science from

---

55. Leibniz, *Principles of Nature and Grace*, §7–8.
56. Felipe et al., "Georges Lemaître's 1936 Lecture," 162.

the Bible is as absurd as trying to derive religious doctrines from the binomial theorem in mathematics. Therefore, he also distanced himself from those who believe that there are details in the Bible about nature that support science. This was something he himself had believed when he was younger, but over time he reached clarity on this point.

Lemaître's groundbreaking science combined with his humility in not promoting himself is inspiring, and his thoughtful reflections on the relationship with faith are challenging. Since he lived relatively recently, these thoughts are still relevant.

To better understand what Lemaître meant, we can ask what would happen if we could conduct a thought experiment where God "turned himself off"?[57] Would natural laws gradually become less reliable and eventually stop functioning, as they need God to keep them going? Or would there be less charity and increased immorality?

It's easy to think too small about God in this question, as if God resided within creation, like the Greek and Norse gods did. The biblical worldview states that God, who exists outside the natural world, created it from nothing. This contrasts with the Greeks' eternal world, which was in chaos, but out of which the gods created order. In the Greek mindset, "nothing comes from nothing," so the world must always have existed, and the gods didn't create it.[58]

God is therefore much more than just someone who keeps the wheels turning, even though he does that as well. This idea has been developed by philosophers over the centuries, perhaps especially by Thomas Aquinas in the thirteenth century. He argued, as noted, that even the universe of the best science of his time, Aristotle's eternal universe without a beginning, needed the Bible's creator. That is, a creator who does not need an external reason to exist because he is the only one who exists in himself. Even the common Christian creeds from the first centuries say this, particularly the abbreviated form of the Athanasian Creed:

> The Father is uncreated, the Son is uncreated, the Holy Spirit is uncreated.
> The Father is immeasurable, the Son is immeasurable, the Holy Spirit is immeasurable.

---

57. Bube, *Putting It All Together*, 176.

58. In Latin, the saying is "creatio ex nihilo"—creation from nothing, in contrast to the Greeks' eternal world that was based on "ex nihilo nihil fit"—nothing comes from nothing.

> The Father is eternal, the Son is eternal, the Holy Spirit is eternal.[59]

This creed is an attempt to formulate thoughts found in the Bible. We perceive here that God, the uncreated, exists without any cause other than himself and that it has always been so. The creed sheds light on the statement "I am who I am" (Exod 3:14), which is already found in the second book of the Bible. No human can say this about themselves, and these words run like a red thread through the Bible until the last book, which summarizes them with, "I am the Alpha and the Omega, . . . who is, and who was, and who is to come, the Almighty" (Rev 1:8).

The act of creation shows that God is the source of all existence. Nothing else, not life, plants, animals, or humans, not the Earth, Sun, planets, or galaxies exists without him. So, if God were to "turn himself off," the Bible gives us some glimpses of what might happen. It says, "You alone are the Lord . . . You give life to everything" (Neh 9:6). Paul says something similar in his speech to the Greek philosophers at the Areopagus council: "He Himself gives everyone life and breath and everything else. . . . For in Him we live and move and have our being" (Acts 17:25, 28). If God were to "turn himself off," there would no longer be anything to sustain all life.

It is even clearer when words from the book of Job are brought into the discussion: "If it were his intention and he withdrew His spirit and breath, all humanity would perish together, and mankind would return to the dust" (Job 34:14–15). We would notice it immediately as everything would end abruptly. It is difficult to imagine how this would manifest, but everything that exists would cease to exist, and everything that is would no longer be. Augustine had clearly grasped this when he said, "God is working until now in such a way that if his working were to be withheld from the things he has set up, they would simply collapse."[60]

Perhaps such matters had slipped Pius XII's mind in November 1951, and, unfortunately, he had not consulted Lemaître. Fortunately, the misunderstanding was clarified in a meeting between Lemaître and the pope a few months later, and the pope did not directly link creation and the big bang in such a way after that.

---

59. Wikipedia, "Athanasian Creed," sec. Protestantism, para. 4.

60. From *Literal Interpretation of Genesis*, in Ortlund, *Retrieving Augustine's Doctrine of Creation*, 36.

Measuring Distant Stars

What made Lemaître's big bang theory gain traction relatively quickly was that it corresponded with measurements showing that the farther away a star is, the faster it is moving away from us. As noted, Edward Hubble was able to demonstrate this result after measuring objects up to 5 million light-years away. The velocities he found were up to 1000 km/s.[61]

When an ambulance with its siren on speeds past, one can hear how the pitch changes from high to low. This is called the Doppler effect, which we also use in ultrasound imaging to measure the speed of blood flow through heart valves, thus enabling diagnoses. The Doppler effect can also be measured in the light from stars. The gases in the star absorb certain "tones" or spectral lines that are unique to the material the star is made of. A common substance is hydrogen, and its lines are determined by the properties of the atom. These lines can be ultraviolet, infrared, or visible light, and have been known since the early 1800s. If these lines are slightly redder than expected, it means the star is moving away from us. Therefore, measuring velocity is not so difficult.

Distances, however, are another matter. In the 1800s, it became possible to measure the distance to the nearest stars using parallax, the phenomenon where stars appear to be in slightly different positions as the Earth moves in its orbit around the Sun. This was discussed in the previous chapter. Bessel's first measurement in 1838 was accomplished by observing a star that was only eleven light-years away from Earth. When using telescopes on Earth, this method works for stars up to a few hundred light-years away. If we didn't have to look through Earth's atmosphere, the results could be improved tenfold. However, this is almost negligible compared to the distances Hubble measured.

The key to these measurements lies in a type of pulsating stars called Cepheids. American astronomer Henrietta Swan Leavitt (1868–1921) analyzed measurements on such stars in the Small Magellanic Cloud. Assuming that all the stars in the cloud were at the same distance from us, she published data for twenty-five of them in 1912 and showed that there was a direct relationship between brightness and how slowly these stars pulsated.

Today, the relationship between brightness and the frequency of pulsation of stars is called Leavitt's law, and it has become the standard for measuring great distances. Others measured pulsating stars close enough

---

61. Kirshner, "Hubble's Diagram and Cosmic Expansion."

to us that the distance could also be calculated by parallax measurements. In this way, Leavitt's method could be calibrated and used to measure distances to stars much farther away from Earth. A few years later, Eddington came up with a theory for how helium in a star could explain the pulsation, thus strengthening confidence in the method. Unfortunately, Leavitt died of cancer at the age of fifty-three. The importance of her discovery increased over time, and she was even proposed as a candidate for the Nobel Prize three years after her death; the proposer, however, did not know she had already passed away.

There is little biographical information about Leavitt, but an obituary describes her as "steadfastly loyal to her principles, and deeply conscientious and sincere in her attachment to her religion and church."[62] It would indeed have been interesting to know what thoughts she may have had about the relationship between God and the vast universe she measured.

In the 1920s, Hubble, based on Leavitt's law, had discovered that the universe is larger than our own galaxy, the Milky Way. The most visible galaxy is the Andromeda Nebula. Another is the Small Magellanic Cloud, which Leavitt had observed. Hubble also found that the farther away a star is from us, the faster it is moving. In hindsight, it has been shown that Hubble miscalculated the distances and that they were only one-seventh of the actual distances. Despite this, he demonstrated that distance and speed are related. Lemaître referred to Hubble's measurements in 1927 when he first calculated the expansion of the universe. The fact that they matched observations, as noted, made his hypothesis much stronger than if it had been purely a theoretical result.

Atheists with Alternative Theories

Lemaître consistently maintained a clear distinction between religion and science to avoid accusations that he was driven more by theology than physics. Nevertheless, other scientists were quick to accuse him of this. One such scientist was American Nobel laureate Robert Millikan (1868–1953), who once interrupted Lemaître by saying, "No, not that, that suggests too much the creation," when Lemaître suggested that cosmic rays, which Millikan was an expert on, might be remnants from the

---

62. Bailey, "Henrietta Swan Leavitt," 197.

big bang.[63] Considering that Millikan himself was a Christian, this may seem peculiar. Einstein, initially critical of the big bang, quickly became convinced by Hubble's measurements of the redshift in distant stars. Likely, Einstein's strong grounding in philosophy helped him avoid the conflation of religion or metaphysics with science, a confusion that both Pius XII and Millikan made.

Due to Hubble's initially underestimated distances, the universe's age was estimated to be only 1–2 billion years, which was less than geological dating of Earth suggested. Hence, there were those who raised purely scientific objections against the big bang. Over time, dating of the Earth and measurements of the size and the age of the universe have been reconciled. When two independent measurement techniques support each other like this, it increases confidence in the results and strengthens our belief that natural laws have been unchanged over millions and billions of years.

British astronomer Fred Hoyle (1915–2001) proposed a competing theory in 1948 for an expanding universe without a beginning, called the steady-state theory. It posited that hydrogen was continuously "created" in the void between stars, fueling the expansion of the universe—a theory developed in collaboration with Thomas Gold and Hermann Bondi. The continuous creation of hydrogen conflicted with the crucial principle in physics that mass and energy cannot suddenly appear from nothing as the steady-state theory required hydrogen to create itself. It is also worth noting that all three astronomers were atheists. Hoyle emphasized this in popularizing his theory, once stating in a BBC interview, "The reason why scientists like the 'Big Bang' is because they are overshadowed by the Book of Genesis."[64] Hoyle, therefore, faced the same criticism of conflating worldview and science as Lemaître, demonstrating that such accusations can go both ways.

Hoyle is also credited with coining the term *big bang* for Lemaître's primordial atom theory, likely meant derogatorily. Despite implying a loud noise—which is very inaccurate as there was no atmosphere to carry the sound—*big bang* has become an established scientific term well-known to many. Despite their differences, Lemaître and Hoyle had a good enough relationship to vacation together in the Alps.

63. Farrell, *Day Without Yesterday*, 83.
64. Wikipedia, "Fred Hoyle," sec. Rejection of the Big Bang, para. 2.

More overt criticism of the idea of a beginning came from Soviet communist Andrei Zhdanov, Stalin's chief ideologist, who in 1947 accused Lemaître and his followers of being pseudo-scientists aiming to resurrect the theory of the universe's creation from nothing.[65] Although he was wrong about Lemaître's intentions, he correctly noted that the big bang theory is a clear departure from Aristotle's eternal universe and resembles the creation narrative. Thus, the theory has revitalized the classical kalām argument for God, which posits that everything that begins must have an external cause. The argument has roots in a Muslim theological tradition known as *'ilm al-kalām*—the study of the spoken word.

Lemaître became isolated when Belgium was occupied during World War II, disappearing from public view. He did little work on the primordial atom hypothesis after this. Ukrainian American George Gamow (1904–1968) and his collaborators developed the hypothesis further, concluding that the primordial atom was very hot, not cold as Lemaître had imagined. They speculated that remnants of this heat might be observable. This afterglow, or cosmic microwave background radiation, was discovered shortly before Lemaître died, measuring only about three Kelvin. The measurements were so compelling that a Nobel Prize was eventually awarded to the discoverers in 1978, thereby establishing Lemaître's big bang as reputable science, overshadowing both Aristotle's eternal universe and Hoyle's steady-state theory.

Does the Big Bang Require a Creator?

In recent decades, a new generation of physicists, in many ways Hoyle's successors, has emerged. They give the impression of being able to explain the big bang and suggest the theory may not be as solid as once thought. Like Hoyle, they likely find the notion of the big bang too reminiscent of the creation narrative and seek to explain the origin differently.

One such physicist was Stephen Hawking (1942–2018), a very distinguished physicist. I once counted and found he had published about fifty-five articles in the world's leading physics journal, compared to my solitary one.[66] However, I have often asked friends and colleagues why

---

65. Kragh, *Entropic Creation*, 224.

66. This is *Physical Review Letters* and our paper is Lambert et al., "Bridging Three Orders of Magnitude."

the world's most famous physicist never got a Nobel Prize. Few can adequately answer.

In his later years, Hawking enjoyed contemplating grand ideas about the big bang. In his alternative creation narrative, he suggested that numerous universes were created from nothing without supernatural intervention, arising naturally from physical laws. He explained that, because there is a law like gravity, the universe can and will create itself from nothing.

This illustrates Hawking's theoretical approach, as he seems to assume that laws and mathematics are able to create. The notion of multiple universes is also an untestable idea; if it was testable, it would by definition concern our own universe. However, Hawking had as much faith in elegant theories as in experimental validation. The idea that one can think about how the world is certainly plays a role in modern physics since all theories begin this way. But if theory becomes everything, it echoes prescientific Greek physics, where the idea of eternal, perfect cycles was so essential that planetary orbits just had to conform to beautiful circles. When they didn't match observations, adjustments were made, resulting in circles upon circles, an example of intellectualism discussed in the next chapter. Hawking's most famous theory, about radiation from black holes, is indeed beautiful. But since this theory is unconfirmed, and may never be confirmed, he never received the Nobel award. The Nobel Committee has wisely resisted the temptation to reward elegant theories unconfirmed by observation.

When Stephen Hawking spoke about questions outside the realm of physics, he was often listened to as a philosopher. For example, he asked,

> Where did all this come from? Did the universe need a creator? Most of us do not spend most of our time worrying about these questions, but almost all of us worry about them some of the time. Traditionally these are questions for philosophy, but philosophy is dead. Philosophy has not kept up with modern developments in science, particularly physics. Scientists have become the bearers of the torch of discovery in our quest for knowledge.[67]

Philosopher Derek Parfit responded to such statements by saying,

> That first event, some physicists suggest, may have obeyed the laws of quantum mechanics, by being a random fluctuation in a

---

67. Hawking and Mlodinow, *Grand Design*, 1.

vacuum. This would causally explain, they say, how the Universe came into existence out of nothing. But what physicists call a vacuum isn't really nothing. We can ask why it exists and has the potentialities it does. In Hawking's phrase, "What breathes fire into the equations?"[68]

A philosopher will easily see the contradiction in Hawking's statement, but many others are swept along by Hawking's speculations. For "a law of nature like gravity" or "the laws of quantum mechanics" are not "nothing." Something must exist for there to be a law of nature. So, Hawking and physicists who support him in this regard have deceived themselves.

This point is further illustrated when Hawking, in his book, quotes Albert Einstein's statement mentioned in chapter 1 that the most incomprehensible thing about the universe is that it is comprehensible. Hawking, however, responds with a banal truism: "The universe is comprehensible because it is governed by scientific laws; that is to say, its behaviour can be modelled."[69]

Here, Hawking reveals his rather shallow philosophy. For him, natural laws had become the cause of everything, and they have almost replaced God. Einstein was wondering what the origin of natural law could be and how it can be that these laws are such that we humans can understand them. Unfortunately, it never seemed that Hawking even grasped this issue.

While some people might give the impression that modern physics is on the verge of explaining the big bang in a natural manner, we are far from it. Physicists can form hypotheses about how the big bang started and from what, but physics has nothing to contribute to the really big question: how can it be that anything exists at all?

The account of the relationship between the big bang and the creation of the world has highlighted the importance of the philosophy of science. As noted, Pope Pius XII and the Nobel laureate Robert Millikan are examples of people who seemed to have a problem separating the big bang and creation from each other, while Albert Einstein and Georges Lemaître, who both were better versed in philosophy, managed to do it. This is even more important when we come to evolution and human origins in later chapters, and for that reason, the next chapter will deal with philosophy of science.

---

68. Parfit, "Why Anything? Why This?" 1.
69. Hawking and Mlodinow, *Grand Design*, 87.

5

Philosophy of Science

> The study of philosophy is not that we may know what men have thought, but what the truth of things is.
>
> Thomas Aquinas, *Exposition of Aristotle's Treatise*

It is a paradox that when facing seemingly difficult issues such as biological evolution, many manage to reconcile them with Christian faith while others believe them to be irreconcilable. The theme of this book has so far mostly revolved around physical science, such as the history of life and the discovery of the big bang. The interpretation of the big bang and whether it is the same as the Bible's creation from nothing is a subject where the need for philosophical reflection started to become apparent.

In this chapter, I will lay a foundation that will assist in understanding the varying views on evolution among Christians. This is only possible if we examine the philosophy that consciously or unconsciously lies behind the views. Some may find it a bit tedious to delve into philosophy, but listen to what the articulate G. K. Chesterton said:

> Philosophy is merely thought that has been thought out. It is often a great bore. But man has no alternative, except between being influenced by thought that has been thought out and being influenced by thought that has not been thought out. The

latter is what we commonly call culture and enlightenment today. But man is always influenced by thought of some kind, his own or somebody else's; that of somebody he trusts or that of somebody he never heard of, thought at first, second or third hand; thought from exploded legends or unverified rumours; but always something with the shadow of a system of values and a reason for preference. A man does test everything by something. The question here is whether he has ever tested the test.[1]

To think clearly, we must consciously address which thoughts and values we are influenced by, and against which we evaluate different views. Therefore, we cannot avoid some philosophy. Such an approach has historical roots, as the study of nature was indeed once called natural philosophy. Some would argue that philosophy is unnecessary, and that natural science alone has all the answers. Such a view is both superficial and ahistorical.

Here we will look at why we think that science is even possible. Then we will address Aristotle's four explanations that underpin antiquity's and partly the Middle Ages' scientific views. Two of these, *form* and *purpose*, were downplayed in the early modern era and replaced with a mechanistic view of nature, yet a nature that was assumed to be governed by divine laws. Gradually, these laws of nature have been disconnected from the lawgiver and considered as independent causes. Behind most of these views lies the assumption that it is possible to understand nature. This is something we take for granted today, but it has not always been self-evident.

IS SCIENCE POSSIBLE?

How do we know that it is possible to uncover deeper relationships in nature? In the previous chapter we saw that the Greek view tended to attribute divine properties to nature. This particularly applied to space, the part of the universe that was beyond the Moon, which was considered easier to understand than the Earth, since it followed a sort of divine logic. In antiquity, nature was readily given animistic traits because physics and biology were not distinguished properly. Even solid substances like metal were assumed to have natural tendencies, almost like instincts

---

1. Chesterton, "Revival of Philosophy," 176.

in animals. History, as we saw, was also assumed to repeat itself in a cyclical view of history.

One aspect is how we view nature. Another equally important factor is how we view the possibility for us to understand nature. Johannes Kepler's statement from chapter 3 that the laws of nature are within our grasp because God created us in his own image is one of the strongest statements there is about man's ability to decipher nature. Our creation in God's image is often repeated in this book for that reason. It is unique as no other creation stories say anything close to this.

Its consequence, that all humans are of equal worth, is not found by studying nature. On the contrary, there is much in nature that suggests the opposite. A Greek philosopher like Aristotle, for example, believed that some people were born to be slaves. The idea of equality comes from the Bible, not from nature, as historian Tom Holland explains. He tells how the idea that we are all equal before God motivated Gregory of Nyssa (335–395) as well as his brother Basil of Caesarea (330–376) to establish one of the very first hospitals for the poor. They were inspired by their elder sister Macrina (327–379). During a period of food shortage, she would regularly visit the dumps in Cappadocia to pick up baby girls who had been abandoned by their parents. The fate of the girls would either be to die there or, at best, to be picked up by someone to be slaves or prostitutes. Macrina, on the other hand, treated them as if they were her own children. Similarly, the Quaker William Penn (1644–1718) could assert that there is no ranking of people based on skin color, and that therefore no one was born to be either slaves or masters.[2]

Kepler's statement above explains why many early scientists considered science to be possible. At the same time, we have our natural inclination to promote self-interests and even evil, as the Bible from the beginning paints a picture of a creature that opposes God and promotes itself. We are tempted to take shortcuts if it benefits us. We often have too much faith in our own abilities and are offended by criticism. We often overlook what does not fit our own theories. This can make one wonder if it is possible to discover truths about nature at all. All experience suggests that we can find out a lot, but in recognition of human arrogance and selfishness, it is central in science that all ideas must be tested.

Nobel laureate Richard Feynman (1918–1988) put it well: "Science is a way of trying not to fool yourself. The first principle is not to fool

---

2. Holland, *Dominion*, 159–83, 413–39.

yourself, and you are the easiest person to fool."[3] It is not enough to have clever ideas about nature, the ideas must also match reality. This has elements in it that may remind us of Montesquieu's principle from 1748 about the division of power when governing a nation. Power should be divided into a legislative, an executive, and a judicial branch so they can control each other, thereby preventing abuse. The very first modern constitutions, such as the American one from 1787 and the Norwegian constitution from 1814, are all based on this very realistic acknowledgment that people will always seek to gain power. The principle of division of power is also in the British constitutional system, which has roots back to the Magna Carta of 1215, which reduced the king's power, the executive power. Montesquieu considered the independence of the courts the most important. In the same way, experiment and observation are what ultimately determine whether a scientific theory is correct.

One of the best examples of testing by observation is the general theory of relativity from 1915. When it was launched, it was just a beautiful mathematical theory, and it was incomprehensible to most people—and still is, for that matter. Relativity could explain a problem that physicists had struggled with since 1859, which relates to a small deviation in the orbit of Mercury. During the solar eclipse in 1878, many astronomers tried to find Vulcan, a hypothetical planet between the Sun and Mercury, as this was one of the best candidates to explain the discrepancy. But it was not possible to calculate Vulcan's orbit unambiguously and, more importantly, Vulcan was never observed. Then came Einstein, who said that since Mercury is so much under the influence of the Sun's gravitation and moves so quickly, Newton's theory is not accurate enough. With Einstein's improved theory, however, theory and practice were in harmony. Another prediction was that light should be deflected twice as much by gravity as Newton's theory suggests. This was confirmed during yet another solar eclipse in 1919, and this confirmation was important for making Einstein a celebrity. Such predictions are necessary for a theory to be accepted as more than just beautiful mathematics or elegant principles, but as a theory that indeed says something true about nature.

---

3. Feynman and Leighton, *Surely You're Joking, Mr. Feynman!*, 343.

Whatever Will Be, Will Be

A colleague of mine shared a story from a marriage where one of them had grown up in Norway, but in a foreign cultural context. When the couple arrived at Oslo Airport for a trip abroad, the question arose whether their luggage was insured. It quickly became clear that the answer was no. The thought was completely alien to the foreign-cultured individual who believed that whatever happens will happen anyway. Many such reactions are subconscious, but our thinking can be a result of a culture shaped by the idea that God meticulously controls all things. This, in turn, can blend into determinism, where the belief is that our fate is predetermined and that everything that happens is a direct expression of God's will.

This way of thinking had its proponents in seventeenth-century Europe as well, especially in France. It is called occasionalism. The concept comes from the notion that there might be an occasion that precedes a result, which, without being the true cause, is the occasion for which it occurs. If the luggage in the example above were lost, the theft would not be the explanation because it was just an occasion God used to express his will. Islamic theology is to some extent characterized by this, especially since the Ash'ari tradition took over from the rationalistic Mu'tazilah tradition in the twelfth century.

Primary and Secondary Causes

The most crucial marker against occasionalism was the distinction introduced in early medieval times between primary and secondary causes. Both Guillaume (William) de Conches, who worked in Chartres in France (figure 29) and Thomas Aquinas played crucial roles. It would make it possible to entertain the two thoughts that God is in charge of nature, yet nature largely behaves rationally and is possible to explore.

De Conches rejected the idea of a deistic God who retreated after creation was complete. But he did not go along with the idea of a God who micromanages everything. He argued that there might be two reasons why something happens. The primary cause is God—without him nothing could happen. It is easy to think that the primary cause is the first thing that happens in a long chain of causes, such as the big bang at the establishment of the universe. But the primary cause goes even further; it is simply the reason why anything exists at all. It has its root in the uncreated God, the only one who exists in himself. The primary cause is also behind events that do not follow natural laws, such as Jesus's resurrection from the dead and his ascension.

Figure 29. The Cathedral of Chartres; construction began in 1045 and was completed around 1220. Guillaume (William) de Conches (ca. 1085–1154) came from Conches in Normandy but worked at the cathedral school in Chartres and possibly also in Paris. He wrote about how Plato could be reconciled with the Bible.[4]

For Thomas Aquinas, the idea of the primary cause was crucial to say that God is behind creation even if the world is eternal, as discussed

---

4. "Chartres 1," image courtesy of Atlant, CC BY 2.5, Wikimedia Commons.

in the previous chapter. The primary cause cannot be explored with natural science, precisely because it is the cause for natural science to be possible at all.

So how do things happen in nature? Well, by the laws or regularities that express how nature always acts in the same way. This is the secondary cause, and it can be explored with natural science. De Conches stressed that God is faithful and not capricious, and therefore these laws hold firm. The firmness of the laws makes it meaningful to explore nature.

The influence from de Conches can be found in *The King's Mirror* from the mid-thirteenth century, as mentioned in the introductory chapter. The author of *The King's Mirror* asks whether volcanoes come from the country's nature or have a spiritual origin—that is, are they due to a secondary or a primary cause?

The establishment of this distinction was a first step toward making modern, experimental natural science possible in Europe in the Middle Ages. Another crucial step was a new understanding of the Greek view of cause and effect from Aristotle.

ARISTOTLE'S FOUR EXPLANATIONS

Aristotle explained a phenomenon with four complementary explanations.[5] This way of thinking played a significant role during the Middle Ages but also encountered increasing opposition. Aristotle's ideas were further developed by Muslim interpreters such as Persian Avicenna (Ibn Sina, ca. 980–1037) and Spanish Moroccan Averroes (Ibn Rushd, 1126–1198). Thomas Aquinas, who called Aristotle "the philosopher" and Averroes "the commentator," united these ideas with Christian theology in the aftermath of what is called the Renaissance of the twelfth century.

The four explanations are easiest to understand with a concrete example of something man-made, like a dining table:

1. The dining table is made of wood, and that is the *material* explanation or cause.

2. The dining table is based on an idea of what makes it a dining table, answering the question, "What is it?" This includes dimensions such

---

5. I am using the word *explanation* here rather than the more common word *cause*, as cause usually is restricted to an explanation in the past as in Hocutt, "Aristotle's Four Becauses."

as how long, wide, and tall it should be. This is the *formal* cause or explanation and can also be called the idea, description, or blueprint.

3. A carpenter shapes the wood according to the design. This is the *efficient* cause. It answers the question, "What brought this into existence?" It is a cause that usually lies in the past.

4. The table was ordered because someone needed it for a big feast. This is the *final* cause, which has to do with purpose or intention. Explanation in terms of final causes is called *teleology*. It is often a cause that lies in the future, and it answers the question, "What is it for?"

Let us now consider the two of these which seem the most foreign to us, but which played a crucial role in the development of natural science. These are the concepts of *teleology* and *form*, items four and two in the list.

Purpose or Teleology

In the dining table example, *teleology* concerns a purpose that is imprinted on the materials from outside by a human being. The wood materials themselves do not have anything in them that points toward a purpose, and if they were placed in a pile, they would never form a table by themselves. The intention comes from the person who ordered the table. This is an example of so-called Platonic teleologism, which comes from outside—is extrinsic—and is the form of teleology that is easiest to understand.[6] In the example, the purpose comes from the person who ordered the table, but purpose can also be associated with a deity. *The King's Mirror* provides examples of such teleology used as an explanation for natural phenomena as in this statement about the volcanoes of Iceland:

> And God has made such great and terrifying things manifest upon Earth to man, not only that men may be the more vigilant, and may reflect that these tortures are indeed heavy to think upon, although after they depart this life, they will have to suffer those that they see while still on Earth.[7]

Here it is evident that nature is meant to teach us about what God intends.

---

6. The distinction between different forms of teleology is due to Feser, "Teleology," who uses the name *Platonic teleological realism* for what others call *Platonic teleologism*.

7. Larson, *King's Mirror*, 131.

Aristotle did not need such an extrinsic purpose.[8] For instance, a heart has the function of pumping blood around the body. That is the purpose of the heart, and it wouldn't be a heart if it didn't do that. Although Aristotle did not have the modern understanding of a heart's function, he would probably have agreed that the purpose thus comes from within—is intrinsic—and lies in the heart's nature, regardless of whether a god has arranged it that way or not. When you watch a nature program on television or hear a biologist speak, it doesn't take long before such explanations appear. This is often called *teleonomy* instead of teleology.[9] The term is especially used about organisms and thus denotes an intrinsic purpose. The distinction between teleonomy and teleology is meant to make it clearer that intrinsic purpose is different from extrinsic purpose.

This distinction also says something about the limitations of the machine image that is often used for an organism.[10] Throughout the ages, images from current technology have been used to characterize organisms. They have been compared to a clock where each gear is finely tuned to play together as a whole (seventeenth century), a steam engine (eighteenth century), and a chemical factory with a series of reactions that work together (nineteenth century). More specifically, the brain has been compared to a telephone exchange that connects distant parts (twentieth century), and in our time it is compared to a computer that handles information from a multitude of sensors.

These images continue a tradition all the way back to Nicolas Steno, whom we met in chapter 4. He commented that the brain is like a machine and further said in a lecture in Paris in 1665,

> There are two ways only of coming to know a machine: one is that the master who made it should show us its artifice; the other is to dismantle it and examine its most minute parts separately and as a combined unit.[11]

Here he formulated the reductionist program for brain research based on the machine metaphor. Although this has provided much insight, these comparisons are no more than images and have their limitations. Unlike

---

8. Von Glasersfeld, "Teleology and Concepts of Causation."

9. Teleonomy from Greek *telos* which means "goal" or "purpose" and *nomos* which means "law," while teleology derives from *logos* which means "a branch of learning."

10. Nicholson, "Organisms ≠ Machines."

11. Swanson, "Quest for the Basic Plan," 357. See also the preface of Cobb, *Idea of the Brain*.

machines, the brain's and organisms' internal steering toward purposes have an independent self. They organize and regulate themselves, and they repair themselves to some extent. Machines such as clocks, steam engines, factories, telephone exchanges, and computers must be organized, regulated, and repaired by the one who made them, external to the machines themselves.

Machines are always designed to be good for something outside of themselves, like a clock that tells the time for its user. The intrinsic purpose of organisms, we could say, is to live on, because life will reproduce itself. In a machine, each part is designed in advance to contribute to the whole. In an organism, the relationship between parts and the whole is much less clear. No part is really anything in itself, and they are not even the same all the time. The cells in the body are continuously recreated, and the cells I have today are not the same I had a few years ago—but still, I am the same person. In studies of the brain, it also turns out that it is not possible to precisely locate where things take place, unlike in a clock where each gear has a specific function. The brain has the ability to reorganize itself. The difference between machines with an extrinsic purpose and organisms with an intrinsic purpose is crucial, but still, the comparison with a machine remains a very useful, albeit limited, picture of how organisms and life function.

Form

The second foreign concept from Aristotle is *form*. This is probably the hardest of the four explanations to understand. We find a remnant of the idea in the word *inform* which originally means to transfer form, nature, or essence to something. This is also easiest to understand when it comes to living beings. *The King's Mirror*, for instance, says about a species of whale that "sea-faring men fear it very much, for it is by nature disposed to sport with ships."[12] It becomes more incomprehensible to us today when *The King's Mirror* also says that "these northern lights have this peculiar nature, that the darker the night is, the brighter they seem."[13] An explanation by reference to its nature does not seem to explain anything at all to us for a natural phenomenon like the northern lights.

---

12. Probably bowhead, also called Greenland whale. Larson, *King's Mirror*, 121.
13. Larson, *King's Mirror*, 149.

The central place of nature or form meant that discovering the "original" universal form behind a phenomenon was important in the Middle Ages. The external manifestations are just a kind of raw material for the intellect to find the universal form. As an example, there are many kinds of horses: strong workhorses and fast racehorses, brown and white, tall and short, but the central question is what the essence is of being a horse. This was something for the intellect to figure out. Thought processes were therefore at least as important as observations for the pursuit of natural philosophy.

In Aristotle's thinking, the form of all things has to do with the essence of things, that which makes it what it truly is. For all living beings, plants, animals, and humans, the soul is the form-explanation. The natural tendency of things also has to do with form, such as a stone seeking toward low ground and a flame seeking upward.

Aristotle distinguishes between natural and unnatural motion. The natural motion of a mass is either straight-line, when it falls, or it is circular, like the Moon going around the Earth. An unnatural motion is what is imparted on a cannonball as it is shot out. A corresponding example from the animal world of unnatural motion is the behavior an animal exhibits in captivity as opposed to under natural conditions. Everyone knows that it is almost impossible to learn anything about the wild behavior of animals by studying them in captivity. Therefore, it was not as obvious to them as it is to us that studying the behavior of a stone under controlled experiments would say much about how a stone truly behaves on its own. An enforced unnatural motion did not indicate anything about the stone's natural motion and its true nature. This animistic view of nature meant that there was not much value seen in conducting experiments. This attitude was a hindrance that held Greek science back. Observations, on the other hand, where what was studied was not influenced, such as in astronomy, were a different matter and an area where the Greeks excelled.

Aristotle's logical fourfold division is useful even today. It can help to distinguish between different types of causes and explanations. And it is important to understand how we have moved away from these four explanations, especially in the field of natural science. People in the Middle Ages used knowledge of nature in a different way than we do today. This was in particular evident when it came to purpose, which often was associated with moral teachings. Think of the pelican, which often lets its large beak rest on its chest. This action is probably the origin of the Greek legend that the pelican could peck itself to bleed to feed its young. In this way, it became an image of Christ, who gave everything for us, and therefore the pelican was used in coats of arms from the Middle Ages.[14]

Goals and Purposes Exist Outside of Science

Most people today would agree that the *efficient* explanation, like the carpenter in the table example, is primarily what we associate with cause. Second comes the *material* explanation, like the wood material the table is made of. These two explanations may be thought of as energy and mass respectively, and they are the only ones that can be described precisely with mathematics. The other two seem a bit irrelevant.

We are influenced by a way of thinking that philosopher and statesman Francis Bacon, among others, advocated for. Bacon says that

> the handling of final causes, mixed with the rest in physical inquiries, has intercepted the severe and diligent inquiry of all real and physical causes, . . . to the great arrest and prejudice of further discovery.[15]

Bacon encourages us to forget the teleological explanation, or the purpose of the table. That only leads to speculation. Narrowing the focus to the efficient explanation became central in natural science and one of the reasons for its success. When we think of cause today, it is therefore always the material and efficient explanations we have in mind.

At the same time, unfortunately, many take this too far. The absence of the study of purpose only means that teleology is of a different character than other explanations. It does not mean that there are no purposes, but nature is not so simple and unambiguous when it comes to understanding them. Therefore, purpose cannot be studied and understood in the same way as other causes. They simply belong to other areas, such as philosophy and theology. Bacon also clearly says that teleological explanations exist:

> I had rather believe all the fables in the Legend and the Talmud, and the Alcoran, than that this universal frame is without a mind.[16]

---

14. Harrison, *Territories of Science and Religion*, 61–62.
15. Bacon, *Advancement of Learning* 7.7.
16. Bacon, "XVI. Of Atheism."

He believed in a mind behind the universe—that is, purpose and teleology. In the terminology of philosophy, we can say that the lack of teleology is epistemological, not ontological. There is teleology, mind, thought, and design behind nature, but natural science is not the tool to gain knowledge about it. Something similar is said in the preface to the second edition of Newton's *Principia* from 1713. It was written by the mathematics professor Roger Cotes, who had assisted Newton with the publication of this edition:

> This most beautiful system of the Sun, planets, and comets could only proceed from the counsel and dominion of an intelligent and powerful Being.... This Being governs all things, not as the soul of the world, but as the Lord over all. And on account of his dominion, he is wont to be called Lord God or Universal Ruler.[17]

Bacon, Newton, and Cotes all have quite clear ideas on what is behind it all, what the teleological explanation is. It is God himself who has willed it so, and, in that sense, the three are advocates for a form of Platonic teleologism.

Form Explanations Are Replaced by Natural Laws

Natural laws are so central to modern science that we don't think much about where the term *natural law* comes from. Laws have not always played a central role, for although regularities have been observed at all times, people thought that they were an expression of natural inclinations. The regularities were expressions of *form* or soul, whether it applied to animals or objects. In *Opticks* (1704), Newton only expressed something that had already become a common way of thinking when he rejected that a thing's *form*, which here is called occult in the sense of hidden and incomprehensible, has any value:

> Such occult qualities put a stop to the improvement of natural philosophy, and therefore of late years have been rejected. To tell us that every species of things is endowed with an occult specific quality by which it acts and produces manifest effects, is to tell us nothing.[18]

---

17. Quoted in Koperski, *Divine Action*, 75.
18. Quoted in Koperski, *Divine Action*, 70.

It is worth noting here that there is a difference between what happened with Aristotle's formal cause explanation and with the final cause explanation. Form was deemed worthless and completely abandoned, at least when it comes to dead objects. Final cause explanations, on the other hand, were set aside and regarded as impossible to study with natural science. But they were there all the same. It is only in our time that natural scientists can bring themselves to believe that there is no purpose and meaning in nature since such purpose and meaning is not found in science.

A typical example is the statement by American theoretical physicist and Nobel laureate Steven Weinberg (1933–2021) that "the more the universe seems comprehensible, the more it also seems pointless."[19] One can wonder what criterion Weinberg would have deemed sufficient to conclude otherwise. Francis Bacon would have responded that since purpose or point cannot be found in physics, this view is a philosophical view. The quote is a worldview statement, reflecting Weinberg's atheism, disguised as a scientific statement. Weinberg's view of purposelessness represents unfortunately a very common misunderstanding of science in our time.

LAWS OF NATURE

The Greeks used concepts such as *inherent properties*, *nature*, *tendencies*, or *form* rather than *laws of nature*. Guillaume de Conches and Roger Bacon (ca. 1210–ca. 1292) were early among those who talked about laws. Roger Bacon wrote about optics and spoke of the "law of refraction." Copernicus talks about laws for planetary orbits. Kepler also uses the term *law* about optics, and as mentioned in chapter 3, he explained that he gained insight into the Creator's thoughts when he studied the laws for how planets behaved.[20]

Natural Laws in the Early Modern Period

In the 1600s, and especially with Descartes, laws of nature were clearly formulated as an expression of God's will. Aristotle's form concept was now completely abandoned.[21] This is expressed in the quote above from

---

19. Weinberg, *First Three Minutes*, 149.
20. Ruby, "Origins of Scientific 'Law.'"
21. This topic is more thoroughly discussed in Henry, "Metaphysics and Origins,"

Roger Cotes in Newton's *Principia*, which continues to refer to God as the source of the laws of nature:

> From this source, then, have all the laws that are called laws of nature come.[22]

Here it is clear that natural laws are related to the belief that there is a legislator behind nature. The Irish natural philosopher Robert Boyle (1627–1691), who is behind the law that the volume of a gas is inversely proportional to the pressure, agreed with Newton and said that

> nature is not to be looked on, as a distinct or separate agent, but as a rule, or rather a system of rules, according to which these agents and the bodies they work on, are, by the great Author of things, determined to act and suffer.[23]

Furthermore, the English philosopher and priest Samuel Clarke (1675–1729) says in defense of Newton that

> the course of nature, truly and properly speaking, is nothing else but the will of God producing certain effects in a continued, regular, constant, and uniform manner.[24]

Philosopher of science Jeffrey Koperski sums this up by stating seventeenth-century philosophers found "substantial forms were useless intermediaries between God and creation," and instead, "laws are nothing more than patterns within God's will for how nature must behave. They were not thought of as autonomous agents that God created in order to govern nature."[25]

Many believe that the science revolution of the 1500s and 1600s was a rediscovery and continuation of Greek science from antiquity. Newton and many of his contemporary natural philosophers disagreed, emphasizing that with the new view of natural laws, they broke with antiquity and created something completely new.

---

and in Koperski, *Divine Action*, 69–85.

22. Quoted in Koperski, *Divine Action*, 75.

23. The word *suffer* has changed meaning and *endure* may be a more appropriate modern term.

24. Both Boyle and Clarke are cited in Koperski, *Divine Action*, 73.

25. Koperski, *Divine Action*, 99.

Thinking or Experimenting?

Roger Cotes, in Newton's *Principia*, continues by discussing how natural laws can be explored:

> From this source, then, have all the laws that are called laws of nature come, in which many traces of the highest wisdom and counsel certainly appear, but no traces of necessity. Accordingly, we should not seek these laws by using untrustworthy conjectures but learn them by observing and experimenting.[26]

Natural laws, says Cotes, do not derive from some underlying principle that can be thought out—a conjecture—and it is not by necessity that they are the way they are. Nature could be organized in many ways, for God can do what he wills. This view is called *voluntarism*.[27] Here we see a break from the resistance to experiments found in the animistic explanation of form and the distinction between natural and unnatural movements, as previously mentioned. Instead, observation and experiments have now become necessary to find out how God, in his sovereignty, has willed to arrange nature. This cannot be understood by thought alone. The germ of such reasoning is already found in the condemnations of parts of Aristotle's thoughts from 1277, which the bishop of Paris was behind. The condemnation consisted of 219 propositions and emphasized, for example, that God can create multiple worlds, and that God can create something entirely new.[28]

Cotes says that the laws do not necessarily have to be the way they are, and that we cannot find them out from assumptions. He distances himself from the opposite of voluntarism, which is pure *intellectualism* or *rationalism*. In this view, the act of creation is primarily an expression of God's thoughts. Kepler's argument from 1597 that the planets' orbits seemed to fit in between the five Platonic solids (see chapter 3) has a strong element of such intellectualism. It is reminiscent of the Greek idea that the planets' orbits must be circles because they were simple and beautiful. Behind this was a belief that God has characteristics that make him prefer such elegant theories. However, Kepler later got access to Tycho's accurate observational data and had to revise his ideas when it turned

---

26. Quoted in Koperski, *Divine Action*, 75.
27. From the Latin word *voluntas*, which means will.
28. Propositions 34 and 48 are discussed in Grant, *Foundations of Modern Science*, 78–80.

out that nature, or God, did not quite fit into this beautiful model. Nature gave different answers than those Kepler initially concluded, based on assumptions about how God had arranged it. Nevertheless, Kepler's first book on Platonic solids came out in a revised edition in 1621, so he was probably fascinated by this view all his life.

Thus, even for Kepler it was the empirical data found by experiments and observation that was decisive. The voluntaristic view of Cotes and Newton is therefore usually called *empiricism*, and it is this perspective, as opposed to intellectualism, that has been the underlying idea in natural science since the seventeenth century. Even more accurate is to say that it is a combination of the two that applies. New theories may indeed be thought out intellectually, but it is confirmation through experiments and observation that makes science what it is today.

Unfortunately, we now find examples of some trying to make such confirmation less important again. This is particularly true for string theory, which concerns the very smallest elementary particles. It is also the case for inflation theory, which may be one description for the expansion of the universe immediately after the big bang. Inflation theory has been launched as a hypothesis for how the universe could have expanded so rapidly that it split into independent "bubbles" and formed separate universes. This is the multiverse theory, which some rely on when claiming that our universe is just one of many that have come about by chance. Cosmologists George Ellis and Joe Silk are right when they say that it undermines science when some try to exempt such speculative theories about the universe from observational or experimental confirmation. They urge to "defend the integrity of physics," which is also the title of their article, and they go against colleagues who claim that if a theory is sufficiently elegant and has enough explanatory power, then experiments are not needed.[29] Science writer John Horgan calls this type of speculative science "ironic science," and emphasizes that a science that cannot be confirmed cannot arrive at any form of truth. Horgan has been critical of this for a long time and rightly says that exemptions from experimental confirmation blur the lines between real science and pseudoscience.[30]

---

29. Ellis and Silk, "Scientific Method: Defend the Integrity of Physics."
30. Horgan, *End of Science*, which was reissued in 2015.

To What Extent Does God Interfere with the Course of Nature?

Natural laws in the seventeenth century for physics and mechanics were considered expressions of how God acts in nature. The laws did not have an independent role and were not causes of something happening. But gradually this understanding has been changed and become the opposite, as expressed by Albert Einstein who said that natural laws exclude that God can be involved:

> The man who is thoroughly convinced that the law of cause and effect operates universally, cannot for a single moment entertain the idea of a being that interferes in the course of events.[31]

Many today believe the same, and that there is no room for a God in nature. The universe runs like clockwork and is determined by laws. Einstein was a *noninterventionist* to such an extent that it is doubtful whether he believed that God had any role at all in maintaining creation. His God was not the God of theism, but a pantheistic and deistic god.[32] Einstein seemed to believe that involving God meant that everything would then be micromanaged, nothing would run regularly, and nature would be impossible to understand.

The medieval division into primary and secondary causes is a kind of middle way in viewing God's role in nature. Newton and other early natural philosophers saw the secondary causes as expressing that most of nature follows regular laws. Nevertheless, there are degrees of difference in the view of how much God interferes in nature, even for theists like them. It concerns many things, from views on the operation of natural laws to the question of whether God answers specific prayers or not. This is a large and complicated issue that I can only touch on here.

As an example, Newton and Gottfried Leibniz (1646–1716) disagreed as Newton, on the one hand, was an interventionist who believed that God sometimes could and had to break the natural laws. God needed, for instance, now and then to "nudge" the planets into place because gravity would otherwise pull them too close to each other. Leibniz, on the other hand, was a noninterventionist. Leibniz is thus closer to being a

---

31. Einstein, *Ideas and Opinions*, 39.

32. Theism is concerned with a God who is active in creation, but different from it as opposed to pantheism where God is in everything and everything is God. Deism is the view that God created the world and then withdrew, leaving the world to operate according to rational laws, but where there is no room for intervention of any kind, including revelation through the Bible.

deist but probably did not consider himself one. He believed that if God needed to fix nature, it would mean that he had not managed to create the world well enough the first time. Leibniz thought such incompetence was incompatible with God's character. Similar dividing lines exist today.

Natural Laws Today

Einstein saw it as impossible to accept a capricious God who tampered with nature. But such a problematic understanding of God's relationship to nature was already resolved in the medieval period when they, as mentioned, distinguished between primary and secondary causes. It is also worth noting that Newton and Cotes had the opposite problem: how can we justify natural laws if there is no lawgiver?

The way we view natural laws today has something self-contradictory about it: there are laws, and they can also be the cause of something happening, but there is no one behind them. In a mysterious way, Nature-with-a-capital-N dictates itself what happens and how things can happen. One way to avoid this contradiction is not to take a stance on why nature follows rules, and to say instead that natural laws just describe what happens. This is often considered the position of the philosopher David Hume (1711–1776). But this view is not without its problems. For example, we were convinced that it was possible to say how gravitation works on planet Mars long before any spacecraft had been there. We had no experiments from Mars to point to, and if we were to follow Hume to the extreme, we would not be able to express ourselves on this matter. But the fact is that we consider Newton's and Einstein's laws so universal that they also apply to other planets, and we do not depend on travelling there to check.

On the one hand, Einstein and many with him stand for the idea that the laws require nature to act in a certain way. On the other hand, Hume stands for an alternative that says the laws just describe what happens; he does not take a position on what lies behind. A third way is to abandon the whole idea of laws. The American philosopher of science Nancy Cartwright (b. 1957) says it like this:

> I think that in the concept of law there is a bit too much of God. We try to finesse the issue. . . . But in the end the concept of a law does not make sense without the supposition of a law-giver.[33]

---

33. Cartwright, "Is Natural Science 'Natural' Enough," 299. See also Cartwright,

This is a confirmation of Newton's view of the need for God as a lawgiver as the source for natural laws. As an alternative, Cartwright is a proponent of a view that vaguely resembles Aristotle's concept of form. I find it hard to see that this has anything to contribute to sciences like physics, mechanics, and chemistry, but it is easier to see that it can have something to offer in parts of biology and medicine. These fields have more complex connections within them and resemble more Aristotle's original model for causes, which was inspired by biology.

Natural Laws Are Not Causes

I would rather advocate the original seventeenth-century understanding of natural laws in subjects such as physics, mechanics, and chemistry and problematize today's ideas on natural laws as causes. Cartwright is right that it is hard to imagine natural laws if there is no legislator. The old saying that God "has arranged all things by measure and number and weight"[34] also points toward a lawmaker. Chemistry professor Peter Waage from the University of Oslo was known to quote it, as mentioned in the introduction. Like many other researchers, he saw it is the assumption of God, more than anything else, that supports the belief in the lawfulness of nature.

In the physical sciences, the most fundamental laws and equations are today called "governing" equations. I don't really like this term because it gives the impression that natural laws are causes, as many in our time believe. A comparison with completely different kinds of laws can clarify what I mean. It is not difficult to find examples of governing laws, but these are not laws of nature. I grew up less than a two-hour drive from Sweden and, as a child, I always found it amusing every time we came to the border where the road went like an X. From here, you had to switch from driving on the right-hand side to the left-hand side. In 1967, Sweden decided to switch. Early in the morning on September 3, at 4:45 a.m., all cars stopped and remained still for a quarter of an hour before they switched over and continued driving on the right-hand side. This was the result of a decision by the Swedish Parliament on May 10, 1963. The example illustrates how a law was the cause of what happened more than four years later. The law set the norm for how people were supposed to behave. It was *normative*, as it's called.

"No God, No Laws."

34. Wis 11:20 (NRSVUE).

With natural laws, it is completely different. According to the original idea, they express how God has arranged nature. They have not been decided by an authority that can punish those who decide to violate them. In fact, they cannot even be broken. Therefore, natural laws are not laws in the legal sense, but descriptions of patterns—they are *descriptive*, not normative. Natural laws also provide limited insight into how nature really works at its deepest level, like the primary cause.

The eighteenth-century interpretation of the mechanical model of the universe, inspired by Newton's laws, went too far. Earlier natural philosophers like Pierre-Simon Laplace (1749–1827) believed that if they only knew the initial conditions, they could calculate absolutely everything that would happen later. The universe was like a clockwork, and all the rules were completely unveiled. They therefore believed that the laws explained how nature really is at the profoundest level, not just that they described our observations of nature.

The height of such belief was perhaps when deviations in the orbit of Uranus, the sixth planet, which had been found in 1781, could be explained with a seventh planet. The new planet's path was calculated, and Neptune was found in 1846, as the first planet to be discovered based on a calculation. It is understandable that this could give rise to a certain arrogance and a belief that it was possible to predict everything.

Modern physics has strengthened us in the belief that we cannot really explain the deepest secrets of the universe, although there is no shortage of those who would like to tell us that we can. Therefore, I cringe a little every time I see a headline saying that "Physics Require . . .," because this is a very superficial way of thinking about natural laws, which confuses cause and effect. Once, during a lecture, I was asked to explain where gravitation comes from. Of course, I couldn't. Newton himself said in an appendix to *Principia* from 1713 that he would not make any hypothesis about it.[35] Today we know more about gravitation than Newton did through Einstein's general theory of relativity and quantum physics. Gravitation may be described by the curvature of space, and there may be a particle called graviton. But these are primarily better descriptions, not explanations that tell us why gravitation exists in the first place. So, the question of origin is still open, and some of these questions are probably beyond what can be studied with natural science.

---

35. Newton used the expression *hypotheses non fingo* in Latin.

Although biology and evolution cannot be so easily described with simple natural laws, Darwin himself used the term *natural law* about evolution. He also distinguished between primary and secondary causes. He wrote that,

> To my mind it accords better with what we know of the laws impressed on matter by the Creator, that the production and extinction of the past and present inhabitants of the world should have been due to secondary causes, like those determining the birth and death of the individual.[36]

WHAT IS SCIENCE?

This chapter has shown that there is a limit to what natural science can tell us about extrinsic intentions or teleology that are imposed on nature from the outside. Intentions are nevertheless clearly incorporated into nature as in the intrinsic teleonomy. In themselves, they may point toward a creator, but do not have to, and we are leaving the field of natural science in contemplating that.

At this point it is time to state more exactly what science is. One of the first things that comes to mind is that science is a special method for finding things out. That captures some of the essence, but it is not a definition of science per se, but rather how scientific knowledge is found. Here is a better definition that encompasses much of what has been said earlier in this chapter:

> Nothing which is non-quantitative is the business of science. But everything which is quantitative is its business. Non-quantitative aspects of existence, such as purpose, freedom, design, honesty, cannot be handled by science because they are not quantitative propositions. But every bit of matter is quantitative and therefore the business of science.[37]

This is a quote from Stanley Jaki who continues by explaining how quantities are different from other concepts, such as qualities. Only for the latter is it meaningful to apply the phrase, "more or less." Jaki says, "Goodness can be realized in various degrees, more or less. Alertness too.

---

36. Darwin, *Origin of Species*, 488.
37. Jaki, "Biblical Basis of Western Science," para. 34; see also Jaki, "Power and Poverty of Science."

Any food can taste good, more or less. But it is not possible to state about the number five that it is more five or less five."[38]

Jaki's statement is a good starting point, but to avoid the misunderstanding that science is only about the "how" of juggling numbers, it needs to be explained. Science is also about understanding in the form of relationships between phenomena, often mathematical. Jaki's statement may also be interpreted to mean that the focus on quantities means that science consists of precise and timeless truths. To avoid this, I like to add that science ultimately is a creative process of exploring the unknown, implying that theories and understanding will be revised.

To conclude this chapter, an understanding of the possibilities and limits of science, as well as conscious or unconscious thinking about natural laws and intentions will have a decisive impact on how we think about a topic like evolution, as the next chapter will discuss.

---

38. Jaki, "Biblical Basis of Western Science," para. 36.

6

Evolution and Purpose

> Another source of conviction in the existence of God...follows from the extreme difficulty or rather impossibility of conceiving this immense and wonderful universe, including man with his capacity of looking far backwards and far into futurity, as the result of blind chance or necessity. When thus reflecting I feel compelled to look to a First Cause having an intelligent mind in some degree analogous to that of man; and I deserve to be called a Theist.
>
> CHARLES DARWIN, AUTOBIOGRAPHY

FOR MANY YEARS, I have had a beautiful, polished fossil on my desk. It is an ammonite from Morocco, a kind of extinct squid with an external shell shaped like a beautiful spiral with a diameter of four to five centimeters. It is dated to the Devonian period, which is considered to have lasted until 359 million years ago. The ammonites were extinct along with the dinosaurs 66 million years ago. Every time I look at it, I wonder what life on Earth might have been like when it was alive, and also how much or how little we know about what has happened since then.

Questions on evolution are certainly a topic I have struggled with myself. For a long time, I felt uncomfortable every time a nature program on TV claimed that "evolution has made it so," that "chance has led to this," and that everything, including us humans, therefore just happened to be the way it is and there is no deeper meaning behind it all. It seemed to me that the commentators were making evolution a kind of God-replacement. On the other hand, it was a bit strange that the same programs could say "because of gravity, so . . ." without me feeling the same discomfort.

Personally, I have tried to deal with evolution in several ways. There was a short period when I believed that it was classical Christian belief to read the first part of the book of Genesis literally as an account of what had happened in the last then thousand years. It gradually became difficult for me to believe that science, with its basis in the belief of an ordered, God-given creation, should give such confusing results that major features came out completely wrong.

I have adopted the point of view of C. S. Lewis here. At the age of fifty-two he wrote, "I don't see how at my age, I can start making myself a good enough Biologist to reply to the Darwinians."[1] Lewis was humble enough to view evolutionary theory as an outsider, like me, and as long as scientists consider it to be the best theory, he would follow them. This is the example I follow here also. Biological theories are complex and more or less informed opinions from outsiders carry little weight. The emphasis here is on explaining current theories and referring to those who are closer to the field than me, in order to explain their limitations.

In this chapter, we will therefore look at evolution from both a scientific and a philosophical standpoint, and in the following chapter specifically at humankind. These chapters are largely based on the previous one about the philosophy of science, especially regarding the discussion of purpose.

EVOLUTION IS NOT WHAT YOU THINK IT IS

Several different terms are used for evolution, such as *Darwinism*, and *neo-Darwinism*. The different terms can have a precise scientific meaning, but some of the terms also have broader meanings that touch on worldviews.

---

1. Ferngren and Numbers, "C. S. Lewis on Creation and Evolution," 30.

Figure 30. Charles Darwin (1809–1882), English naturalist who proposed the theory of evolution in the book *The Origin of Species* in 1859. The book introduced the principle of "natural selection" as opposed to the "artificial selection" that occurs in animal breeding. *The Descent of Man*, published in 1871, also deals with human origins. Darwin had a complex relationship with the Christian faith he was raised in and eventually identified as an agnostic. Nevertheless, his 1859 book has many references to the Creator. Since Darwin's time, there are few scientific works that include such references.[2]

We may use the term *Darwinism* for Charles Darwin's (figure 30) original explanation from 1859 and the following years. For some reason, the other originator of the theory, Alfred Russel Wallace (1823–1913),

---

2. "Charles Darwin by Julia Margaret Cameron," Art Institute of Chicago, Wikimedia Commons.

is nearly forgotten. Darwin and Wallace presented their theories at the same meeting in London on July 1, 1858, and Darwin published his influential book the year after. It was as much biogeography as fossils that convinced them about evolution. Biogeography deals with the distribution of animals and plants on Earth and the observation that certain species are found only in some places and not others. Darwin's expedition with the ship *Beagle* to South America, New Zealand, and Australia in the period from 1831 to 1836 was significant as biogeography is most evident in the southern hemisphere. In the more contiguous land masses of Europe, Asia, and North America, wildlife is far more uniform. Wallace's name is especially associated with the discovery of the dividing line between the flora and fauna of Borneo, Bali, and the rest of Indonesia and Asia on the northwest side of what is now called the Wallace Line, and Australia, New Guinea, and Sulawesi on the other. On the Indonesian side, there are Asian animals like elephants, rhinoceroses, and orangutans and on the other side kangaroos and other marsupials. This suggests that life has taken a very different avenue and has a different history on the more isolated Australian side than on the Asian side.

The theory of evolution was modified with time, mainly from 1920 to 1950, leading to neo-Darwinism. The term *Darwinism* is used today for several concepts. On the one hand, it is a historical term that encompasses Darwin's original theory. On the other hand, it is used for the updated view that should more accurately be called neo-Darwinism. But in some circles, Darwinism generates strong associations with an atheistic and materialistic view of life that denies any purpose. Such lack of clarity can quickly make the discussion about evolution heated and can lead to people talking past each other. In the scientific community, the term *Darwinism* is rarely used at all, as it does not reflect the breadth and depth of modern evolutionary theory. To avoid misunderstanding, I will therefore avoid using the term *Darwinism* here.

Even the more neutral term *evolutionary theory* evokes quite different thoughts in people. Below, I have listed some potential elements in a definition:

1. The beginning of life on Earth about 3.5–4 billion years ago.
2. All life is related and has developed from simpler to more complex forms.

3. Natural selection guides development, which means that offspring differ slightly from parents. This leads to random changes where those that are best adapted survive.

4. There is neither purpose nor meaning in the development of nature or the universe at large.

5. Society is also subject to evolution, and the best adapter survives, as summarized in the term *social Darwinism*.

Different understandings of the term *evolution* can lead to apparent conflicts, exemplified by black/white assertions such as "Evolution as a theory is in crisis." Others frame apparent dichotomies such as "No to God. Yes, to Darwin" or "Evolution or creation?" It's possible that those who say this may have a very broad definition of evolution in mind, even encompassing the seven points of cosmic evolution from the list in chapter 2 (see p. 44), as well as the five points listed here. On the other hand, you have individuals like the prominent British atheist Richard Dawkins (b. 1941), an evolutionary biologist himself. He has stated that "Darwin made it possible to be an intellectually fulfilled atheist."[3] Clearly, this conflicts with what Charles Darwin himself wrote in the quote at the beginning of this chapter as well as in the last sentence of *The Origin of Species*: "There is grandeur in this view of life, with its several powers, having been originally breathed by the Creator into a few forms or into one."[4] Although Darwin may not have considered himself Christian, he certainly was not an atheist. The statement about the Creator can be found in all editions from the second in 1859 to the sixth in 1871. Sadly, it is absent in many versions of Darwin's book—for example, in the latest Norwegian translation, as it is based on the first edition. They follow a practice from Ernst Mayr starting in 1964 who wished to present Darwin at his "most revolutionary," thus underplaying Darwin's own revisions, and obscuring his clarifications.[5]

To have a meaningful discussion, we must clarify what is meant by evolution in a scientific sense. It will become apparent that several of the five points listed above can be excluded.

---

3. Dawkins, *Blind Watchmaker*, 6.
4. Darwin, *Origin of Species*, 429.
5. Priest, "Revisiting the Origin of Species."

Evolution According to Science

One of the first things that struck me was that science has a different and much narrower definition of evolution than what is conveyed by popular culture. When Darwin spoke of evolution and natural selection and titled his book *The Origin of Species*, it clearly only pertains to life. What separates life from all else is the ability to reproduce and pass on genetic material. Thus, cosmic development is not part of Darwin's theory.

I then read a leading textbook on evolution written by American evolutionary biologist Douglas Futuyma (b. 1942).[6] Futuyma defines biological evolution as change in the properties of populations of organisms over many generations. The book *Evolution for Dummies* states that evolution is the process that causes populations and species to change over time.[7] This has to do with the relationship between species and change within species, and thus we are only talking about the fact that all life is related and natural selection means the best adapted survive, items two and three in the list on pages 167–68.

What may surprise some is what is not included. Specifically, evolution doesn't explain how life began. Futuyma writes that life started over 4 billion years ago, and that the start isn't that important. It's clear that what matters is studying life as we know it. Also, he notes that the lack of an explanation concerning the origin of life is an argument used against evolution. This lack of clarity likely arises because, for instance, science documentaries on television often conflate the origin of life with the evolution of life and are rarely successful in distinguishing established science from speculation. The start of life is thus easily portrayed as something we understand, even though we actually know very little about how it might have happened.

An example from a review paper will clarify this. It has the title "The Origin of Life: What We Know, What We Can Know and What We Will Never Know" and it states that "until the principles governing the process by which life on the Earth emerged can be uncovered . . ."[8] This carefully worded statement by scientists really says the same as science writer John Horgan, after having followed the field for decades, says directly: "Pssst! Don't Tell the Creationists, but Scientists Don't Have a Clue How Life Began." Since I am not a biologist myself, this illustrates my approach in this

---

6. Futuyma, *Evolutionary Biology*, 4.
7. Krukonis and Barr, *Evolution for Dummies*.
8. Pross and Pascal, "Origin of Life," 1.

chapter. I will state my point of view through what leading scientists in the field have to say, rather than try to argue from my necessarily limited understanding of biology.

Just like the big bang theory really is about what happened after the origin of the universe in a presumed big bang, evolution also refers to the development of life, after life had begun. Nonetheless, it cannot be overlooked that how life started is an immensely interesting field of research. But evolution presupposes the existence of life. Therefore, there often exists a discrepancy between what the public believes evolution to be and what biologists mean by the term. For a meaningful discussion, we need to be on the same page. Evolution is an explanation of how life has become so diverse, but it's not an explanation for the origin of life. This eliminates the first point in the list on pages 167–68.

Similarly, the fourth point concerning the absence of plan or purpose is also not part of Futuyma's definition, even though this doesn't prevent many biologists from having strong opinions about lack of purpose, with some authors discussing it in their books. I will return to this point later. Crucially, whether any potential lack of plan or purpose is included or not makes little difference to how evolutionary scientists perform their work and for evolution as a scientific concept.

The same holds true for social Darwinism, the last point in the list. Like most other academics today, the vast majority of evolutionary biologists reject this view. This perspective has several origins, but one major contributor was English philosopher Herbert Spencer (1820–1903), who used the concept of evolution to apply to everything from biology and human consciousness to society. He proposed that evolution progressed in stages toward the perfect human in the perfect society. He was also the one who coined the term *survival of the fittest*, which Darwin himself began to use. In social Darwinism, this has been misused to justify that the strongest should rule over the weak. This concept has been used as the basis for race theories, ideas about "racial hygiene," and eugenics, which is the misuse of science to promote dubious ideologies. The racial theories propagated by the Nazis and the atrocities that resulted during the Second World War opened our eyes to where social Darwinism can lead.

Now we're left with these two points from the five-point list on pages 167–68:

2. All life is related.

3. Natural selection leads to the survival of the fittest.

These points represent the core of what biological evolution is. It is first a story of how life has evolved from a common ancestor and second a description of the mechanism(s) for how life evolves. It is important to separate the two as the former is much easier to agree on than what the specifics of the mechanism are.

Neo-Darwinism

The "how" of evolution is a field where new knowledge has been constantly established since Darwin's time. The occurrence of evolution—that is, the relationship between species—was established as good science even before Darwin entered the arena. This was a result of all the fossil findings in the early nineteenth century and the growing understanding that life had a long history, as chapter 4 showed. What Darwin did was to introduce the mechanisms of natural selection and sexual selection. The best adapted, or those who succeeded best in finding a mate, could live on through their offspring.

So how does one get variation that gives rise to better adaptation for some individuals than for others? One of the factors that contributed to this knowledge was the discovery of the suitability of the theories of the Austrian monk Gregor Mendel (figure 31) about thirty-five years after he first presented them. What are now called Mendel's laws deal with principles and rules of inheritance.

Darwin himself shared his contemporaries' views that characteristics acquired by an individual during its lifetime could also be inherited. This idea is linked to the French zoologist Jean-Baptiste Lamarck and is therefore called Lamarckism.

In the 1880s, German August Weismann postulated that the inheritance effect is one-way. What he meant was that germ cells control the other cells in the body, but there is no influence from the other cells back to the germ cells. This is called the Weismann barrier, and it is an argument against Lamarckism. British Francis Crick also emphasized this in his central dogma from the 1950s. Then Dutchman Hugo de Vries discovered mutations, which are changes in a gene or chromosome, in the early twentieth century. Subsequently, population geneticists discovered the processes behind genetic drift,[9] gene flow,[10] and recombination—that is, the mixing of genes from two cells during sexual reproduction. The "modern synthesis," or neo-Darwinism, combines all these mechanisms, along with Mendel's laws and natural and sexual selection.

Figure 31. Gregor Mendel (1822–1884), Augustinian monk who worked in the St. Thomas Monastery in Brno, which is today in the Czech Republic, at that time part of Austria. Between 1856 and 1868, he conducted hybridization experiments with pea plants, which he presented as "Versuche über Pflanzen-Hybriden" (Experiments on plant hybrids) in 1865. His work remained almost unknown until it was rediscovered in the early twentieth century.[11]

9. Genetic drift is random variation that does not affect survival, and which is particularly important where there are small populations, as it often reduces genetic variation.

10. Gene flow is the exchange of genes and occurs when individuals migrate between different isolated populations. It prevents the formation of new species.

11. "Gregor Mendel," Wikimedia Commons.

Today, the modern synthesis is considered by many to be a sufficient explanation for most aspects of biology and paleontology. This is certainly the case when it comes to variation within a species, as in artificial selection or breeding with the goal of creating livestock that give more milk or less fatty meat. Many regard the modern synthesis as a good enough explanation for evolution from one species to another as well, but as we shall see, not all do. Here one has to consider that there may be multiple mechanisms playing a role. These are discussed under the term *extended evolutionary synthesis* later in this chapter.

Chance and Lack of Purpose

A central idea in neo-Darwinism is that mutations in genes occur entirely at random. These mutations are not conscious; they do not know which changes are advantageous. Therefore, evolution appears as a gamble where occasionally someone draws a lucky lottery ticket.

These chance occurrences are the origin of the idea about the lack of purpose, meaning, and direction in evolution, which is the fourth possible element in the definition of evolution in the five-point list on pages 167–68. Many scientists have advocated this, including American biologist Jerry Coyne (b. 1949) who says that we, "like them [other creatures], are also the product of blind and impersonal evolutionary forces."[12] Paleontologist G. G. Simpson (1902–1984) stated that "man is the result of a purposeless and materialistic process that did not have him in mind. He was not planned."[13] Futuyma also maintains that we find no traces of purpose or goals in the living world. Hence, he concludes that, since there are no purposes or design in nature, blind uncaring processes prevail.

The formulation on the web page of the Natural History Museum at the University of Oslo is less categorical. It states that "it is beyond the realm of science to prove that this process has any goal and planned control, and it must be up to each individual to fit the theory of evolution into their own worldview and religion."[14] In saying this, they imply that science has limitations, and I would also interpret the formulation to mean its negation, that it is not possible to scientifically prove the absence of a goal or direction.

---

12. Coyne, introduction to *Why Evolution Is True*, xvi.
13. Simpson, *Meaning of Evolution*, 344.
14. Naturhistorisk Museum, "Evolusjon" [Evolution], para. 7.

Coyne's, Simpson's, and Futuyma's arguments presuppose that randomness equates to a lack of purpose, meaning that neither any intelligence nor God is behind evolution. As a response to such statements, some attempt to show that central parts of the theory of evolution, such as the formation of new species, are simply incorrect. Others prefer to try to show that things are not as random as they appear to be. The main argument is to try to demonstrate that when structures are complex enough, they could not have arisen by chance.[15]

In addition, there is a development within the field of biology itself that suggests pure chance may play a lesser role than previously thought. The classic thought experiment is to rewind evolution a few billion years and start it again. Would we get the same animals, and would we be the same? This therefore also concerns the uniqueness of humans. I will address this scientific approach to chance and purpose later. As we will also see, there is a much better way to argue. It suggests that randomness does not have to mean there is no purpose behind it, and that purposes cannot really be explored with science. This will be a philosophical way of arguing but first let me review some limitations of evolutionary theory that even prominent scientists discuss.

The Inexplicability of Evolutionary Transitions

C. S. Lewis made a remark at the end of the 1940s where he distinguished between the biological theory of evolution and what he called the Great Myth: "In the science, Evolution is a theory about changes: in the Myth, it is a fact about improvements."[16] This distinction between change and improvement Lewis had learned from John B. S. Haldane (1892–1964), one of the founders of neo-Darwinism and a professed atheist and secular humanist. It will be evident that C. S. Lewis's and Haldane's view is not so different from the view held by many evolutionary biologists and geneticists even today.[17]

The challenge for evolutionary theory is still to explain *change*—that is, the apparent progress over the history of life, assuming that "[b]y any sensible measure of complexity, one is likely to conclude that biological

---

15. As in, for example, Behe, *Darwin Devolves*.
16. Lewis, "Funeral of a Great Myth," 85.
17. Most of this section builds on Holm, "Learning from C. S. Lewis's View on Evolution."

units of evolution in certain lineages got more complex through the 3.5 billion years of evolution."[18] The apparent progress in the history of life is marked by distinct evolutionary transitions.[19] Note that these transitions are different from the imprecise terminology *microevolution* and *macroevolution*. The latter usually means evolution at the order, class, or phylum level in the Linnean system—that is, within the same body plan. The transitions are at an even higher level. They are often expressed in highly technical terms, but a recent list of the major transitions in a more popular vocabulary is:[20]

1. The emergence of protocells, a self-organized collection of independent replicators or genes—that is, the building blocks of life

2. First life consisting of prokaryotic cells—that is, cells without a nucleus, such as bacteria—some 3.5–4 billion years ago

3. Eukaryotic single-celled organisms, characterized by cells with a nucleus (protists) about 2.5 billion years ago, such as yeast and amoeba

4. Plastids, organelles inside the eukaryotic cells, such as chloroplast for photosynthesis that is vital for plants to take up energy, probably around 1.5 billion years ago; an example is algae

5. Multicellularity, plants, animals, fungi, 800 million years or more ago

6. Solitary individuals that form colonies—that is, among ants, bees, and termites

7. From primate societies to human societies with natural language or the ascent of man

---

18. Szathmáry, "Toward Major Evolutionary Transitions Theory 2.0," 10104.

19. Szathmáry and Smith, "Major Evolutionary Transitions," and Smith and Szathmáry, *Origins of Life*. John M. Smith (1920–2004) studied under Haldane and as an atheist was a supporter of Humanists UK. Humanists UK, "John Maynard Smith."

20. Szathmáry, "Toward Major Evolutionary Transitions Theory 2.0."

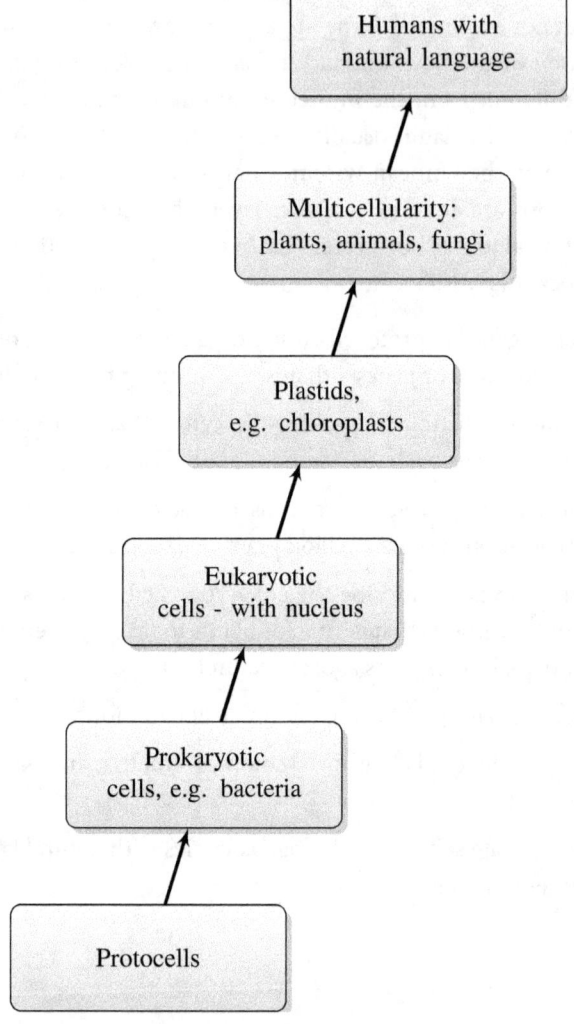

Figure 32. The major evolutionary transitions in biology depicted as a progression leading to humans.

The transitions are shown in figure 32. Note that the two first stages denote what we call the origin of life, which as noted is really a prerequisite for biological evolution. A paper in the prestigious journal *Nature* starts by wondering,

> There is no theoretical reason to expect evolutionary lineages to increase in complexity with time, and no empirical evidence

that they do so. Nevertheless, eukaryotic cells are more complex than prokaryotic ones, animals and plants are more complex than protists, and so on.[21]

The same authors say something similar in their book written for a popular audience:

> The theory of evolution by natural selection does not predict that organisms will get more complex. It predicts only that they will get better at surviving and reproducing in the current environment, or at least that they will not get worse.[22]

This echoes what Lewis said about change versus improvement. Szathmáry and Smith very honestly ask,

> Why did natural selection, acting on entities at the lower level (replicating molecules, free-living prokaryotes, asexual protists, single cells, individual organisms), not disrupt integration at the higher level (chromosomes, eukaryotic cells, sexual species, multicellular organisms, societies)? The problem is not an imaginary one: there is a real danger that selection at the lower level will disrupt integration at the higher. . . . We cannot explain these transitions in terms of the ultimate benefits they conferred.[23]

The big question is not whether these transitions have happened or *how* they happened, but the question *why*, as indicated by the quotes above. The *how* question is better understood, and the book explains the major transitions and the major hypotheses for what took place. This is a complex subject, and a cursory reading of popular books may indicate that the mechanisms have been uncovered and are well understood.

As an example, one of the mechanisms is symbiosis, long-term interaction between two different species. It is likely that two prokaryotic cells joined, one becoming the nucleus of the other, in forming the eukaryotic cell in stage 3. This particular form of symbiosis is called endosymbiosis. Similarly, endosymbiosis is thought to have occurred in stage 4 with one cell becoming the chloroplast of the second. These are examples of collaboration, in many ways the opposite of survival of the fittest and competition. The 1967 paper that first proposed endosymbiosis was rejected by fifteen journals before being published. Some of the difficulty can be

---

21. Szathmáry and Smith, "Major Evolutionary Transitions," 227.
22. Smith and Szathmáry, *Origins of Life*, 15.
23. Szathmáry and Smith, "Major Evolutionary Transitions," 227.

explained by the sheer length of the paper, fifty pages, but a good part of the reason is that the idea was unexpected and contrarian at the time.[24]

In support of the view that there are inexplicable transitions, it is appropriate to repeat the quote from the introduction about what one may consider to be the most important of the transitions—namely, one and two combined and seven: "Two other major and largely unsolved problems . . . are the origin of the basic features of living cells and the origin of human consciousness."[25] They then add: "[T]here is nothing in the theory of evolution by natural selection to suggest this [i.e., progress in evolution] is inevitable, and of course bacteria are still one of the most abundant and successful forms of life."

Many scientists seem to have a hard time accepting that there is this inexplicable progress in evolution. One reaction is to think that it will probably be possible to understand it sometime in the future. Another is to consider evolutionary changes to be just variation and not progress. This is probably the most common view. It is a view that may lead to a low view of humans.

EVOLUTION AND PHILOSOPHY OF SCIENCE

We now have a background in the historical development of evolutionary theory, as well as some insight into the limitations of what it can explain. I have touched upon chance and purpose, and here this will be expanded upon. I claim that the best way to understand evolution is through philosophy. Let's now apply the ideas from the previous chapter about purpose and natural laws to evolution, keeping in mind the main thesis of that chapter, which is that it is not really possible to study or uncover purpose by means of science.

"Absence of Evidence" Is Not "Evidence of Absence"

A few generations ago, the question arose as to whether infant formula was a fully adequate alternative to breastfeeding. Researchers believed that they had complete knowledge of everything that matters in breast milk, and that it was therefore possible to create fully adequate replacements. There was an "absence of evidence" of benefit for breast milk compared

---

24. Schaechter, "Lynn Margulis (1938–2011)."
25. Charlesworth and Charlesworth, *Evolution*, 125.

to substitutes. Thus, it was claimed, we had "evidence of absence" of the benefits. This conclusion laid the foundation for a large industry that has subsequently been accused of exploiting poorly educated mothers. Surprisingly, it has turned out that infants who only receive infant formula have a higher risk of problems than children who are breastfed naturally. It is estimated that over eight hundred thousand children worldwide die each year due to lack of breastfeeding.[26] The standards used to analyze breast milk were simply not good enough. The inference from "absence of evidence" of benefit to the stronger "evidence for absence" of benefits was not valid.[27]

Nevertheless, this is exactly what happens in the evolution debate. There is an absence of evidence for intentions or purpose behind evolution, but this is not the same as evidence of absence. There may be intentions behind evolution that biology cannot discover. In the previous chapter, we saw that intentions, which are one of Aristotle's four explanations, were purposely eliminated from science in the seventeenth century. This was important for making modern natural science based on experiments possible. Therefore, it is a contradiction to say that there is evidence of absence for intentions in natural science, and even more so to say that it means that such intentions do not exist. A more inquisitive attitude would instead be open to the fact that science is not a suitable tool for finding them. This is what came out of the discussion of intention in the previous chapter, and it is the type of argument that has been most useful to me personally.

What Is the Alternative to Randomness?

Randomness is a scientific concept, while *intention* deals with something that lies outside science and points toward a goal in the future. Randomness is an expression for the possibility of prediction of future events, and its tools are statistics and probability.

It is easy to conclude that randomness means a lack of intention, but that is actually a philosophical short circuit. The English theologian and biochemist Arthur Peacocke (1924–2006) says that "chance often has

---

26. Victora et al., "Breastfeeding in the 21st Century."

27. Criticism of this way of drawing conclusions, and more illustrations of the phenomenon, can be found in the highly readable Taleb, *Black Swan*, 50–61.

been apotheosized into a metaphysical principle."[28] The English statistician David Bartholomew (1931–2017) says that "at the center is the question of whether our treating elements of the physical world as random in some respects is because they are too complex to describe in full detail or because there is intrinsic unpredictability in nature." He then adds: "In technical language: Is uncertainty epistemological or ontological?"[29] In other words, is it our lack of knowledge about the world that makes us see it as random, or is it fundamentally random in its nature?

What is really the alternative to randomness? It would have to be that the result of evolution was predetermined—that is, the process is deterministic. However, in a deterministic universe, human freedom and responsibility would also disappear. One can argue that randomness can play a creative role in achieving God's purpose.[30]

The Bible has some narratives that bring out exactly this point. When Jesus heard about "the eighteen who were killed when the tower in Siloam fell on them," he asks if "they were more guilty than all the others living in Jerusalem?" (Luke 13:4). It is clear here that disasters like this, whether they are due to irresponsible craftsmen or come from nature itself, are something God allows to happen without any connection to those affected by it. The same applies to diseases. Consider the example of Jesus meeting a blind man. The disciples asked, as one would naturally do, if it was the blind man himself or his parents who had sinned, as he was born blind. Here it seems that Jesus rejects a determinism that provides easy explanations when he says that neither the blind man nor his parents are at fault for this (John 9:1–3).

Coincidences in the form of natural disasters or diseases can obviously strike at random. Nevertheless, the idea that God may be involved in our lives is central in the New Testament. The same can be said about our own origin. I am created by God, yes, but I am also a result of my parents. The exact timing of my conception has a lot to do with exactly who I became. Thus, I am also a result of when my parents were conceived, my grandparents, etc., back in time. It seems that a random process has led to who I am. In the Bible, there is never a conflict between the idea that I am created by God and that I was conceived naturally. Belief in creation is not a theory that competes with scientific explanations even when they involve randomness.

28. Peacocke, "Chance and the Life Game," 301.
29. Bartholomew, "Probability, Statistics and Theology," 148.
30. Ewart, "Necessity of Chance."

Purpose Explanations in Biology

As we saw in the previous chapter, biology often has purpose explanations like Aristotle's original teleonomy. In terms of explaining an organ such as the eye, this becomes a purely functional explanation. The eye can see so that the animal can find food or detect enemies—otherwise, the animal would not have survived.

But how can it be that all living things have such an intrinsic purpose? It is a paradox that biologists must remind themselves not to be "fooled" by what they see. In other sciences, it is precisely observations and experiments that drive science forward. Just listen to what Francis Crick says: "Biologists must constantly keep in mind that what they see was not designed, but rather evolved."[31] Richard Dawkins is even more specific:

> Natural selection is the blind watchmaker, blind because it does not see ahead, does not plan consequences, has no purpose in view. Yet the living results of natural selection overwhelmingly impress us with the illusion of design and planning.[32]

Crick and Dawkins do not believe in any underlying cause for the purposefulness they observe and apparently have to remind themselves not to think too much about it.

Let's now look closer at these statements and the statements from Coyne, Futuyma, and Simpson that "we are the result of blind and impersonal forces," that there are no traces of intention or purpose in the living world, and that "man is the result of a purposeless and natural process that did not have him in mind." These scientists believe that the selection and mutation mechanisms are the result of coincidences, and that it points toward a lack of intentions. As mentioned earlier, an addition or lack of the point that there is no meaning or direction in evolution will not change anything on what the theory of evolution can explain. This is the fourth point from the list on pages 167–68, and as argued it does not contribute anything to this being a scientific theory. As seen in the previous chapter, much of the success of natural science is due to the realization that it could not provide explanations for underlying intentions. When some modern researchers observe coincidences and still conclude that there are no intentions, they therefore make a logical misconception.

---

31. Crick, *What Mad Pursuit*, 138.
32. Dawkins, *Blind Watchmaker*, 21.

Francis Bacon said that a "little philosophy incline[s] man's mind to atheism, but depth in philosophy bring[s] men's minds about to religion."[33] I think Bacon is right, and that although they can be deep in their science, these researchers are all the more superficial in their philosophy. The author G. K. Chesterton aptly expressed the issue in 1922: "Unfortunately science is only splendid when it is science. When science becomes religion it becomes superstition."[34]

Geneticist Theodosius Dobzhansky (1900–1975), one of the founders of the modern synthesis, reached another conclusion. He is often quoted by biologists for his article titled "Nothing in Biology Makes Sense Except in the Light of Evolution." The statement is surprising in many ways. The article was written at the end of Dobzhansky's life, and as one of the few scientific articles, it has its own page on Wikipedia. The title is incredibly well formulated and known far beyond the article itself. However, when a few years ago I took the time to read the entire article, I was surprised as Dobzhansky also wrote this:

> I am a creationist and an evolutionist. Evolution is God's, or Nature's, method of creation. Creation is not an event that happened in 4004 BC; it is a process that began some 10 billion years ago and is still under way. . . . Does the evolutionary doctrine clash with religious faith? It does not. It is a blunder to mistake the Holy Scriptures for elementary textbooks of astronomy, geology, biology, and anthropology.[35]

When Dawkins has to deny his own observation that nature gives an overwhelming impression of design and planning, it reveals that his worldview overrides his science. Evolution has become evolutionism and has been elevated from a scientific theory to a worldview that explains all there is. Evolutionism is naturalism plus evolution, or naturalism disguised as science. This is what C. S. Lewis called the Great Myth.

Long before anyone thought of evolution and independently of theories about how nature has come about or evolved, Thomas Aquinas formulated a different and very useful way of interpreting intrinsic purpose.

33. Bacon, "XVI. Of Atheism."
34. Chesterton, "Separation of Science and Popular Science," 355.
35. Dobzhansky, "Nothing in Biology Makes Sense," 127, 129.

Thomas Aquinas's Fifth Way

Aquinas combined Aristotle's thoughts with a Christian worldview. He also gave an explanation for why there could be intrinsic purposefulness in all of life. He did not accomplish this by stating that purposefulness was directly imposed on all things by a deity, as in Platonic thought. In a clever way he justified Aristotle's idea of intrinsic purposefulness by saying that there must be a reason for such ubiquitous purposefulness. This is the topic of the last of the five ways (see chapter 2), known as "the teleological way." Since this argument about purpose is often confused with the argument that complexity points toward God, it is worth quoting in full here:

> We see that things which lack intelligence, such as natural bodies, act for an end, and this is evident from their acting always, or nearly always, in the same way, so as to obtain the best result. Hence it is plain that not fortuitously, but designedly, do they achieve their end. Now whatever lacks intelligence cannot move towards an end, unless it be directed by some being endowed with knowledge and intelligence; as the arrow is shot to its mark by the archer. Therefore some intelligent being exists by whom all natural things are directed to their end; and this being we call God.[36]

This applies to all non-intelligent objects and beings, which for Aquinas meant everything except humans.

Aquinas asserts that since there are beings with these inclinations—these purposes—built into them, we can conclude that there must exist a God who is the reason for the very existence of purpose. In modern language, we might say that life has built-in information that has the codes required for this very purpose.[37] But the purposefulness is more than just information; it is such an integral part of life and every organ, whether we understand it scientifically or not, that life without it is inconceivable. It is not something that needs to be added from the outside in each individual case. Aquinas says that this points beyond each individual being to God as the source of this purposefulness.

This argument differs from a complexity argument. All life, whether complex or what we regard as simple, possesses this intrinsic

---

36. Aquinas, *Summa Theologica*, pt. 2, question 2, art. 3, in Kreeft, *Shorter* Summa, 63.

37. This way of interpreting Aquinas's fifth way corresponds to "scholastic teleological realism" in Feser, "Teleology."

purposefulness which indirectly points to God. Nevertheless, Aquinas's fifth way is often interpreted narrowly to mean that just complexity points to God; but it is much wider than that.

As mentioned earlier, an argument about purpose resides outside the realm of science, whereas arguments based on complexity mean scientific investigation. When complexity is used to try to prove or suggest purpose and thus the existence of God, very great expectations are placed on what science can find out, beyond what I understand it to be capable of.

Why Does It Go "Upward"?

If we look beyond individual phenomena, it may seem as if the trend points "upward" in the history of life, such as with cosmic development as described in chapter 2. The evolutionary transitions described earlier in this chapter also demonstrate how the evolution of life has had a direction toward an ever-higher degree of organization and complexity. In parallel, the plants had a development that started in water with algae and then came land plants. Among them, mosses came first, then ferns, and then conifers. Finally came the flowering plants, which include 90 percent of all plant species on Earth. Here, too, one sees ever greater diversity over time.

The evolutionary mechanism, which is based on random mutations and natural selection, does not really have a good explanation for this, as mentioned. One can ask where the amazing property of life comes from that allows it to adapt to changes in the environment. There is a wonderful balance between stability and adaptability that looks "just right" in life. The stability lies in the fact that life does not collapse because the offspring are so different from the parents that the species are not fixed. The adaptation lies in the fact that most species adapt to small changes in the environment, even if the climate changes of our time may be too big for that.

The question of why it is this way is worth reflecting on. Can we see God's finger in the apparent trend toward the more complex, more organized, and more advanced—what has culminated in intelligence and consciousness?

This is an argument which resembles that of Darwin's friend and popularizer in the US, botanist Asa Gray (1810–1888). He argued that if one takes one step back, it is evident that the mechanisms for evolution and the evolutionary process bear all the marks of having been designed.[38]

---

38. Kojonen, *Compatibility of Evolution and Design*.

Darwin wavered back and forth, but he also wrote that "life, with its several powers, having been originally breathed by the Creator."[39] In this way, he is not so different from Newton and his attitude toward where gravity comes from. The agnostic Darwin did not want to make hypotheses about where life comes from. Both Darwin and Newton seem to agree that one of the definitions of God is precisely that he is the source of all existence, whether it is life itself or a condition for life, such as the force of gravity is.

The Complex Complexity Argument

A different way of arguing is found in American biochemist Michael Behe's (b. 1952) book on "irreducible complexity." It had a big impact on me when it first came out, and I found the argumentation quite persuasive.[40] With time, however, I began to question some of its assumptions which are also those of the intelligent design (ID) movement.

The ID movement makes these claims, as far as I understand:

1. That there is intelligence behind creation. Unless you are an atheist, this is not controversial. All Christians who confess the Apostles' Creed say, "I believe in God, the Father almighty, Maker of Heaven and Earth . . .,"[41] and believe that the Creator's intelligence is reflected in creation.

2. That neo-Darwinism with genes and mutations cannot explain all aspects of life. As discussed in this book, this is a belief even held by secular scientists, and it has been easier to justify it in recent years. The extended evolutionary synthesis of the next section is based on a somewhat similar analysis of the shortcomings of neo-Darwinism. However, proponents of the extended evolutionary synthesis specifically distance themselves from any talk of a divine creator. This is probably because they disagree with the next claim.

3. That natural science can be used to determine if something is designed or not. Terms like *irreducible* or *specified* complexity have been used. Irreducible complexity means that, for example, an organ consists of several parts that have no function individually, while

---

39. Darwin, *Origin of Species*, 429.
40. Behe, *Darwin's Black Box*.
41. Wikipedia, "Apostles' Creed," sec. Text, 1.

specified complexity denotes specific unlikely patterns.[42] These arguments may be made quantitative by setting threshold values for probability so that a small enough probability indicates design. Arguments from information theory are now also common and may be based on the complex linguistic structure found in, for example, DNA. Information theory comes from the field of communications and says that a high information content is the same as a small probability, as I learned it as a young student.[43] A high information content is an indication of design.

It is only the third point that is specific to ID, and which is controversial. It should be emphasized here that it is the use of *natural science*[44] that is controversial. It is not controversial at all among believers that there are philosophical, theological, and indeed common-sense arguments for design in nature, and indeed design due to God. I have earlier commented that both the cosmic evolution shown in figure 13 and the major evolutionary transitions in biology of figure 32 are evidence of intention, and indeed God's purpose. Although these figures are clothed in the language of science, their interpretation in terms of purpose represents a philosophical view of evolution, not a scientific one, in my view.

The third point has to do with the sometimes-difficult demarcation line between what is science and what is not. Those who are sympathetic to ID seem to make these assumptions:

1. Detection of design can be separated from identification of the designer.
2. Such "impersonal" design is in a separate category from purpose. Design may thus be detected and quantified with science while purpose may not.

First, it is agreed in the ID movement that natural science cannot be used to "prove" God. Therefore, it is claimed that it is better to look for an "intelligent designer" instead of God. This would ease the burden

42. Both irreducible and specified complexity have their own Wikipedia articles where more in-depth explanations are found.

43. This is Shannon information theory, which is also referred to in ID literature such as Thorvaldsen and Hössjer, "Fine-Tuning of Molecular Machines and Systems."

44. It should be emphasized that with natural science is meant what in German and Scandinavian languages is called *Naturwissenschaft* as opposed to *Wissenschaft*. Social sciences and humanities, which are not quantitative sciences, are thus not part of natural science.

of proof, as it only needs to imply a minimal ability to create and not all other characteristics that we normally associate with God. An intelligent designer could be God, but it could also be something completely different, like alien civilizations from other solar systems. I am probably not the only one who has trouble not thinking of God every time the term *intelligent designer* is mentioned. Especially when it comes to biology, I find it hard to think of any credible alternative to God as the "designer."

Second, it follows that if the designer can be made "impersonal," purpose and design are two separate things. I find this problematic as purposeless design to me is a contradiction. The definition of science quoted at the end of chapter 5 also puts design in the nonquantifiable category outside of natural science. It could be argued that that definition of science should be broadened to include detection of design, but this is not something I would be comfortable with, even though this is what those who affirm that evolution demonstrates lack of purpose in nature implicitly do.

It is nevertheless my hope that pointing out these differences in assumptions may lead to a more understanding and a more fruitful and civil dialogue between the various factions in the science-theology debate.

I am sympathetic to most aspects of the agenda of the ID movement. The ID movement's focus on pointing out that God is the creator and their criticism of evolution as a worldview is important, as is their questioning of whether mutations and natural development can really accomplish as much as the proponents of evolution would have it. Likewise, their emphasis on the wonders of the natural world is something we all can learn from. This is "intelligent design light," which many can agree to. "Hardcore intelligent design" seems to me also to use science, which deals with nature, and stretches it beyond its validity to be a direct argument for the supernatural.

BEYOND NEO-DARWINISM

Many biologists believe that evolution is neither as random nor as centered on genes as the modern synthesis or neo-Darwinism would have us believe. Their scientific arguments are well worth considering, even though they may not carry the same weight as the philosophical ones.

As has been shown earlier in this chapter, important phenomena like the major evolutionary transitions cannot be explained well within the neo-Darwinist paradigm. This also shows that there is a need for other explanatory models.

British physiologist and biologist Dennis Noble (b. 1936) is critical of the view of Francis Crick that the gene is the "secret of life," and of the deterministic image conveyed by Richard Dawkins's statement that "DNA neither cares nor knows. DNA just is. And we dance to its music."[45] Any parent of children with identical genomes—that is, identical twins—like me, also feels intuitively that there must be more to what determines what a human is than genes alone. The message of Noble's book is that the gene now has been dethroned as a uniquely privileged level of causation. In his view, the interaction between cells and the organism is central, or as he says, "A cell is vastly more than its DNA, and an organism is vastly more than a collection of cells."[46] It is popular to compare humans and chimpanzees as we share from 96 to 98.8 percent of the genome. We also share 60 percent of the genes with fruit flies. Based on this new view of causation, such comparisons are almost as meaningless as drawing far-reaching conclusions from the fact that we are made from the same chemical elements, as science writer Philip Ball (b. 1962) remarks.[47]

Likewise, paleontologist Ian Tattersall says, in a discussion of the role of brain size in evolution, that this field has been under "the gradualist dictates of the Evolutionary Synthesis because a large brain is a necessary, but not a sufficient condition to explain what is uniquely human."[48]

Important questions about the limits of reductionism and the gene-centered theory of evolution, and the lack of a description of purpose are now more openly discussed.

Reintroduction of Purpose?

The focus on efficient and material causes in science constitutes what is called *methodological naturalism*—that is, that the method of science is about natural causes only. It does not mean that nature is all there is, such as in Weinberg's *ontological* or *metaphysical naturalism* of the last chapter, only that our method is limited to investigating natural causes.

---

45. Dawkins, *River Out of Eden*, 133.
46. Noble, *Dance to the Tune of Life*, 64.
47. Ball, *How Life Works*, 268.
48. Tattersall, *Masters of the Planet*, 129.

The implied machine view of nature is in particular a limitation when it comes to the study of life, and it has become evident now that the lack of consideration of purpose in science limits what it can say. Dennis Noble says that goals are central to living organisms and cannot be ignored, thereby trying to reintroduce the study of teleology.[49] Likewise, Philip Ball reacts to Weinberg's expression of how the universe is pointless and wonders if not the remark itself is meaningless, and a category error. On the contrary, Ball says that one of the definitions of life is that it is a "meaning generator" and laments the lack of a theory of meaning in science and the "related concepts of purposes, goals, and intentions." Ball devotes a chapter in his *User's Guide to the New Biology* to agency and how life gets goals and purposes. He discusses Schrödinger's *What Is Life*, which was discussed here in chapter 2, and also touches upon teleonomy and teleology and asserts that "denying biology any agency denies its very nature" and that "it is really only at the cellular level that biological agency fires up," suggesting that biology needs to be better connected to physics.[50]

I find it interesting that it is finally admissible to wrestle with questions such as agency and purpose in biology as real properties and not just dismiss them like many have done. A rigorous theory of purpose and meaning, like those for the efficient and material causes, seems, however, to be far away. Without connecting it explicitly to the study of purpose, Ball comments that the "popular view that science is the process of studying what the world is like needs to be given an important qualification," and then goes on to say that, in reality, it is much simpler as "science tends to be the study of what we can study."[51] As said in the previous chapter, early scientists found that purpose could not be studied by science. This may not be a once-for-all verdict, but there is a very real possibility that it is in the nature of science that purpose cannot be grasped.

A more modest goal is to realize that current theories are limited in what they can describe. This is a very important insight by itself, regardless of whether a rigorous theory for teleology can be developed or not. This is also the essence of the movement called the Third Way of Evolution. Its supporters, like Denis Noble, believe that neo-Darwinism ignores much contemporary evidence and builds on some unsupported assumptions about the nature of hereditary variation. They have called it

49. Noble, *Dance to the Tune of Life*, 45.
50. Ball, *How Life Works*, 42, 44, 421–23.
51. Ball, *How Life Works*, 189, 204.

the Third Way because neither do they consider the option for explaining the origins of biological diversity inherent in "Creationism that depends on intervention by a divine Creator."[52] This statement includes more than young Earth creationism and may very well include the intelligent design movement also, in the view of the Third Way.

The Third Way emphasizes some new developments in biology over the last few decades that may point the way.

Convergence

One who believes that if evolution were to start over it would yield roughly the same result is the Christian British paleontologist Simon Conway Morris (b. 1951). It was almost unavoidable that humans would arise once life existed, claims Morris, yet the emergence of life is extremely rare.[53] He suggests that the evolutionary process is more ordered and directional than one might think, and that the intelligence of humans was a highly probable outcome. Morris justifies this with examples of convergence, where the same structure arises in entirely different creatures.

An example is how the camera-like eye of creatures as disparate as the octopus and humans bears many similarities. There is nothing to suggest that their distant common ancestors had eyes, yet both have ended up with similar solutions. The laws of nature impose such strong constraints on what functions as an eye that there are only a few ways to create a well-functioning eye.

Another example is the remarkable ability of dolphins and bats to navigate using ultrasound. I've worked with ultrasound for many years, and I'm still impressed every time I hear the sophisticated sounds of bats. They analyze the echoes of their own sounds to avoid collisions and to locate insects. I have bats by my house in the suburbs of Oslo, probably Northern bats, and I can listen to them with a bat detector. I cannot stop being fascinated when I go out at dusk, hear their sounds, and often see the bats as they hunt for insects, then note how the sound changes at the moment of capture. They switch to much faster emissions to better track the prey's movement. Dolphins have similar echolocation abilities. However, the common ancestors of these mammals could not perform

---

52. thethirdwayofevolution.com, para. 1.

53. This thesis is evident from the title of his book *Life's Solution: Inevitable Humans in a Lonely Universe*.

such ultrasound echolocation, so these skills have evolved independently of each other.

Until now, it was believed that such convergent evolution was due to completely different genes in bats and dolphins mutating. Echolocation requires the ability to emit ultrasound, to hear it, and not the least to interpret what is heard. To take hearing as an example, it turns out that it may be due to the same gene in the two species. In both cases, the change has occurred in the protein prestin, which is found in all mammals and enhances sound in the outer hair cells of the cochlea in the inner ear. What led researchers to this conclusion is that mutations in prestin lead to a loss of high-frequency hearing in humans. Therefore, the same mutation in the same gene seems to have occurred at least twice independently in two completely different species.[54]

Such convergent evolution is the rule rather than the exception, and the potential for it lies hidden in the genome. This is just one of many examples of convergent evolution that Conway Morris and others have uncovered, and it shows that evolution is not free to take any random direction. There are external boundary conditions that set narrow limits for what is possible.

Extended Evolutionary Synthesis

I have great sympathy for biologists, as I believe they—like few other scientists—experience that their science is being attacked. While physics and chemistry have been able to work undisturbed, there has been a storm of discussion surrounding biology. It is possible this causes biologists to protect their established science and possibly place more explanatory power in it than there is justification for. We see this in Futuyma's textbook on evolutionary biology as well. I was surprised when I found separate sections in his book that dealt with attacks from young Earth creationists. I have never seen anything like that in textbooks in other subjects.

In our time, however, criticism comes from science itself, and then there is greater hope that it will be considered. Several researchers doubt that neo-Darwinism has enough explanatory power for macroevolution. An important concern for the criticism is that the modern synthesis is just one of several mechanisms for this, and that the reductionist view underlying it is insufficient. There, everything is explained with the basic

---

54. Pennisi, "Hear That?" and Pennisi, "Bats and Dolphins."

units of biology, which are the genes, and how these give rise to a slow and gradual evolution.

We see an interesting development among a group of biologists who promote what they call an extended evolutionary synthesis, EES. The synthesis has led to a discussion of whether evolutionary theory needs to be rethought. Some biologists answer yes and that it is urgent. Others, in turn, answer: No, everything is fine because today's theory can incorporate new discoveries and ideas.[55]

Those who believe it is urgent say that organisms are constructed as they develop; they are not just "programmed" to evolve based on genes. This is an organism-centered view of evolution as opposed to a gene-centered view. Living beings do not just evolve to fit into preexisting environments, but construct and develop together with the environment. In that process, they change the structure of the ecosystem; something that in turn leads to changed conditions for life.

Much suggests that evolution has occurred in fits and starts. Neo-Darwinism, on the other hand, presupposes that there has been a smooth and gradual evolution. In reality, there have been long periods without much change and then major changes over quite a short time. The clearest example is the emergence of flowering plants about 100 million years ago. In a letter in 1879, Darwin wrote, "The rapid development, as far as we can judge, of all the higher plants within recent geological times, is an abominable mystery."[56] This is particularly true of the dicotyledonous flowering plants (seeds with two embryonic leaves), which include all common flowers as well as all deciduous trees (trees that seasonally shed leaves) and fruit trees. In Darwin's time, it was believed that dicotyledonous plants were developed from monocotyledonous plants (seeds with a single embryonic leaf), which include grains, grasses, orchids, bananas, pineapples, and tulips, and which were considered much older. Such mysteries are often resolved over time, but here the opposite has happened, and the mystery has only grown larger. Both types of flowering plants turn out to be equally young.[57]

Such evolution in fits and starts is better described by the extended evolutionary synthesis. It emphasizes:

---

55. See interesting discussion between Laland et al., "Does Evolutionary Theory Need a Rethink? Point Yes, Urgently," and Wray et al., "Does Evolutionary Theory Need a Rethink? Counterpoint No, All Is Well."
56. Buggs, "Deepening of Darwin's Abominable Mystery," 1.
57. Buggs, "Deepening of Darwin's Abominable Mystery."

- How organisms modify the environment (niche construction), and that this then affects further evolution. Examples include termites and their mounds, beavers that build dams, and the symbiotic relationship between flowers and insects, but also humans and our culture.
- How the environment directly shapes the properties of organisms (phenotypic plasticity), and that this in turn can change genes in what is called cultural inheritance.
- How evolutionary developmental biology ("evo-devo"), which deals with how species develop from the fetal stage, affects the formation of variation (developmental biases) in surprising ways. Convergence, as discussed earlier, is one aspect of this.
- How organisms can pass on more than genes from generation to generation. This is called epigenetics, and it affects how genes are expressed, not the genes themselves. It is a limited version of Lamarckism from the early nineteenth century and means that the Weismann barrier and the central dogma are not as absolute as supposed in neo-Darwinism.

The difference is that in standard evolutionary theory, where these phenomena are also studied, they are just considered results of evolution, while in the extended synthesis they are also causes. This can also be understood as a "back to Darwin" movement, since Darwin recognized more mechanisms than those included in what Dennis Noble calls "dogmatic forms of neo-Darwinism."[58] Futuyma, who I have referred to earlier, is quite critical, but doesn't reject EES. Surprisingly, he also says,

> I do not think all advocates of an EES are impelled by emotional distaste for the utter lack of purpose and agency in evolution by natural selection, but it may be useful to ask if our views of evolutionary theory are affected by extra-scientific values.[59]

Futuyma is afraid that some supporters of the extended synthesis are driven by motives he does not like. But does he also feel that his own atheism is threatened? As mentioned earlier, I believe that those who tie their atheism to evolution, precisely "are affected by extra-scientific values."

---

58. Noble, *Dance to the Tune of Life*, 120–59.
59. Futuyma, "Evolutionary Biology Today," 9.

It is not easy to say what the fate of extended evolutionary synthesis will be. Is the resistance due to the old school's dislike of new ideas? Or is it just a matter of small details that today's theory can easily incorporate? We must leave it to the biologists themselves to conclude, but calling this a revolution is probably going too far. At least it seems that the idea that more than just random mutations are required is here to stay. This might, perhaps, eventually give us a humbler evolutionary science, which can more easily see the limits of what it is able to explain. Physics has gone through such a development, and therefore it is interesting to compare with the development of physics from the eighteenth century to the twentieth century.

Biology's Parallel to Dark Matter

Newton's law of gravitation was a breakthrough because it united the large and small. It could describe everything from how stones fell on Earth, to the stability of planetary orbits. The world seemed to work like a clock, just like the early mechanical clocks. The prime example is the one from 1386 in the cathedral in Salisbury, England, which is the world's oldest functioning clock. This mechanistic view of nature took over from the more organic view that the Medieval Age had from Aristotle. It played a crucial role during the Enlightenment of the eighteenth century, when Laplace also came up with a description of how a planetary system could form. In principle, everything could now be calculated, if the initial conditions were known. It was believed that these laws not only described nature but also explained *why* nature works. They had forgotten the insight of Newton, Boyle, Kepler, and Galileo that the laws were just describing how, not the *why* of the universe.

In the twentieth century, the belief in determinism in physics was challenged. This was particularly true of quantum theory. In quantum mechanics, Heisenberg's uncertainty principle says that it is not possible to know both the velocity and position of a particle. This is not because we have poor measuring instruments, but it is a fundamental fact about nature. Quantum uncertainty applies at the micro-level, and we can probably ignore it when we talk about larger objects like stones and planets and even brains. However, over the past few generations, it has become clearer that even for such phenomena, there can be uncertainty. According to chaos theory, certain complex systems are so sensitive to small changes in the initial conditions that it is impossible to calculate what the future will be. The weather is a good example. We currently work with a limit of a week or two on how far into the future the weather can be predicted with some certainty. It's possible that this period can be extended with better models, but it seems that there may still be a limit to how far into the future we can predict something as chaotic as the weather.

In cosmology, building on Einstein's relativity theory, it is also understood that the big bang marks a first event, and that it is impossible to say anything about what may have been before that. Even time started then. If we are to believe the measurements, there are indications that the universe is expanding faster and faster as time goes by. This requires the existence of an unknown dark energy with negative gravity that "rips" the universe apart. There is also something called dark matter, which is the invisible mass needed to describe why galaxies behave the way they do. Dark matter only affects gravitation, not electromagnetic waves like light, and is therefore impossible to detect with ordinary instruments.

The point of this is to show that physics has moved from a mechanical view of everything, to realizing that there are limits to how accurately we can predict the future. Physics has also shifted from believing that it has complete oversight to having to reckon with both dark energy and dark matter, where "dark" is just a nicer word to express that this is something we don't know about and cannot observe directly.

Biology, with the central role of neo-Darwinism, may be where physics was during the Enlightenment: everything is determined by genes, and humans are "nothing more than" genes ensuring their survival. It reminds me of the confidence of the mechanistic physicists in the generation after Newton when a present-day biologist can bring himself to say that "evolutionary theory is the best-understood theory in science, the best justified, and the best documented."[60] Hopefully biology will grow up, just as physics has had to do, to a more mature and humble view, and maybe the extended evolutionary synthesis will show the way.

---

60. In a popular book by biologist and atheist Erik Tunstad: Tunstad, introduction to *Darwins teori* [Darwin's theory], 13–14.

7

Man and Evolution

> We do not need to be expert zoologists, anatomists or physiologists to recognise that there exist some similarities between apes and man, but surely, we are much more interested in the differences than the similarities. Apes, after all, unlike man, have not produced great prophets, philosophers, mathematicians, writers, poets, composers, painters, and scientists. They are not inspired by the divine spark which manifests itself so evidently in the spiritual creation of man and which differentiates man from animals.
>
> ERNST BORIS CHAIN (1906–1979)
> NOBEL PRIZE IN PHYSIOLOGY OR MEDICINE 1945

THE EVOLUTION OF HUMANS concerns us personally in a much more profound way than other big questions surrounding science and the Bible. Are we the result of impersonal forces only that by chance ended up with us? Or are we the result of God's desire to create us in his image so that we could have fellowship with him and be creative like him? The concern is now where our consciousness, which is one of the most unique things about humans, can come from. Thus, this question is different from questions about the development of life before humans, about the Earth's place in the universe, or about the big bang. These topics also concern us, but not on such a personal level.

Let us begin with an overview of the most important events in the history of life and humans according to science. The details here are constantly changing, but the big picture is quite well established. Some of the important events in the history of life are:

- The beginning of life 3.5–4 billion years ago, about 1 billion years after the formation of the solar system.
- Multicellular organisms that existed before or around the Cambrian explosion about 540 million years ago.
- The extinction of the dinosaurs about 66 million years ago.

The history of humans is short in comparison:[1]

- Humans and chimpanzees are considered to have a common origin between 4 and 13 million years ago.
- There are findings of *Homo erectus*, which begins to resemble modern humans, which are estimated to be at least 1.6–1.9 million years old, and the first consciously designed stone tools are dated to the same time.
- The first evidence of fire and fireplaces is 790,000 years old.
- The first findings of wooden spears and tools consisting of a rock mounted on a handle, as well as traces of constructed shelters, are 400,000 years old.
- A human, anatomically similar to modern humans—*Homo sapiens*—but with a smaller brain, can be traced back 200,000 years in Africa.
- Modern humans with their large brains are estimated to be 60,000–70,000 years old. They then travelled out of Africa and must have had the ability for symbolic thinking and language. The argument for dating language to that time is that these were ancestors to all humans today, and that we all have the same ability for language.
- Neanderthals disappeared 30,000 years ago. There is much evidence to suggest that there was interbreeding between modern humans and Neanderthals. If that is the case, it is also likely that

---

1. Partly based on Tattersall, introduction to *Masters of the Planet*.

Neanderthals had similar language abilities as modern humans. But there are also those who believe they did not.

Figure 33. Extinct mammoth with tusks and hair, from cave painting in Font-de-Gaume in the South of France, dated to approximately 17,000 BC.[2]

After the advent of modern humans, cultural development is primarily what has taken place. Humans don't only learn as individuals, but collectively. Spoken and written language are central to this process, but our early history is "complex territory, and riddled with controversy."[3] However, some key points are:

- The oldest trace of inscriptions, a cross-hatched pattern drawn with an ochre crayon from Blombos cave in South Africa, is about 73,000 years old.[4]

- The oldest small sculptures and cave paintings date back to about 40,000 years ago. When we see a picture like in figure 33, we understand that a human similar to us made it, and not an animal. Both art and language are therefore sure signs of our special position in creation.[5]

- The oldest agriculture began around the end of the last Ice Age—that is, around 9000–8000 BC.

2. "Mammoth Font de Gaume," by Henry Fairfield Osborn, Wikimedia Commons.
3. Baker, "Christians Should Reject," 202.
4. Henshilwood et al., "Abstract Drawing."
5. A reflection on this is found in Chesterton, *Everlasting Man*, 13–31.

- At approximately the same time, we began to keep domestic animals, such as goats and sheep, for food. There are traces of domesticated dogs from at least 13,000 BC.

- In Göbekli Tepe in eastern Turkey, near the border with Syria, something that is considered to be a sanctuary or temple has been found. There is no full agreement on this interpretation, but if it turns out that the sanctuary is as old as from 10,000 to 8000 BC, it would imply something about how long and how important religion has been to us.

- The oldest findings of symbolic inscriptions are from 6000 to 5000 BC, while writing in our modern sense is from around 3600 BC.

Population development is difficult to know for certain, but an estimate for how many people lived at certain key points, and the sum of all born up to this time, is as follows:[6]

- 50,000 BC: 2 million—number born up to this time: 7.9 billion
- 8000 BC: 5 million—number born up to this time: 9 billion
- Year 1: 300 million—number born up to this time: 55 billion
- 1200: 450 million—number born up to this time: 82 billion
- 1650: 500 million—number born up to this time: 94 billion
- 1850: 1.3 billion—number born up to this time: 102 billion
- 1950: 2.5 billion—number ever born up to this time: 108 billion
- 2022: 8 billion—number ever born up to this time: 117 billion

There are three surprises here: The first is the large number of people who are considered to have been born up to 50,000 BC. The second is that almost half of all who have ever lived, lived before year 1. Finally, it is also surprising that only about 7 percent of all who have ever lived, are alive today.

---

6. 2022 estimates from Kaneda and Haub, "How Many People."

INTELLECT, RATIONALITY, AND INTENTION

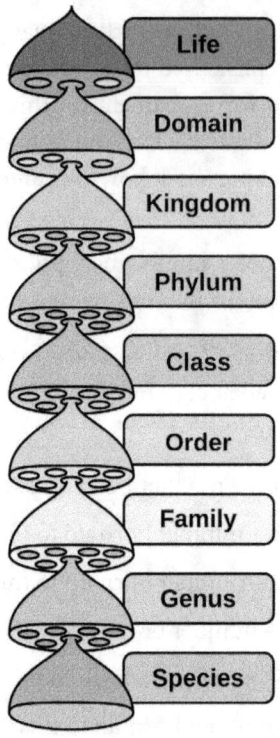

Figure 34. Levels of biological classification.[7]

What really sets humans apart from other species? In the eighteenth century, Swedish Carl Linnaeus organized all known plants and animals into a hierarchical system as shown in figure 34. He placed our species, *Homo sapiens*, in the genus *Homo* along with apes in the family Hominidae, order Primates (originally denoting the primary and highest order of animals), class Mammalia, phylum Chordata (from string, usually a backbone), and kingdom Animalia. It is surprising that Linnaeus placed us with apes because he, for a large part of his life, was convinced that each species was unchangeable and created separately, although he eventually expressed doubt about the immutability of individual species. The biological rationale for giving humans this place is the small anatomical

---

7. "Biological Classification," by Peter Halasz, Wikimedia Commons.

differences between humans and apes as pointed out in the initial quote from Ernst Boris Chain in this chapter. But the differences that exist are still important:

- Humans have a pelvis that allows us to walk more efficiently on two legs.
- We have a much more versatile hand for precision work, which naturally lends itself to tool production, but it is not so good for climbing and hanging from branches.
- We have a shoulder joint which is not designed to hang from trees, but that allows us to throw with precision. This is important for hunting. Additionally, we have unparalleled coordination between the eye and the hand.
- To produce our rich variety of speech sounds the vocal tract's vertical and horizontal parts need to be approximately equally long, a feature which is unique to humans.[8]
- We control fire.
- We sweat through the skin and do not have body hair. This gives us more endurance than many other species.
- We are almost omnivorous and adapt our diet to what is available. Cooking and roasting help us with this, and therefore we use less energy on our digestive system, which is much smaller than that of apes. Instead, we use much more energy on the brain.

The Brain

The human brain is incredibly complex:

- Today's best estimate is that it contains approximately 86 billion nerve cells or neurons. This is more than in other species, but not noticeably more.[9] The number of neurons is only slightly less than the number of stars in our galaxy, the Milky Way, and approximately the same as the number of galaxies in the universe.

---

8. Hauser et al., "Mystery of Language Evolution."

9. Although other species have larger brains than humans—for example, whales and elephants—they probably have fewer nerve cells, as primates have the most nerve cells per kilogram of brain. Herculano-Houzel, "Remarkable, Yet Not Extraordinary."

- The nerve cells have thousands of connections to other nerve cells, totaling about 100 trillion connections. Collectively, the nerve fibers have a length equivalent to the distance to the Moon and back, making it clear that the brain is the most complex organ that exists.
- Even though the brain weighs only about 1.5 kg—which is 2 percent of an adult's weight—it uses a full 20 percent of the human body's energy. No other species uses such a large proportion for the brain.

The brain is central to the crucial difference between humans and other species, namely our capacity for language. Although some of our closest relatives in the animal kingdom in theory may produce a subset of the sounds we produce, it doesn't appear that the brains of these animals have the same control over their muscles.[10] Apes can learn many words using tangible objects or sign language, and can respond to questions, but they don't grasp sentence construction very well.[11] A human child starts asking questions at an early age, but apes don't seem particularly inclined to inquire. It doesn't seem as though the ape species has an awareness of their own lack of knowledge and the need for more information.

The building blocks, matter, which make up the brain and indeed a human being, essentially do not act with any kind of purpose or meaning. Yet our consciousness has intentions, it's purposeful, and operates rationally. It is everything that the material is not.

Consciousness is something we have always struggled to understand, which is not so strange considering we must use our own consciousness to research consciousness. No other field has such a close connection between the subject under study and the researcher. It is not possible to read off data in an objective way in an experiment involving a person's thoughts. It is only the person himself who can convey his thoughts. In experiments that do not involve the mind, one can take an objective third-person perspective, but when it comes to the private and subjective phenomenon of consciousness, we can only have a first-person perspective.[12]

On the one hand, we have our experiences and personal perceptions of what we see and hear, what thoughts we have about it, and the wonder about whether my colleague right beside me is experiencing

---

10. Dunn and Smaers, "Neural Correlates of Vocal Repertoire."

11. Premack and Premack, *Mind of an Ape*, 29. The gorilla Koko is said to have asked a question once, according to its own Wikipedia page.

12. Blackmore, *Consciousness*, 1–16, and Chalmers, "Problem of Consciousness."

the perceptions in the same way. On the other hand, there is a physical world which is the origin of these experiences. The challenge is that these two sides of existence are so different from each other. This is the mind-body or soul-body problem particularly associated with Descartes in the seventeenth century. There is almost an insurmountable chasm between what we can observe with objective measuring methods for brain activity and these subjective experiences.

Brain Measurement

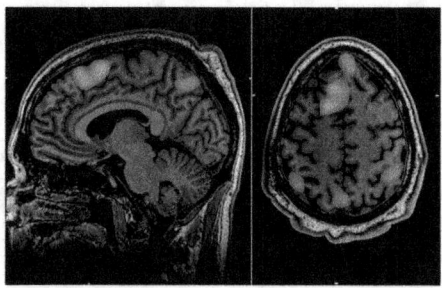

Figure 35. Functional MRI (magnetic resonance imaging) of the brain during testing of short-term memory.[13]

Although we may measure brain activity electrically (EEG) or perform functional imaging to see which areas in the brain are activated by different kinds of activity (functional magnetic resonance imaging—fMRI), these measurements do not really capture consciousness in itself. Some years ago I attended a lecture by Japanese researcher Seiji Ogawa (b. 1934), who first discovered the effect behind fMRI more than thirty years ago (see figure 35).[14] He concluded his lecture by expressing a hope that it would be possible to discover what the brain is really doing. So far, fMRI and other methods only reveal where activity takes place, but not the information contained in the neurons. To understand how far away we are from this goal, we must look at how coarse-grained an MR image is. The temporal resolution is only a couple of seconds and each volume element (voxel) in such an image is an average of the information from over 5 million

13. "FMRI Scan," by John Graner, Walter Reed National Military Medical Center, Wikimedia Commons.

14. Ogawa et al., "Brain Magnetic Resonance Imaging."

neurons.[15] Other methods may be more fine-grained, but they can only depict what happens on the surface of the brain. Thus, we are miles away from the desire to read off what individual neurons are doing.

These limitations are made even more evident in a remarkable study where brain research methods were used in an attempt to find out how a microprocessor works. The processor was the one found in an Apple I computer from 1976, and which is today considered a simple and primitive processor (see figure 36). The researchers tested a simulator for the processor while it was used for video games. In brain studies, attempts are made to understand how nerve cells are connected. The method consists in removing parts to see the effect, while activity in individual cells and in larger areas is observed. All of this was attempted on the microprocessor by studying its geometry, disconnecting individual transistors, or observing their activity, or trying to observe activity in slightly larger areas. But no matter the method, the researchers could not figure out how the processor worked. They were dealing with a man-made component that is simple compared to today's processors and much simpler than a brain, yet the experiment failed.[16] Therefore, it is likely that we would not even have discovered the existence of consciousness with today's methods for studying the brain.[17]

Studies like these demonstrate how little we know about the brain. There is good reason to be skeptical of sensational headlines that state otherwise. As an example, work is now being done to create a wiring diagram for all the brain's trillions of connections, but it is uncertain whether we will be any wiser from it. Neuroscientist Jeff Lichtman at Harvard University asks what it really means to understand something. He compares it to a city like New York and questions if it makes sense to say, "Now I understand New York." In principle, we already have a full overview of how New York is connected and how its parts fit together, yet the statement does not make much sense.

---

15. Logothetis, "What We Can Do," predicts a decrease in voxel size by a factor of one hundred or more.

16. Jonas and Kording, "Could a Neuroscientist."

17. Hart, *Experience of God*, 159, is one of the best descriptions of the uniqueness of consciousness that I am aware of.

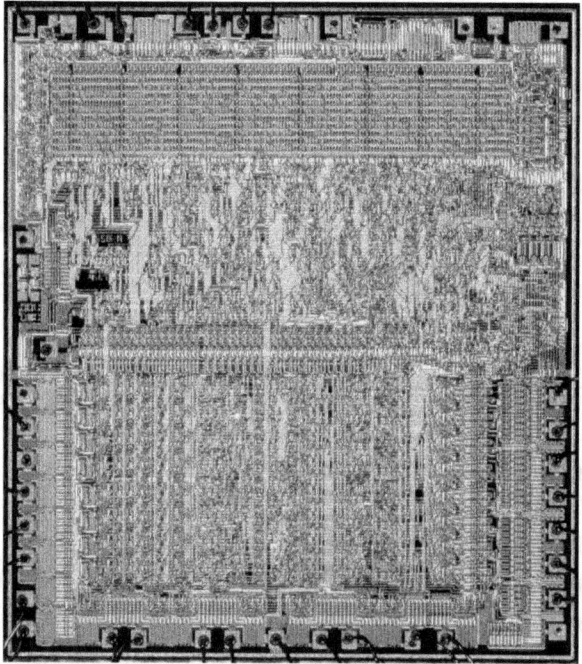

Figure 36. The silicon chip in a 6502 processor of size 3.9 x 4.3 mm. It contains about thirty-five hundred transistors, while modern processors have tens of billions of transistors.[18]

Tripartite Division of Consciousness

There is a vast difference between how scientists and philosophers approach the issue of consciousness. A philosophical tripartite division comes from Thomas Aquinas—who in turn had it from Aristotle:[19]

1. We have automatic physiological functions, such as heartbeat, breathing, and metabolism. This also includes the instinct to ingest nutrients, and to ensure the propagation of the species through reproduction.

---

18. "MOS 6502 Die," image courtesy of Paul Rautakorpi, CC BY 3.0, Wikimedia Commons.

19. This division into three originates in Aristotle's highly readable book, *On the Soul*, bk. 2, pt. 3.

2. We respond to sensory impressions, such as from the five senses: touch, taste, sight, hearing, and smell. In addition, we have perception, memory, and the ability to control motion.

3. We have intellect and rationality that enable us to consider concepts like grace, justice, and abstract mathematics. We also have the will, which causes abstract ideas to induce us to act, and we have self-awareness and can reflect on our own experiences and states.

Aquinas calls the first two in the list vegetative and animalistic, because we roughly share them with plants and animals, respectively. The last one primarily characterizes humans.

As I wrote this, I was waiting for back surgery under general anesthesia. The goal of the anesthesia is to disable the intellect and sensory abilities, but not the automatic functions. The nightmare vision in surgery is that touch, hearing, and vision are still functional while the rest of my body is paralyzed. Then I would feel pain but not be able to express it.[20]

I have myself participated in brain imaging studies with MRI.[21] Typical for many such studies is that they start with mice studies. We measured the natural reflex when the mouse received a small electric shock in the hind legs, thereby registering sensory and motor responses. This is the most common measurement, not least because such functions are shared by animals and humans. It is much more difficult to measure qualities that are unique to humans, such as intellectual or rational brain activity, although traces of these can also be registered.

Here is where we begin to approach what is most distinctive for humans. It is evident in our ability to make advanced tools—everything from the stone age flint blades to today's sophisticated technology. We have a sense of art and music, and we practice complicated burial customs. Aquinas says that since the concepts and ideas involved are not material things, these are immaterial qualities. They need a physical brain to become real, but the brain is not their cause.

---

20. Without the staff at Drammen Hospital in Norway and the grace of God, who together made the operation successful, I do not know if this book would ever have been completed.

21. I am part of an international research group that has done studies in functional MR elastography. It registers the brain's response to vibrations instead of traditional functional MRI which responds to blood flow. There are indications that phenomena register after only 0.1 seconds of stimulus instead of 2–3 seconds as in fMRI. See Patz et al., "Imaging Localized Neuronal Activity."

Another good characterization of the mental comes from the German philosopher and psychologist Franz Brentano (1838–1917), who pointed out that it is "intention" that is central. Intention is something completely different and more than just reacting to sensory impressions. All thoughts we have are about "something," such as what to eat or the act of traveling somewhere. This "something" has an inner existence within us. A physical object, on the other hand, like an apple or a bicycle, cannot be about "something." Admittedly, we can use a physical object like a pencil to express our thoughts, but it is the thought and not the pencil mark that is about "something," and which shows intentions. In contrast to the mental, physical objects are only themselves; they do not point toward anything else.[22]

The Hard Problem

But how can a physical brain give rise to the nonphysical? This question is colored by the fact that the person asking it essentially only believes the physical to be real. Let us rather think like Aquinas and ask how it is that a network of neurons can contain conscious experiences, while a network of computers does not. There are many theories here, but no consensus. The distinction between sensory qualities and intellectual properties, or consciousness and self-consciousness, correlates quite well with what today is called the *easy problem* in contrast to the *hard problem*. This division comes from the Australian philosopher David Chalmers and the hard problem is really only hard for those who only regard the material as real.[23]

Self-consciousness has to do with subjective experience and one's own experience, as opposed to what is physical and objective. These subjective experiences can be anything from the experience of the smell of sour milk to the experience of the property red by looking at a barn wall. Another aspect of self-consciousness is that we can ask ourselves what it is like to be someone. The American philosopher Thomas Nagel wrote a well-known article in 1974 about what it is like to be a bat, although he was not the first to use this image.[24] Bats are very different from us. They fly in the dark and hang upside down when resting. The most fascinating

---

22. Brentano's thoughts can be found in Egnor, "Why Consciousness Shows."
23. Chalmers, "Problem of Consciousness."
24. This paper is still an enjoyable read: Nagel, "What Is It Like to Be a Bat?"

aspect is that they use ultrasound to navigate. But is there something special about being a bat, something subjective? If we answer yes to that question, it implies that bats must be self-conscious. Even though we have learned a lot about how the bat's sonar works, we know very little about the bat's consciousness. In the same way, we can ask if there's something special about being another human, a baby, or a small child, and even about being a computer or an algorithm for artificial intelligence. There's a great gap in understanding between the *how* of physiology, and the *why* of subjective experience. Despite progress in many fields, it doesn't seem that this particular gap is getting much smaller.

The Mystery of Language Evolution

Explaining our language abilities is a major part of the hard problem as language plays an essential role in our collective learning and our self-consciousness. There is no lack of theories for how we, as the only species, came to have complex language. It is sobering to read the following abstract of a much-cited review paper by some of the most prominent researchers in the field:

> Understanding the evolution of language requires evidence regarding origins and processes that led to change. In the last 40 years, there has been an explosion of research on this problem as well as *a sense that considerable progress has been made*. We argue instead that the *richness of ideas is accompanied by a poverty of evidence* [my italics], with essentially no explanation of how and why our linguistic computations and representations evolved.

The authors go on to say:

> We show that, to date, (1) studies of nonhuman animals provide virtually no relevant parallels to human linguistic communication, and none to the underlying biological capacity; (2) the fossil and archaeological evidence does not inform our understanding of the computations and representations of our earliest ancestors, leaving details of origins and selective pressure unresolved; (3) our understanding of the genetics of language is so impoverished that there is little hope of connecting genes to linguistic processes any time soon; (4) all modeling attempts have made unfounded assumptions, and have provided no

empirical tests, thus leaving any insights into language's origins unverifiable.

In conclusion they say:

> Based on the current state of evidence, we submit that *the most fundamental questions* about the origins and evolution of our linguistic capacity *remain as mysterious as ever* [my italics], with considerable uncertainty about the discovery of either relevant or conclusive evidence that can adjudicate among the many open hypotheses.[25]

These researchers have studied the language ability of animals, looked at fossils and archaeological evidence, studied genetics, and used modelling. They are honest enough to conclude that the impression of considerable progress in our understanding that many have is not founded on evidence. No wonder the paper is titled "The Mystery of language Evolution." The study supports the statement already mentioned that the origin of human consciousness is a major and largely unsolved problem in evolution.[26]

Abstract Mathematics Is Not Physical

Language is also the main tool for expressing abstract mathematics.[27] I'm not talking about concrete calculations like adding prices in the store or subtracting a discount. This is arithmetic, which is only a tiny branch of the abstract and logical structure that is mathematics. Take, for example, the number pi or π (shown in figure 37), which is the ratio between the circumference and the diameter in a circle. Although we know that π has something to do with circles, it is an abstract object that does not exist in space or time. The number π has never been the cause of anything. It simply exists by itself.

---

25. Hauser et al., "Mystery of Language Evolution," 1.
26. Charlesworth and Charlesworth, *Evolution*, 110–27.
27. I am indebted to Professor Martin Herdegen, who works with financial mathematics at the University of Stuttgart, for inspiration for this section.

Figure 37. The symbol for the number pi.[28]

Interestingly, there are only a few digits in π that are concrete enough to be determined by measurement. Chinese Zu Chongzhi (Tsu Chung-chih) (429–ca. 500) impressively found the first eight digits already in the fifth century as 3.14159265.

The number π, on which so much of science depends, is therefore something that cannot be fully determined experimentally. The existence of π is something we see primarily from mathematical proofs, which themselves are abstract concepts. It is these proofs that allow us to determine the number π with the trillions of digits that are known.

Philosophy professor Øystein Linnebo writes the following about the fact that mathematical objects are abstract and exist independently of the human mind, or what he calls mathematical Platonism:

> If the view is true, it will put great pressure on the physicalist idea that reality is exhausted by the physical. For platonism entails that reality extends far beyond the physical world and includes objects that aren't part of the causal and spatiotemporal order studied by the physical sciences.[29]

Therefore, one cannot simultaneously believe that π exists and that all that exists in the world is physical, because π is not physical. The physical covers the external world, but we also have an internal world, our consciousness. But the number π is not simply a creation of my consciousness. Indeed, thoughts, like the concept of π, are expressed in words and sentences, and we grasp them with the mind. But truth and logic are not created by human language or psychology, nor are they something that only exist in our consciousness. The reason for this is that there are not

---

28. "Pi symbol," by Marian Sigler, Wikimedia Commons.
29. Linnebo, "Platonism in the Philosophy of Mathematics," §1.2.

just two, but three kinds of realities, as the German philosopher Gottlieb Frege (1848–1925) stated it:[30]

1. The outer world of material objects that we know through the senses, but π is not here.

2. The inner world of impressions, mental images, emotions, inclinations, and desires. It is characterized by this:

    a. Unlike the material world, which is public, the inner world can neither be sensed with eyes, ears, smell, or taste nor can it be touched. It is private. Everyone can see the physical tree stump I may happen to kick, but only I feel the pain in my toe.

    b. We have sensory impressions, emotions, and moods. They are something we have in our consciousness, and they cannot exist otherwise, such as the pain from kicking the tree stump. On the other hand, material things exist independently of us.

    c. The inner world needs someone to exist in, a bearer. Pain in a toe cannot exist without a being's consciousness. By comparison, material things in the outer world exist independently of a bearer.

    d. The inner world has only a single bearer and cannot be shared. Two people do not have the same inner world. We cannot feel the pain that another experiences, even though we can feel empathy.

3. Thoughts, ideas, or conceptions. Here we find π. It is tempting to think that π corresponds to the inner world, since π cannot be sensed and is thus not physical. But in contrast to impressions in the inner world, π does not need a bearer, for π is not dependent on my mental state. Otherwise, we would risk that my π and your π were different, but a concept like π exists independently of me and everyone. If truths like the one about π were purely subjective, then objective science would not be possible.

But how is it that advanced mathematics, such as the number π, partial differential equations, and complex numbers that are not physical and cannot cause anything in the physical world, can still describe the physical world with such great accuracy? This is Wigner's paradox of the

---

30. Frege, "Thought."

"unreasonable effectiveness of mathematics in the natural sciences" as noted in the introduction. Could this point to a rational thought behind the physical universe, as Einstein wondered about, and Kepler was convinced of? Or is it just evolution that has caused us to see patterns that help us master the world? There is much to suggest that something more than such an evolutionary psychology explanation is needed. For how can we explain that human consciousness can discover and understand precisely this connection between such abstract concepts and the physical world? All this points to our consciousness being more than purely material.[31]

HUMAN NATURE AND CONSCIOUSNESS

Are the body and consciousness two different entities, or are they one? This has implications for how we may think that humans and evolution can coexist. Many models have been proposed over time.

Aristotle's Form-Matter Model

Aristotle thinks that the soul is the very principle of life. In his four-part explanatory model, which was mentioned in chapter 5, the soul is the form explanation that describes human nature. The soul or form gives life to and permeates the body, which is the material explanation. In early modern times, as we touched on, this way of thinking was abandoned in physical sciences as the form concept was not so fruitful. Aristotle's model for man consists of two parts, but they are very closely connected. Often, man has been thought to consist of two parts that were more separated than this.

Dualism's Dichotomy

Dualism comes from the Greeks, especially Plato, who believed that the soul had a self-sufficient existence independent of the material. However, dualism is best known from René Descartes (1596–1650). He made a distinction between material and mental causes in science. Since intention is one of the things that characterizes consciousness, it was natural to think that consciousness did not fall under natural science—it simply

---

31. The arguments of Frege were instrumental in convincing the philosopher Edward Feser of the inadequacy of materialism: Feser, "Road from Atheism."

did not fit in, as explained in chapter 5. As in Aristotle's form explanation, dualism has no problem with the uniqueness of humans, and that is its strength. The weakness of dualism is that consciousness is not directly observable. Only its effect and not consciousness itself can be scientifically examined.

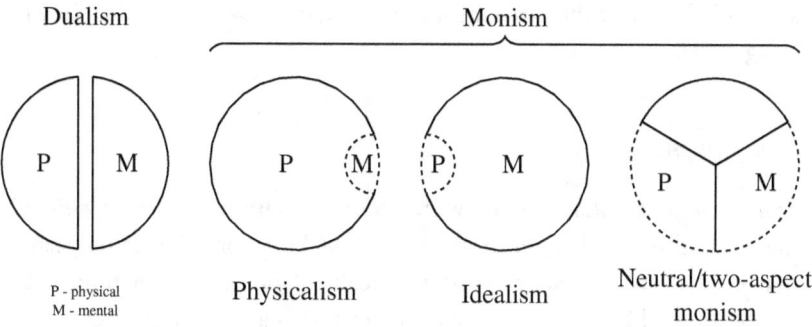

Figure 38. Dualism and three forms of monism.

Central to this dualism is that the body and consciousness are two completely separate entities, as shown far left in figure 38.[32] The challenge then is to explain how they interact. Descartes thought the center of the soul was the small pineal gland in the brain, which was believed to only exist in humans. But the pineal gland turns out to exist in most vertebrates.[33] Because of the insoluble problem of how body and soul play together, dualism is abandoned by many today. On the other hand, the whole point of dualism is to state that consciousness or soul is something other than the material. It is somewhat paradoxical then to demand that it should be possible to examine it scientifically with physical concepts such as energy and mass.

Monism: We Are One

It is common today, especially among natural scientists, to characterize humans by some form of *monism*—that is, that we only have one nature.

---

32. I am discussing here only *substance dualism* where the soul is a separate entity that will live on after the body is dead. This is not the case in *property dualism*, where the soul is more connected to the body.

33. The pineal gland (*glandula pinealis*) produces melatonin, which plays a role in maintaining the circadian rhythm.

This is more in line with today's brain studies that clearly show the intellectual and the rational cannot take place without a brain. Studies of electrical activity, studies with functional magnetic resonance imaging, and, not the least, studies of people with different types of brain damage show this. This would support monism, where there is more connection between soul and body than in dualism. Monism comes in many versions—let's look at the three most important ones, which are also shown in figure 38.

Materialism

Many scientists today operate with a monistic and *materialistic* view of man. It is also called *physicalism*. Strictly speaking, materialism only says that everything is matter, while physicalism includes everything that can be studied in physics. Beyond matter this is also energy, forces, and space-time. For simplicity, I equate them with each other here, so that materialism also gets a wider definition. In materialism, physical reality is therefore the only thing that exists, and the problem is then to explain self-consciousness from a physical brain. This is exactly the hard problem mentioned earlier. Therefore, self-consciousness is considered to be something that somehow just appears out of the blue with a larger and more complex brain. It is, in other words, an epiphenomenon. Imagine that you are going to light a bonfire. The goal is to get heat, but you get smoke as well, even if that was not intended. Similarly, self-consciousness just happens to appear. The German doctor and atheist Carl Vogt was onto this as early as the 1870s when he noted that "all the properties that we designate as activity of the soul, are only the functions of the cerebral substance, and to express ourselves in a coarser way, thought is just about to the brain what bile is to the liver and urine to the kidney."[34]

In its extreme, consciousness is eliminated and the tough problem disappears. This is referred to as *eliminative materialism*, which is a natural consequence of a fully materialistic view of humanity, but not all are so consistent that they will say so. Free will also disappears, and we are just a product of our genes. Old-fashioned astrology, which claimed that we were determined by the movement of the planets, has been replaced by a modern "astrology" in miniature, where the movements of the atoms or randomly composed genes are decisive. This removal of the special

---

34. Vogt, *Physiologische Briefe* [Physiological letters], 355.

position of consciousness contradicts many people's self-understanding and can easily be perceived as absurd. But it also shows how decisive our idea of a phenomenon is. If my model of man does not include the uniqueness of consciousness, then this idea wins over my own experience and reduces consciousness to something unimportant.

A modern example is Francis Crick, who received the Nobel Prize in 1962 for the discovery of the DNA's helical structure. He said that "a person's mental activities are entirely due to the behavior of nerve cells, glial cells, and the atoms, ions, and molecules that make them up and influence them."[35] This is the *reductionist materialist* view. Reductionism is easy to recognize in that the explanations use expressions like "are entirely due" or "is nothing but." This "nothing-buttery" view implies that sociology is nothing but applied psychology, which is nothing but applied biology, which in turn is nothing but applied chemistry.[36] In the end comes physics and, in particular, particle physics, which is the most fundamental, and which, in principle, can explain everything—we just haven't figured out how yet.[37]

Supporters of this kind of reductionism may agree that there is much left to explain, but they can get away with adding that it is because the explanations have not yet been found. Philosopher of science Karl Popper (1902–1994) called this *promissory materialism*.[38] Reductionists rely on future discoveries to understand phenomena today. Although this is often dressed in scientific language, it is a philosophical position that cannot be tested with standard scientific methods. Reductionism sounds like an explanation, but it's really an evasion, and it has an element of blind faith, a faith that does not build on scientific facts. I wonder why more people don't see that the mystery of how matter can give rise to consciousness is really just as unresolved as the mystery of how the soul and body can interact, which is what made many people reject dualism.

When attempts at an explanation for consciousness are given, the term *emergence* usually appears. It's a word that denotes that something complex and new can be formed from interactions of the simple. An example of an emergent system is a bird swarm like the one shown in figure 39. Each bird is only affected by its immediate neighbors, but it still

---

35. Crick, *Astonishing Hypothesis*, 271.

36. MacKay, *Clockwork Image*. Chapter 4 is called "'Nothing-Buttery' and Other Hazards."

37. This is a paraphrase of a comic strip: Munroe, "Fields Arranged by Purity."

38. First used by Karl Popper in 1984 according to Gendle, "Philosophy of Mind."

looks like the swarm itself is controlled as if there were a separate swarm intelligence. At the same time, each bird benefits from the swarm, both as protection against predators and for finding food.[39] There is nothing new in emergence, it has been observed for thousands of years and is even described in the Bible. Just think of this observation of the self-organization of ants: "Go to the ant, you sluggard; consider its ways and be wise! It has no commander, no overseer or ruler, yet it stores its provisions in summer and gathers its food at harvest" (Prov 6:6–8).

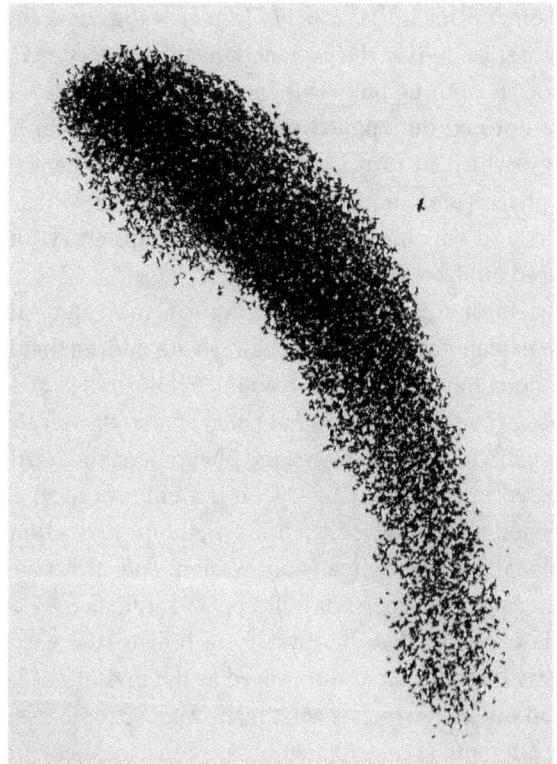

Figure 39. A bird swarm emerging from individual starlings as a response to a bird of prey in the upper right.[40]

39. It is common to explain the behavior of a flock of birds by simply looking at how a bird interacts with its six or seven closest neighbors. But Pearce et al., "Role of Projection in the Control of Bird Flocks," show that it is important for birds deep inside the flock to see what is outside the flock. Therefore, the density of the swarm must also be controlled. How that happens is not fully explained.

40. "Starling Flock with Nearby Predator," image courtesy of Mostafameraji, CC BY-SA 4.0, Wikimedia Commons.

Such *weak emergence* can be used to justify reductionist materialism. *Weak* here means that something unexpected, but not entirely inexplicable, emerges from something simple. The opposite is *strong emergence*, which denotes something new that cannot even in principle be deduced from the properties of the simpler elements that it is based on. As previously mentioned, we would never have guessed from brain measurement that the brain encompasses consciousness, since there are no independent traces of consciousness in the measurements. This is something completely different from just the unexpected. Chalmers believes that there is really only one example of strong emergence, and that is consciousness itself. Everything else is weak emergence.[41] In a materialistic view of humanity, the concept of strong emergence takes on an air of mystery.

Idealism

The opposite of materialism is to consider that the soul dominates over the physical. This is called idealism. It was popular in the eighteenth century, but seems to reemerge today, as a reaction against the barrenness of materialism. Some of the best criticism of materialism therefore comes from various directions within idealism. Computer engineer and philosopher Bernardo Kastrup from the Netherlands has distinguished himself as an eloquent critic. Kastrup points out that we humans cannot actually experience the material directly. We only have the experience of it through our senses and our mind, therefore he says that the mind or the mental is more real than the material. Russian American physicist Andrei Linde (b. 1948) described it in this way in 1998:

> Let us remember that our knowledge of the world begins not with matter but with perceptions. I know for sure that my pain exists, my "green" exists, and my "sweet" exists. I do not need any proof of their existence, because these events are a part of me; everything else is a theory. Later we find out that our perceptions obey some laws, which can be most conveniently formulated if we assume that there is some underlying reality beyond our perceptions. This model of material world obeying laws of physics is so successful that soon we forget about our starting point and say that matter is the only reality, and perceptions are only helpful for its description. . . . But in fact

41. Chalmers, "Strong and Weak Emergence."

> we are substituting reality of our feelings by a successfully working theory of an independently existing material world. And the theory is so successful that we almost never think about its limitations until we must address some really deep issues, which do not fit into our model of reality.[42]

On this basis, Kastrup also concludes that the hard problem is only a problem as long as we have a strictly materialistic view of reality, as I have stated previously. Kastrup asks us to think of a painting and what it depicts. A materialist's attempt to explain what a person is can be compared to someone who asks a painter to paint his portrait. When he receives the finished picture, he forgets who he is and solemnly declares that the portrait is his true self.

In idealism, the idea is that if the material brain is the bearer of consciousness, then all material must also have consciousness. There are many directions within this, but there are two main categories: bottom-up and top-down. In the first view, a person is made up of a large number of small, simple objects or particles with consciousness. Everything has consciousness, and this is called *panpsychism*. A problem for panpsychism is to explain how each individual object's consciousness collaborates to become a person's consciousness. This combination problem can be said to be as difficult as the tough problem of materialism. Kastrup instead prefers a top-down view where one starts with a universal consciousness that then splits and becomes the individual's consciousness. He also limits consciousness to only exist in biology, thus rocks and other dead objects are not conscious. This universal consciousness has in many ways replaced God or has some resemblance to an image of God—without Kastrup, as far as I know, himself using this designation.

Kastrup sets his idealism against the all-too-simple materialistic model and also against the dualistic model, which he thinks is represented by religion. There I think he misunderstands religion. He assumes that consciousness must always have been in nature without any more explanation of how or why. Its origin is a mystery. Kastrup rejects the idea that consciousness could have entered by what he calls "an arbitrary discontinuity in nature."[43] Such a discontinuity could be in his view—for example, that "God created man in his image" (Gen 1:27). Despite these

---

42. Kastrup, *Idea of the World*, 282.
43. Kastrup, *Idea of the World*, 65.

reservations against the pure idealistic view itself, there is much to learn from idealists' criticism of the materialistic view of man.

Another reservation against idealism is that an emphasis on consciousness easily leads to a degrading of the physical, making the physical world something inferior. There is a long tradition for such views clothed in religious language and where material life on Earth is evil and is just preparation for life in heaven. From a Christian point of view, it is counter to the fact that God found life on Earth so valuable that he himself in the form of Jesus Christ became a human with flesh and blood. This is what is called incarnation. The emphasis on identity as more important than biology is also a form of idealism. The idea that some people are "born in the wrong body" is not easy to reconcile with the appreciation of the body that is implicit in the Apostles' Creed which says "I believe ... in the resurrection of the body."[44]

Simultaneously One and Dual

A third monistic standpoint is *neutral monism* or *two-aspect monism*, shown at the far right in figure 38. This is a view that many Christians hold, such as the English theologian and physicist John Polkinghorne (1930–2021).[45] Neutral monism can be most easily explained by an image from physics. In quantum mechanics, an object can be described either as a wave or a particle, and the underlying description of both is the theory of quantum fields. In the same way, matter and consciousness are two sides of the same coin, they are complementary and inseparable, and neither of them dominates over the other, as in idealism and materialism. They are just two ways in which the single substance that exists in the world manifests itself.

Another image is how water can exist as ice, liquid water, or water vapor. Here we have three different descriptions that all show different sides of the same substance. Here, too, we know that they are united in the description of the water molecule. However, such a common designation for matter and consciousness remains to be found. In this respect, we may be no further along than in dualism, where the interaction between body and consciousness also is to a large degree unknown.

---

44. Wikipedia, "Apostles' Creed," sec. Text, 11.
45. Polkinghorne, *Belief in God*, ch. 3, and Baker, "Christians Should Reject."

A disadvantage of neutral monism is that it can be difficult to avoid saying that all matter, not just that which a human is composed of, has consciousness. Then a dead object like a stone also has a form of consciousness. This is panpsychism, as mentioned in the discussion of idealism. It is somewhat similar to Aristotle, who says that stones naturally seek the Earth, implying a form of animism, in which stones, in a sense, have a will of their own.

It is tempting also to remark that two-aspect monism shares some similarity with dualism.[46] Perhaps we can see two-aspect monism as an attempt at a compromise that will preserve the best of both dualism and monism?

It should be mentioned that there are many more models for body and mind than those included here, but the differences are even more subtle, and it can be difficult to distinguish them. The number of models just underscores how complicated thinkers throughout all time have considered this problem to be, and how far we are from any agreement on human nature. This is also a field where it seems unlikely that any scientific breakthrough will soon occur, and it is legitimate to wonder if there exists a scientific solution at all.

The Limits of Science

As we have seen, idealists are strongly critical of the prevailing materialistic view of humanity, so this criticism does not just come from those who want to maintain a biblical view of humanity. The philosopher Thomas Nagel, who wrote the article about what it's like to be a bat, says in the same article that reductionists don't even try to explain consciousness. A few years ago, he published a book with the telling subtitle *Why the Materialist Neo-Darwinian Conception of Nature Is Almost Certainly False*.[47] Nagel calls himself an atheist and believes that the body-soul problem is hopelessly unsolvable; it is a mystery. Therefore, thinkers like Nagel may be called *mysterians*. In a survey, it was revealed that as many as 20–40 percent of those who call themselves atheists do not believe that reductionist materialism is a good enough explanation for humans, so Nagel is not alone in being a mysterian.[48] Another way to put it, and one I prefer

---

46. This is especially the case with the weaker form of dualism, property dualism.
47. Nagel, *Mind and Cosmos*.
48. A survey by Newman University/YouGov from 2017 showed that 19 percent of

over the term mysterian, is that we have reached the limit of what science can discover. For a researcher, this is not a stance you easily accept, but here it may be the only way out.

Charles Darwin must have sensed this as well and was perplexed by it. In a letter to the Christian American biologist Asa Gray in 1860, he wrote that he was not "contented to view this wonderful universe & especially the nature of man, & to conclude that everything is the result of brute force."[49] Furthermore, he wrote in 1871 that "in what manner the mental powers were first developed in the lowest organisms, is as hopeless an enquiry as how life itself first originated. These are problems for the distant future if they are ever to be solved by man."[50] In his autobiography from 1876, Darwin doubted whether "the mind of man, which has, as I fully believe, been developed from a mind as low as that possessed by the lowest animal, be trusted when it draws such grand conclusions?"[51] We also see this dichotomy in him as he transitioned from being a theist to an agnostic. Both the human mind and God seemed to be shrouded in mystery for him.

It is evident that humans possess something unique that we do not share with animals. We have an inner, subjective world we can express through language. Language also enables us to learn as a collective group through culture, rather than just as individuals. Moreover, we have a spiritual thirst that manifests itself in an awareness of something or someone higher than us. We also have a profound need to be seen as individuals, which is expressed by each person having a unique name. We are so dependent on being recognized as persons that this seems to be built into our very nature. Unfortunately, we also have a capacity for evil that is not as easily recognized in animals.

The models for consciousness discussed here, dualism and monism in various forms, are all attempts at understanding ourselves. Particularly popular these days is monism in the form of materialism. But if our bodies are merely the result of an evolution that originated from other creatures, we need an explanation for where our unique properties come

---

atheists in Great Britain and 38 percent in Canada somewhat agree, agree, or strongly agree with the statement "Evolutionary processes cannot explain the existence of human consciousness." Among the religious the proportion increased to 54 percent and 55 percent, respectively. Elsdon-Baker, "Questioning Evolution," and Wilkinson, "Darwin's Theory of Evolution."

49. Quoted in Spencer, *Darwin and God*, 95.
50. Darwin, *Descent of Man*, 36.
51. Quoted in Spencer, *Darwin and God*, 98.

from. The explanation provided by reductionist materialists and naturalists that these abilities essentially are unreal is not very intellectually satisfying. It's just an evasion to say that language and consciousness are nothing more than a sufficient number of brain cells in action.

I think the American theologian David Bentley Hart (b. 1965) hits the nail on the head when he says that we face "an absurd dilemma" between dualism and materialism: "We must believe either in a ghost mysteriously animating a machine or in a machine miraculously generating a ghost."[52]

The human mind is still an enigma, 150 years after Darwin, as is evident when Charlesworth and Charlesworth maintain that the origin of human consciousness is one of the major and largely unsolved problems in evolution.[53] No wonder we cannot understand its origin when we cannot even agree on what consciousness is.

---

52. Hart, *Experience of God*, 167.
53. Charlesworth and Charlesworth, *Evolution*, 110–27.

8

The Perceived and the Real Conflict

> From religion comes a man's purpose; from science, his power to achieve it. Sometimes people ask if religion and science are not opposed to one another. They are: in the sense that the thumb and fingers of my hands are opposed to one another. It is an opposition by means of which anything can be grasped.
>
> Sir William Bragg (1862–1942)
Nobel Prize in Physics 1915

A RECURRING THEME IN this book has been that the assumed conflict between science and God or theology is an imagined conflict. We saw in the introduction how even a neutral statement from the Middle Ages about northern and southern zones on the Earth was turned into a story about a church who supposedly killed those with opposing scientific views. Why do so many still perceive that there is conflict, and even make up one? Where does the conflict thesis come from? And is there another conflict, a real one? To illustrate this, let's turn to the story of what happened to the vast number of manuscripts that Isaac Newton left behind in 1727.

NEWTON OF ALL PEOPLE WAS NO NEWTONIAN

William Blake's portrayal of Isaac Newton from 1795 shows him concentrating on geometrical figures and a compass (figure 40). It is part of the poet and painter Blake's criticism of the one-sided scientific rationality of the Enlightenment. Even Newton's muscles and hands are marked by geometry—with sharp angles and lines. His face is turned toward the Earth and away from heaven, as Newton came to be the foremost symbol of a rationality sharply separated from religion.[1]

Figure 40. William Blake's Newton (1795).[2]

This is how Newton was viewed in the generations after his death. He would be seen as a proponent of a Newtonianism that applied the principle of natural law to areas beyond gravitation, both in the natural and social sciences, and even in philosophy.

---

1. This section is based on Snobelen, "Isaac Newton"; Dry, *Newton Papers*; Jacob, Introduction to *Newton and Newtonianism*; Osler, "New Newtonian Scholarship"; Popkin, "Plans for Publishing Newton's Manuscripts"; and Tour, "Controversial Views of Isaac Newton."

2. "Newton-William Blake," Tate Britain, Wikimedia Commons.

The additions to Newton's *Principia* that came in the second and third editions with the aid of Robert Cotes, quoted in chapter 5 (pp. 153–156), and which talked about God as the creator and sustainer of the universe, were explained away. French physicist and mathematician Jean-Baptiste Biot, in his entry in a French encyclopedia in 1822, had interpreted these additions as the result of a nervous breakdown in 1692–93. Biot described a Newton who before that did all his science and afterward turned to theology. In this way one could create a Newton where rational science was separated from an old man's "irrational" religion. This demarcation is a distinguishing mark of the Enlightenment.

Gradually a different and much richer image of Newton has emerged. Paradoxically, as James Gleick remarked in his biography of Newton, "He of all people was no Newtonian."[3] Newton left behind handwritten notes containing some 10 million words, or the equivalent of more than one hundred novels. At his death, just a few of these notes were made public. An example is where Newton had worked out the possible dates for the crucifixion of Jesus Christ from scriptural and astronomical evidence.[4] The rest of the manuscripts were described as "reams of loose and foul papers." This was partly due to the heretical views of the Trinity that were found there, and which may have been the reason why Newton did not publish this while still alive. The papers were kept by his relatives and ended up in the possession of the Earl of Portsmouth. Almost 150 years after Newton's death, in 1872, the scientific parts were sorted out and donated to Cambridge university.

Due to financial problems, the rest, consisting of some 3.6 million words, was auctioned in 1936. There was little interest for them from British institutions so most of the papers on alchemy were bought by the famous economist John Maynard Keynes. The 1 million or so words on alchemy which are now at Cambridge university shows a Newton who was searching for the key to why some substances could give rise to life.

Professor Abraham Shalom Yahuda (1877–1951) was the one who, in the end, bought the theological papers from various dealers. He was a polymath, public intellectual, and bibliophile, born in Jerusalem, and who had lived in Germany, Spain, and, in the end, emigrated to the United States. His rabbinic training, which had given him deep knowledge of the Old Testament, as well as his linguistic abilities made him uniquely

---

3. Gleick, *Isaac Newton*, 8.
4. These were published in 1733; see Pratt, "Newton's Date for the Crucifixion."

positioned to appreciate Newton's writings on the Bible, theology, prophecy, chronology, and church history. A handwritten manuscript from the Yahuda collection is shown in figure 41.

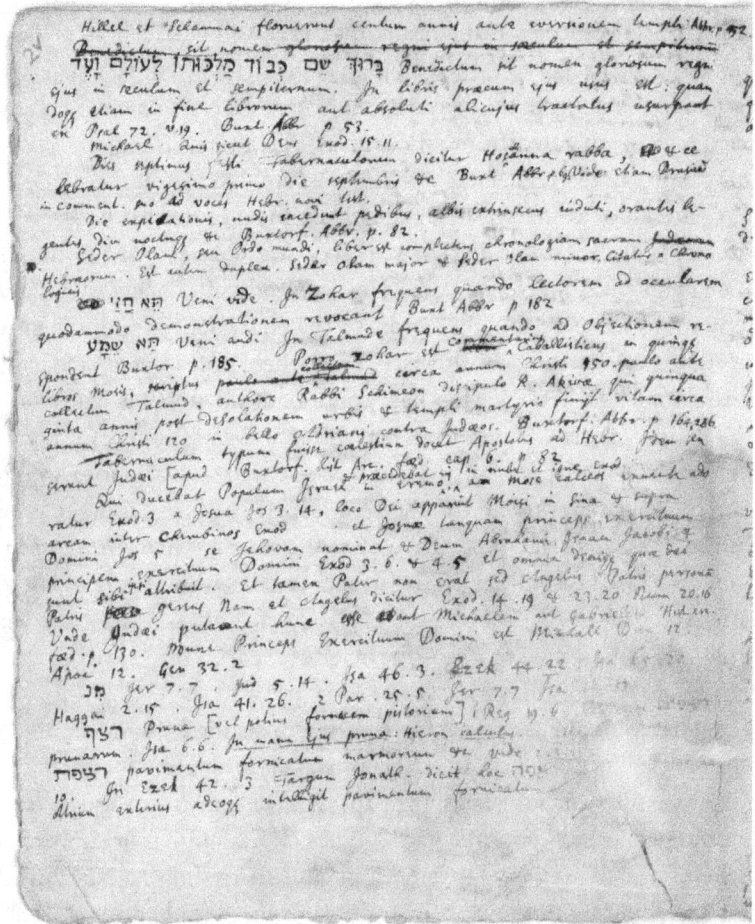

Figure 41. Newton's notes on the Jewish temple based on the book of Ezekiel containing Hebrew writing. Date 1675–1685.[5]

Newton's writings on theological topics amounts to some 2.5 million words of which 1.4 million came from the 1936 auction. Contrary to what Enlightenment thinkers would have us believe they were not the product of an old man's senility but written over a period of at least sixty years.

5. "Notes on the Jewish Temple," National Library of Israel, Wikimedia Commons.

With letters of recommendation from Albert Einstein, Yahuda tried to place these papers with Harvard, Yale, and Princeton universities, but they all refused the material. Since the early 1970s these papers have been in the possession of the National Library of Israel.

There was considerable resistance to the ideas on theology and alchemy found in these papers. Historian of science Margaret C. Jacob recalls the following story:

> I was in the audience in the 1970s when Richard Westfall, speaking at one of the big international congresses in the history of science, presented his early work on Newton's alchemy. There were audible gasps, and under a barrage of hostile questioning, Westfall retorted in exasperation, "I did not write these manuscripts," or words to that effect. Very few in the audience wanted Newton to be a practicing alchemist, as well as a serious religious thinker.[6]

In the 1980s, Newton researchers became aware of the Jerusalem manuscripts and an effort to make them public was initiated. Again, there was resistance. Philosopher and historian Richard H. Popkin tells the story of how he met with the director of historical research at the National Science Foundation in the US who confided that he had told the National Endowment for the Humanities not to fund the project. Evidently, there were people who wanted to preserve Newton's image as a rational scientist and suppress his religious and alchemical opinions.

Despite this, the Newton project has, since 1998, made all his writings available on the internet. Today they offer a view of a Newton who believed in final causes behind nature, who accepted the authority of the Bible and studied it with great devotion, and who believed in the two-book approach to knowledge: nature and revelation. A picture emerges of a Newton who saw his activity as one of uncovering divine activity in the world, whether through science or through ancient wisdom, or in alchemy.

A BRIEF HISTORY OF THE CONFLICT THESIS

The story of the Newton manuscripts demonstrates how the separation of science and faith that we have inherited from the Enlightenment in the belief that this was the view of one of the greatest scientists is false. Newton's life tells us the opposite and gives us instead the image of a scientist

---

6. Jacob, introduction to *Newton and Newtonianism*, x.

who integrated science and belief in God and saw them both as rational ways of seeking knowledge that didn't compete but was complementary.

In the Protestant world, it is not uncommon to trace the conflict hypothesis back to two nineteenth-century books that may be the first to have conflict explicitly mentioned in the titles. The first is the *History of the Conflict Between Religion and Science* from 1874 by the British American researcher John William Draper (1811–1882), based on his earlier writings on similar subjects. The second book is *A History of The Warfare of Science with Theology* from 1896 by American Andrew Dickson White (1832–1918). Here one will find the erroneous argument that the church claimed that the Earth was flat, and this is used as an example of how the church supposedly opposed science. British science historian John Hedley Brooke, one of the most recognized in the field of science and religion, goes so far as to say that White's arguments are deeply flawed.[7]

Nevertheless, both Draper's and White's books continue to be issued in new editions, and according to the statistics quoted in chapter 1 (pp. 18–19) they have indirectly influenced one third of the British population and almost half of Norway's population with the conflict thesis.

As the story about the Newton papers illustrates, they are symptoms of a process that had been going on for a while. As an example, two decades before White's book and the year after Draper's book, Scottish physicists Balfour Stewart and Peter Guthrie Tait published *The Unseen Universe: Or Physical Speculations on a Future State* (1875). As the objective was "to endeavor to show that the presumed incompatibility of Science and Religion does not exist,"[8] the conflict hypothesis must have been a common belief already then. At that time, the criticism was against all forms of Christianity, whether Catholic or Protestant.

It started as a criticism of the Catholic Church, as Milton's account of the meeting with Galileo in the 1630s mentioned in chapter 3 was an example of. It grew with time into what the highly critical and polemical British Enlightenment historian Edward Gibbon (1737–1794) wrote, a century before Draper and White, in *The History of the Decline and Fall of the Roman Empire* (1776–1789). In two chapters he presents his view that Christianity was a major factor in the decline of the Roman empire.

---

7. Brooke, *Science and Religion*, 35.
8. Stewart and Tait, *Unseen Universe*, ix.

He claimed that the church is the enemy of reason, and that Christian theology leads people into intellectual bondage.[9]

Gibbon was influenced by French Enlightenment philosophers like Voltaire (1694–1778), whom he had met in Lausanne where they both lived for a period. Voltaire wrote in a letter to Frederick the Great, king of Prussia, in 1767 that

> ours is assuredly the most ridiculous, the most absurd and the most bloody religion which has ever infected this world. . . . Your Majesty will do the human race an eternal service by extirpating this infamous superstition. . . . My one regret in dying is that I cannot aid you in this noble enterprise, the finest and most respectable which the human mind can point out.[10]

Similar thinking was central to the marquis de Condorcet (1743–1794), philosopher and mathematician, who had written *Outlines of an Historical View of the Progress of the Human Mind*, posthumously published in 1795 as he lost his life during the French Revolution, as mentioned in chapter 3. Here progress was set against Christianity and Condorcet wrote:

> Contempt for the human sciences was one of the first features of Christianity. . . . Even knowledge of the natural sciences was odious to it, because those sciences are dangerous to the success of miracles; and there's no religion that doesn't require its devotees to swallow some physical absurdities. So Christianity's triumph signaled the total downfall of the sciences and of philosophy.[11]

THE REAL CONFLICT

Enlightenment thinkers such as Voltaire could at most accept deism—that is, that the universe was created by a God who is now absent—but there was no room for Newton's active God. The deism of the Enlightenment has developed into today's view that is marked by positivism, belief in progress, and scientism.

Positivism is an approach to knowledge that emphasizes the sensory, empirical basis of human understanding and rejects all metaphysics. The term comes from the French philosopher Auguste Comte (1798–1857),

---

9. Ferguson, "Edward Gibbon on Christianity."
10. Wikipedia, "Voltaire," sec. Christianity, para. 3.
11. Condorcet, *Advances of the Human Mind*, 39.

who started sociology as a field of study. In the beginning of his main work from 1830, he postulated that positive philosophy considers all phenomena to be subject to unchangeable natural laws and therefore that the methods of natural science should apply to all sciences. Comte expected society to develop in a law-like way from a theological phase and move to a scientific phase. Similar ideas of progress can be found in *The Communist Manifesto* from 1848 where society inevitably will move from capitalism to communism.

Scientism is a step beyond positivism. The term was described as follows by the French biologist, philosopher of science, and atheist Félix le Dantec (1869–1917) in 1911:

> I believe in the future of Science: I believe that Science and Science alone will solve all the questions that make sense; I believe that it will penetrate to the mysteries of our emotional life and that it will even explain to me the origin and the structure of the hereditary anti-scientific mysticism that coexists with me in the most absolute scientism. But I am also convinced that men ask themselves many questions that mean nothing. Science will show the absurdity of these questions by not answering them, which will prove that they do not have an answer.[12]

Scientism thus asserts that natural science can solve all mysteries that are of importance. Questions that cannot be answered are meaningless. Science is therefore the only path to truth. Questions about God, meaning, and religion are not just stages we have left behind, they have additionally become meaningless.

Scientism's postulate that everything of importance can be answered by science isn't, by itself, a scientific statement. The paradox is therefore that scientism builds on a claim that according to its own postulate, falls into the category of questions that cannot be answered. In other words, there is something self-contradictory at the very basis of scientism. It claims that everything is natural science, but this claim is a statement that itself cannot be justified scientifically. The same goes for the belief in progress inherent in positivism.

Some of the celebrity scientists of our time, such as Stephen Hawking, Richard Dawkins, Steven Weinstein, and others would more or less openly assert that positivism and scientism are founded on science, not the least because of the similarity between the words. Many people today

12. Original in French: Wikipedia, "Scientisme" [Scientism], sec. Origine du terme, para. 2.

also believe that this is the case due to the authority we place in such celebrity scientists. But this is an example of science overstepping its boundaries.

The real conflict is therefore not between science and theology, but between scientism and theology, or in other words between naturalism and theology. Naturalism asserts that:

- All meaningful questions are scientific, and therefore there are no higher purposes
- Evolution/evolutionism explains everything, and we are merely a higher form of animal subject to blind impersonal forces
- The struggle for existence is a fundamental principle
- The cure for humanity's problems is more enlightenment
- Everything ends with death

These are not just theoretical ideas with little consequences. One example is the fear many have today of artificial general intelligence and how it could lead to a form of transhumanism that may outperform and, in the end, rule over man. Stephen Hawking justified this belief based on his materialistic worldview in this way:

> However, the rapid pace of improvement [in speed and complexity] will probably continue until computers have a similar complexity to the human brain. Some people say that computers can never show true intelligence, whatever that may be. But it seems to me that *if very complicated chemical molecules can operate in humans to make them intelligent* [my italics], then equally complicated electronic circuits can also make computers act in an intelligent way. And if they are intelligent, they can presumably design computers that have even greater complexity and intelligence.[13]

In Hawking's purposeless universe, molecules have miraculously caused life of higher and higher complexity and, in the end, humans. In that light, there is no reason why evolution shouldn't continue and outperform and possibly even threaten man. If man, on the other hand, is the result of having been created in God's image with a purpose, this scenario of the future is not so likely after all.

---

13. Hawking, *Brief Answers to the Big Questions*, 107–8.

There is also something deeply contradictory in the materialistic view, which American philosopher Alvin Plantinga (b. 1932) points out. He goes so far as to say that if everything is fundamentally matter, then I don't know if I can trust my cognitive abilities. If consciousness is just a product of evolution, of the struggle to survive, there is no reason to believe that it is built to find truth. Similarly, we saw at the end of chapter 7 that Darwin wasn't sure if the mind of man, which he believed has been developed from a mind as low as that possessed by the lowest animal, can be trusted.

But if God, who is the origin of all things, exists, he must know what truth is. And if we are made in God's image, we have received a share in this ability to distinguish the true from the false as we do in science. That is what leads Plantinga to conclude that "there is superficial conflict but deep concord between science and theistic religion, but superficial concord and deep conflict between science and naturalism."[14]

If Plantinga is right, which I believe he is, we have been fooled. Just as the "Dark" Ages weren't really dark, the "Enlightenment" wasn't really light. The philosophers of this period have led us astray by their belief than man alone is the measure of all things.

Plantinga's view leads to completely different answers than those of scientism above:

- Science addresses only part of reality
- There is a personal God who has created us and cares for us
- Although God has created us from dust, we have a soul and we are created in God's likeness or image
- Our conscious distancing from God is humanity's problem and the secret to the cure lies in Jesus Christ
- Jesus's resurrection shows that there is hope beyond death and that we will bodily rise again

THE TESTIMONY OF BELIEVER SCIENTISTS

Many scientists would ascribe to the view just outlined. They followed in Newton's footsteps and were not so much influenced by Enlightenment

---

14. This is the claim as stated in the preface of Plantinga, *Where the Conflict Really Lies*.

thinking. In fact, many Christian scientists were instrumental in developing today's science as has been documented in previous chapters. Curiously, there are therefore two parallel streams running through Europe in the eighteenth and nineteenth centuries and up to our time. On the one hand, there is this critical, polemical, and sometimes hateful criticism of both Christianity and the church leading to the scientism of our age. On the other hand, there are the many scientists with a deep Christian faith, living at the same time, and represented today by many scientists even including this author.

One example is André-Marie Ampère (1775–1836) whose father was beheaded during the French Revolution. Ampère discovered that there is a force between two wires when they carry electrical current, and this force was, until quite recently, the standard for quantifying current. For this reason, current is measured in amperes, and you will find units measured in A, for instance, when you read the fine print on your mobile phone charger. Ampère wavered back and forth in his faith, and as a twenty-eight-year-old he wrote this prayer to a friend: "I only find truths, teach me the Truth."[15] Ampère had understood that in the context of the four explanations of Aristotle of chapter 5, scientific truths deal with the efficient and material causes and how they follow natural laws. They are not contrary to truths from the Bible that are mainly concerned with what lies behind science and, in particular, purpose. I'll come back to Ampère at the end of this chapter.

Italian physicist Alessandro Volta (1745–1827) was the first to make a practical battery and therefore we characterize batteries by volts. This can also be seen in the fine print on the phone charger, in statements like 100–250 V for the input voltage. Volta said, "I constantly give thanks to God, who has infused into me this belief in which I desire to live and die, with the firm hope of eternal life. In this faith, I recognize a pure gift of God" (1815).[16]

In Britain, Michael Faraday (1791–1867) discovered how the movement of a magnet will induce a current in a wire. This became the basis for electrical generators and therefore Faraday deserves a thought every time you prepare your morning coffee by means of electricity. Faraday's work led to a theory of matter where forces and fields play an important role. He was skeptical of philosophical theories about the true nature of matter, but

---

15. "Je ne trouve que des vérités, enseigne-moi la Vérité," as quoted in Janin, "André-Marie Ampère," para. 41.

16. Quoted in Kneller, *Christianity and the Leaders*, 117.

in 1844 his experiments led to his, at first, hesitant belief "that particles are only centres of force; that the force or forces constitute the matter."[17]

In the same year, Faraday wrote an interesting note-to-self, which was much more subjective. Here he explained how this view of forces also fitted with his religious world picture. Some consider this to be Faraday's main reason for accepting the new model.[18] Faraday writes "that the Creator governs his material works by definite laws resulting from the forces impressed on matter, and, that matter is that of which we take cognizance by our external senses," and goes on to say, "I cannot imagine physical force without matter, or matter without force." First Faraday expresses a similar conviction to Newton's about the origin of natural law, as we saw in chapter 5. Second, in agreement with his mentor Humphry Davy's conviction that God was always active in creation due to his omnipotence and omnipresence, forces everywhere would be perfectly consistent.

James Clerk Maxwell (1831–1879) expressed Ampère's and Faraday's ideas in mathematics. Most people are at a loss to explain how information enters their mobile phones for them to read the news. It is Maxwell's equations that predict the electromagnetic waves that can transfer such information without wires. Near the end of his life Maxwell said, "I have looked into most philosophical systems, and I have seen that none will work without God."[19] He was also the one who had the text "Great are the works of the Lord; they are pondered by all who delight in them" from Ps 111:2 inscribed on the door of the Cavendish lab as pictured in chapter 2. It is evident that for Maxwell the study of physics was a means of discovering the works of the Lord. A new discovery was not a threat to his faith in God but rather made God greater.

One of my childhood heroes was Guglielmo Marconi (1874–1937), who would make the theoretical waves of Maxwell into something practical. He was awarded a Nobel Prize for this in 1909. Think about him every time you turn on a radio! In my youth I had no idea that Marconi was a Christian, but Marconi said, "I am proud to be a Christian. I believe not only as a Christian, but also as a scientist. Like a wireless device, in prayer the human spirit can send invisible waves into eternity, waves that reach their goal before God."[20] I have always been fascinated by these waves,

---

17. Levere, "Faraday, Matter, and Natural Theology," 100.
18. Levere, "Faraday, Matter, and Natural Theology," 107.
19. Garnett and Campbell, *Life of James Clerk Maxwell*, 426.
20. Speech in Bologna in 1934 as cited in Italian and English in Walsh, *Quotes from Believer Scientists*, 54.

and now I see that just as with Faraday, it is as if belief in the omnipotent God, the Creator of the visible and the invisible, was a help in discovering and accepting the reality of these invisible radio waves.

Light is another manifestation of electromagnetic waves, which Charles H. Townes (1915–2015) clearly understood. He was awarded a Nobel Prize in 1964 for the invention of the precursor to the laser, the maser. The reading of bar codes with a laser in the supermarket should be a reminder about what he said about the scientific process in 1966:

> Faith is necessary for the scientist even to get started, and deep faith is necessary for him to carry out his tougher tasks. Why? Because he must have confidence that there is order in the universe and that the human mind—in fact his own mind—has a good chance of understanding this order.[21]

Townes understood what lies behind science, the theological underpinnings that the early seventeenth-century scientists were motivated by and which they understood much better than most present-day scientists do.

Leaving electromagnetism, I can continue with William Thomson, or Lord Kelvin (1824–1907), whose studies in thermodynamics have led to the unit for absolute temperature being named after him. At zero Kelvin the particles in an atom stop moving. Whenever you check the thermometer on a warm summer day and it reads twenty-seven degrees Celsius or eighty degrees Fahrenheit, bear in mind that this is three hundred Kelvin. Kelvin's advice was that "if you think strongly enough you will be forced by science to the belief in God, which is the foundation of all Religion. You will find science not antagonistic, but helpful to Religion."[22] His faith was one of coherence with science and in dialogue with it according to the classification of chapter 1.

Finally, I would like to point to Georges Lemaître (1894–1966) whom we met in chapter 4 as the originator of the big bang theory. As mentioned in that chapter, his theory was confirmed in the 1960s when cosmic background radiation was serendipitously discovered. According to physicists' preferred temperature scale, the blackness of deep space amounts to an absolute temperature of only 2.7 K. Lemaître said in an interview that

---

21. Townes, "Convergence of Science and Religion," 305–6.

22. In a thank you speech after a lecture on "Present Day Rationalism" in 1903. Thompson, *Life of William Thomson*, 1099.

> I was interested in truth from the standpoint of salvation, as well as truth from the standpoint of scientific certainty. There were two ways of arriving at the truth. I decided to follow them both. Nothing in my working life, nothing in what I have learned in my studies of either science or religion has ever caused me to change that opinion. I have no conflict to reconcile.[23]

Finding Truth and Receiving Truth

The quote from Lemaître echoes the two-book narrative of chapter 1: truth from God's nature and truth from God's grace. This has been a guiding principle in writing this book, as seen in particular in chapters 1 and 2, and the appendix about how the Bible relates to the science of chapters 3, 4, 6, and 7.

First there is truth about God's nature as discovered by science. Ampère referred to it as "finding truths." These truths are uncovered by studying and experimentation. It requires hard work, dedication, and much effort.

The scientific view of nature and man does not, however, give the full picture. I have discussed evolution and models for human consciousness and what might be the origins of consciousness. Here, modern science is strikingly vague, and the word *mystical* is used by many researchers. What we can say for certain is that the Bible challenges the modern tendency to only view humans in a reductionist and materialistic manner. The uniqueness of our mental abilities is so clear that to explain them away as if they are nothing is like sticking your head in the sand. Our consciousness, our language, our rational and intellectual abilities, our thoughts about grace and death, our creativity in art and music, and everything from our drive for beauty and meaning to our abilities in higher mathematics are signs that we are much more. This is what the Bible expresses so beautifully when it says that we are created in God's image—that is, with a purpose.

This brings us to the second aspect of truth that Lemaître talks about. This is God's revelation. A central part of that is "to be created in God's image" as just mentioned. I have tried on several occasions to convey the meaning of this phrase, realizing that no one can fully understand the meaning of this important idea. To fully comprehend it, one would

---

23. Aikman, "Lemaître Follows Two Paths."

need to have a full understanding of who God is, but no human can fully know the mind of God. Therefore, the meaning of the concept "to be created in his image" is also something that we may never fully grasp, but it is something we long to understand. Here we also get a glimpse of the answer to the big questions of the introduction, such as when Einstein wondered that the most incomprehensible thing about the world is that it is comprehensible.

Approaching this kind of truth is very different from the effort required to find truths about nature, as it involves much more of a receptive spirit. God's grace is a gift and requires stillness to fathom. His voice is easy to miss in all of life's busyness. Ampère's prayer was "Teach me the Truth." One needs to listen to the Great Teacher and contemplate what he says to grasp this truth. Without this openness, the Bible will remain closed.

This book therefore ends with a call to consider both aspects of truth and to enter this receptive mood. The core of the Christian faith is not intellectual belief, but a relationship with Jesus Christ who desires above all to become a cornerstone of your life. As a teenager I responded to the following invitation: "Here I am! I stand at the door and knock. If anyone hears my voice and opens the door, I will come in and eat with that person, and they with me" (Rev 3:20). This invitation to a meal is still an invitation to close fellowship and an intimate personal relationship.

If you are a scientist who reads this, this kind of relationship will enrich your science as it did for Ampère, Volta, Faraday, Maxwell, Marconi, Townes, Kelvin, Lemaître, and many scientists living today. And for everyone, it will make your life fuller as you will be able to relate, not only to God's visible cosmos, but also to the invisible world.

Appendix

The Bible and Science

THIS APPENDIX PRESENTS NOTES on various ways the Bible can be interpreted in light of chapters 3, 4, 6, and 7. Little of what is collected here is original, but it gives a record of a non-theologian's attempt to reconcile the Bible with science.

THE BIBLE AND COSMOLOGY

At the time of Galileo, the Catholic Church interpreted the Bible to mean that the Earth stands still and the Sun moves. Luther read this literally in the same way, something that is reflected in his somewhat informal comment on Copernicus's ideas in a table talk as early as 1539, three years before Copernicus's book was published.[1] Today, few read this as scientific description, nor is it considered an "error" in the Bible. This can be explained in two ways.

The first is by stating that the Bible describes the world as it appears and therefore provides a *phenomenological* description. Even today, we say that the Sun "rises." Furthermore, no one feels the Earth moving in everyday life, so for all practical purposes, it seems to stand still.

The second way is by saying that the Bible is adapted to the thinking and science of its time, what is called *accommodation*. Since everyone

---

1. Quoted in Lindberg and Numbers, "Beyond War and Peace," 344–45.

believed that the Earth stood still in prescientific times, the Bible is also written from such a premise. Augustine (354–430) was concerned about this and stated that the Scripture was written based on an adaptation to the "weakness of the little ones."[2]

Let's look at other parts of the view of the Old Testament as well:[3]

1. It indirectly states that the Earth is flat, as the world stands on pillars and is described as a tent with the Earth as the floor.[4]
2. The Earth is a circle surrounded by water.[5] This is not so difficult to understand if we think of a map with the center in ancient Nineveh, near present-day Mosul, Iraq. Then the Mediterranean Sea lies to the west, the Black Sea to the north, the Caspian Sea to the east, the Persian Gulf to the southeast, and the Red Sea to the southwest. There is water practically in all directions.
3. There is a vault with water above the Earth.[6]
4. The Earth does not move.[7]
5. The Sun moves across the sky.[8]

We see that all these points can be read both as phenomenological descriptions and as accommodations to the astronomy and view of other ancient cultures. We can also sense the first three points in the New Testament, which speaks of a tripartite universe that is "in heaven and on earth and under the earth" (Phil 2:10). This is also how the universe was perceived in the Middle Ages. The Bible is also not entirely clear about the water in the vault above the Earth, as the book of Job offers an alternative, described in the form of the water cycle with evaporation and clouds (Job 36:27–28). Practically no one stands for the first three points today.

Items 4 and 5 were central to the struggle around Galileo and were therefore decided in the century after. Therefore, few advocate these five points as science today. It is not possible to claim them without conflicting with very well-founded knowledge and generally accepted science.

2. Ortlund, *Retrieving Augustine's Doctrine of Creation*, 124.
3. Lamoureux, "Evolutionary Creation."
4. Ps 19:5; 104:2, 5; Isa 40:22; Job 9:6.
5. Prov 8:22–31; Job 26:7–14 (esp. v. 10).
6. Gen 1:6–8; Ps 19:1; 104:2–3.
7. Ps 104:5; 93:1; 96:10; 1 Chr 16:30.
8. Ps 19:5–6; Eccl 1:5.

The reading of the biblical texts that many stood for in the fifteenth and sixteenth centuries is therefore abandoned.

Similarly, the physicist James C. Maxwell wrote about the danger of basing one's biblical interpretation too closely on the latest fad in science in a letter in 1876:

> The rate of change of scientific hypothesis is naturally much more rapid than that of Biblical interpretations, so that if an interpretation is founded on such an hypothesis, it may help to keep the hypothesis above ground long after it ought to be buried and forgotten.[9]

It becomes an overly fragile structure if we try to find detailed modern science in the biblical text. Science can be revised before we know it, and then biblical interpretation is left as the loser.

THE BIBLE AND THE AGE OF THE EARTH

When we look at the Bible in light of the scientific discoveries made in the nineteenth century, it is important to keep in mind the concept of God's two books or revelations. The Bible and science are not competitors; they complement each other. The most important thing the Bible tells us about the creation of the Earth is that God is the origin of everything and the foundation of the existence of the universe. This is something all Christians can agree on. However, there may be some differences in the details of how one views that the Earth came to be. The Bible itself gives us a complex portrayal of creation. The two accounts in the first and second chapters of Genesis are different in form, language, perspective, and chronology. Only the first account talks about six days, and in the second account, humans have a much more central role than in the first.

Church father Augustine from the fifth century wrote about the creation account throughout his life.[10] The surprising thing is how non-categorical Augustine is in interpreting the first chapters of Genesis. In one place, he refers to Sirach 18:1 (DRA), which says that "he that liveth

---

9. Quoted in Stanley, "By Design," 63–64.

10. Ortlund, *Retrieving Augustine's Doctrine of Creation*, 13, gives these five sources: *On Genesis: A Refutation of the Manichaeans* (AD 388–89), *The Unfinished Literal Commentary on Genesis* (AD 393–95), *Confessions* (AD 397–401), *The Literal Meaning of Genesis* (AD 401–16), *The City of God* (AD 413–26).

forever created all things together."[11] The word *together* here may be interpreted to be in time—that is, "simultaneously." This is the basis for Augustine's statement that the entire creation could have come into being in an instant.[12]

In another place, Augustine says that the creation of the world, day one, happened in an instant, but he is more open to the idea that the following five days were not necessarily twenty-four-hour days. An obvious difficulty that he points out is that it was not possible to measure what a day is before day four when the Sun was created. It is, after all, the Sun that is the "clock" that defines the twenty-four hours for us. On the fifth day, the animals were created and tasked to multiply and fill the water and the Earth. When it also says, "and it was so" (Gen 1:24), Augustine emphasizes that it meant that they reproduced and filled the water and the Earth. Everyone must understand that this could not happen in twenty-four hours.[13] Augustine also has a pragmatic view of the age of humanity:

> If there had elapsed since the creation of man, I do not say five or six, but even sixty or six hundred thousand years, or sixty times as many, or six hundred or six hundred thousand times as many, or this sum multiplied until it could no longer be expressed in numbers, the same question could still be put, Why was he not made before? For the past and boundless eternity during which God abstained from creating man is so great, that, compare it with what vast and untold number of ages you please, so long as there is a definite conclusion of this term of time, it is not even as if you compared the minutest drop of water with the ocean that everywhere flows around the globe.[14]

Try multiplying six hundred thousand years by six hundred thousand, and you will see that, in comparison, the modern estimate of the age of humanity is insignificant. Even our current estimates of the age of the universe seem so small to Augustine compared to eternity that it is less than a drop in relation to the entire ocean!

Norwegian theologian Børre Knudsen (1937–2014) pointed out the paradoxical fact that in many European languages the days of the week

11. A deuterocanonical work from the period between the Old and New Testaments.
12. Ortlund, *Retrieving Augustine's Doctrine of Creation*, 128.
13. Ortlund, *Retrieving Augustine's Doctrine of Creation*, 138.
14. Augustine, *City of God*, cited in Ortlund, *Retrieving Augustine's Doctrine of Creation*, 122.

are named after gods. In both English and Norwegian, these are Norse gods like Tyr, Odin, Thor, and Frey. These are parallel gods to the Roman gods Mars, Mercury, Jupiter, and Venus, who also have their names on the planets. In addition, we have a day for the Sun, one for the Moon, and one for Saturn.[15] Our seven days come from gods corresponding to the seven wandering celestial bodies. The creation account replaces these gods and their power with the one God. Note that the Sun and Moon are not even mentioned by name in the Genesis account. Instead, the celestial bodies, particularly the "greater light" and the "lesser light" (Gen 1:14–16), are turned into natural phenomena that only serve as "signs to mark sacred times, and days and years." Such was the importance of highlighting that God stands above all these gods that Knudsen says that "if there had been twelve instead of seven of them, the Lord would have created the world in eleven days and rested on the twelfth."[16]

The three main views on how to reconcile the Bible with the new science of the age of the Earth and life in the nineteenth century were young Earth creationism, old Earth creationism, and progressive creationism. The young Earth view is that the Earth is approximately six thousand years old. But Gen 1:1 doesn't really say that heaven and Earth were created on the first day.[17] The text is not specific as to the amount of time between the creation of the Earth in verse 1 and the creation of light on the first day in verses 3–5. In the old Earth or gap theory view, a gap between the creation of the Earth and the creation of life and humans is assumed. Finally in progressive creationism, everything was created over a long period of time that follows the days or order of the creation account, but the days are not twenty-four-hour days. Geologist and theologian William Buckland of chapter 4 went from the gap theory view of old Earth creationism to the day-age view of progressive creationism in the 1840s and 1850s as he struggled with the science of his time, his own and that of others.

These views are all examples of biblical *concordism*, meaning they are attempts to reconcile the creation account with science by aligning the biblical order of creation with what science has found about the Sun,

---

15. The connection between days and planets or gods from French and English is: Sun—Sunday; Moon—Monday; Mars/Tyr—Mardi/Tuesday; Mercury/Odin—Mercredi/Wednesday; Jupiter/Thor—Jeudi/Thursday; Venus/Frey—Vendredi/Friday; Saturn—Saturday.

16. Knudsen, *Grunnsøylene* [Foundational pillars], 18.

17. Lennox, *Seven Days That Divide*, ch. 3.

planets, and life. In the next section, this list will be complemented with more recent perspectives.

Augustine warns against a type of argument that young Earth creationists in particular may be tempted to use. He discusses the firmament above the heavens with water from Gen 1, and the fact that many say that such a thing is impossible because of gravity. Augustine rejects simple arguments to solve these paradoxes:

> Nor should anyone try to refute them by appealing to God's omnipotence, even though all things are possible for him (Mark 10:27) and say that we must simply believe that he can even cause water, which as we know is heavy, to spread across the heavens where the stars have their place.[18]

Augustine would rather take scientific objections seriously than appeal to God's omnipotence. For the same reason, both Tycho and Riccioli rejected a similar argument that God in his power could have made the stars much larger than the Sun in order for Copernicus's theory to make sense (see chapter 3).

It is only in young Earth creationism that Noah's flood is considered to have covered the entire Earth. As early as the seventeenth century, people began to look at the flood with scientific eyes, and calculations showed that there was not enough water to cover all the mountains. This is reflected in alternate views that tend to think that the story of the flood is based on the memory of a local flood or that it is even meant to be figurative. The figurative finds support in that the narrative is poetically formulated as a *chiasmus*[19]—that is, a story where something develops into the opposite and back again. In the story of Noah in Gen 7–8, it concerns the symmetry in the number of days in each phase:

- 7 days to wait for the rain
- 40 days of rain
- 150 days of flood
- 150 days for the water to decrease until the ark grounds
- 40 days to wait in order to open the ark
- 7 days to wait for the earth to dry up

---

18. Augustine, *Literal Meaning of Genesis*, in Ortlund, *Retrieving Augustine's Doctrine of Creation*, 87.

19. A chiasmus, after the Greek letter χ (*chi*), which symbolizes a crossing.

These are the most striking features of the chiasmus in this narrative, but there are even more symmetries as well.[20]

The account of Noah describes a great flood that hid the mountains and wiped out life on Earth. This does not have to mean that the flood covered the entire Earth, as it could just as well be read as a local flood. There are many hypotheses about local floods, from floods in the Euphrates and Tigris to a tsunami due to a meteorite in the Indian Ocean. One of the best-founded hypotheses is a sudden filling of the Black Sea. As the threshold in the Bosporus strait is as shallow as thirty-five meters, it is known that the Black Sea has at times been cut off from the Mediterranean. The sea level has varied with the ice ages, and the present connection between the two is believed to have been opened around 7000 BC. This led to a massive flood, and the Black Sea suddenly rose from being a small, low-lying lake to having the same level as the sea.[21] In support of this, there are remains of settlements in the Black Sea that now lie deep underwater. It could be such a memory that is reflected in the story of the flood, even though the details around this hypothesis can probably never be confirmed.

The three views above on how to align the Bible with science were common before the theory of evolution, and some defend them even today. Lemaître, with the big bang theory, lived in the century after and stood, as we have seen, for *accommodation*, as Galileo and Augustine also did. Lemaître believed that the creation account was adapted to the scientific view of its time, and that the Bible does not teach us anything about the sciences that we are capable of finding out for ourselves. This leads to a more symbolic reading of the creation account. This will be expanded upon in the next section.

THE BIBLE AND EVOLUTION

Evolution gives rise to several new issues when it comes to how creation narratives should be read. The Bible says that:

1. Heaven and Earth are created
2. Species are created separately from nothing[22]

---

20. Lamoureux, "Evolutionary Creation."
21. Ryan et al., "Abrupt Drowning of the Black Sea Shelf."
22. Separate creation of species is mentioned in Gen 1:11–12, 21, 24–25.

3. Humans are created in God's image[23]

Here, the challenge is to balance two considerations, as my friend, professor of theology Torleif Elgvin (b. 1950), emphasizes. On the one hand he says that a literal or "biblicist" reading of the biblical texts struggles to take their human side seriously. On the other hand, one must be critical of those scholars who reduce the Scriptures to historical testimonies alone. Elgvin concludes that it is part of the cultural mandate "to use both reason and science to understand God's world—including the revealed word He has given us through human instruments."[24]

The fact that heaven and Earth are created, the first point above, is an example of a revealed word and it is something that science remains more or less silent about. God's other book, the Bible, complements nature's book here. Why the big bang happened is not something that can be explored with physics, astronomy, or cosmology. The Nicene Creed, which has united all Christian churches since AD 325, summarizes this by stating that "we believe in one God, the Father, the Almighty, maker of heaven and Earth, of all that is seen and unseen."[25] The last point, that humans are created in God's image, is also not something that can easily be explored with science, as it is a revelation about human value and mission.

Earlier we saw that the firmament of water from Gen 1:6–8 was a prescientific concept. Let us imagine that the idea of fixed species created separately is also such a concept. After all, our experience tells us that species are fixed. Even through conscious breeding of livestock, species do not change to the point where we do not recognize them. Species appear immutable, and this is reflected in the Bible's description of them. The seemingly instantaneous creation of species in Gen 1 can even be seen as an adaptation to the idea of spontaneous creation, although this is a bit more speculative. This was the prevailing view of life from ancient times until a couple of hundred years ago, as chapter 4 discusses. The concept of accommodation, which suggests that the creation narrative is adapted to the respective time's understanding of life, can also be applied to species. If this is correct, it provides little basis for a specific "biblical biology" or "biblical zoology" with fixed species, which some indirectly advocate.

23. Gen 1:26–27.

24. Elgvin, "Hvordan lese gammeltestamentlige tekster" [How to read Old Testament texts].

25. Anglican Communion, "Nicene Creed," para. 1.

If we find this to be a radical thought, we should note that we use similar reasoning regarding other statements in the Bible that concern humans. In ancient times, most people believed that the heart and kidneys were central to a person's personality. After all, it is the heartbeat that is visibly influenced by my emotions, not the brain, so there is some logic to this. The Bible has the same view and states that "in their hearts humans plan their course" (Prov 16:9). It also says that "even at night my heart instructs me" (Ps 16:7). In the New Testament it says, "Then all the churches will know that I am he who searches hearts and minds" (Rev 2:23). Yet, no one would think of creating a "biblical physiology" and studying the kidneys and heart based on such assumptions today. This is because it is unproblematic to think that statements about the heart and kidneys are an adaptation to the understanding of ancient times. Similarly, it should be possible to think the same way about the fixity of animal and plant species.

Seven Approaches to Science

The main positions for reconciling science and the Bible are now listed. The first three positions have been briefly mentioned already and were developed before Darwin's time:

1. *Young Earth creationism.* This is the *solar day* theory where the Earth is approximately six thousand years old, and all species were created in six twenty-four-hour days.[26]

2. *Old Earth creationism.* The Earth may be very old, but life and humans were created in six days some six thousand years ago. The *chaos-restitution* interpretation (end of the seventeenth century) puts an unspecified time period between verses 1 and 2 in Gen 1. In the *gap* theory (early nineteenth century), this gap is set to encompass all of geological time.[27]

3. *Progressive creationism.* The Earth is billions of years old, and life, including humans, was created without evolution in a series of steps over a long period of time that follows the days and order of the

---

26. View represented by the Institute of Creation Research and by Answers in Genesis. The latter tend to insist that disagreement with their view undermines the meaning of the gospel. See Anderson, *Heresy of Ham*.

27. Roberts, "Genesis Chapter 1 and Geological Time," and Roberts, *Evangelicals and Science*, ch. 2.

creation account. This is the *day-age* interpretation that was proposed at a time when it was not clear that the order then is different from that of standard science.[28]

4. *Guided evolution.* The Earth is billions of years old, and the history of life is as in mainstream science. God sustains creation and has done things that may never be explained by science, such as the creation of the world, the origin of life, and the emergence of human consciousness. God cares about humans.[29] This view and the next build on a *functional* view of Genesis[30] and/or a *framework* interpretation where the six days are understood thematically or logically rather than chronologically.[31]

5. *Planned evolution.* All the characteristics of life were preprogrammed in the first life, and since then, everything has developed through natural processes. They are sustained by a God who cares about humans by creating the world and nature to be good for us. Otherwise, God does not intervene in the development of nature.

6. *Deistic evolution.* God created the world but has been absent ever since and does not care about humans.

7. *Atheistic evolution.* The Earth is billions of years old, and everything has come about through non-guided natural processes. There is no God.

Theistic evolution is a position which tries to unite a biblical view and the science of evolution. It dates to the time of Darwin. In practice this position encompasses a very wide spectrum of views from deism and pantheism, to planned and even guided evolution.[32] Due to its vagueness, many are therefore hesitant to identify with this label. In recent years, the term *evolutionary creationism* has been given a narrower definition than theistic evolution. This has been done to create distance from a position that may be interpreted as deism. One definition of evolutionary creationism is:

28. Represented by Reasons to Believe.
29. Represented by Biologos.
30. The functional view of creation in contrast to a material one is the thesis of Walton, *Lost World of Genesis One*.
31. The framework interpretation is brilliantly explained in Lennox, *Seven Days That Divide*, ch. 3, as how a surgeon would describe the construction of a hospital compared to how one of the construction workers would do it.
32. Examples are given in Peters and Hewlett, *Evolution from Creation to New Creation*.

It contends that the Creator established and maintains the laws of nature, including the mechanisms of a teleological evolution. In other words, evolution is a planned and purpose-driven natural process. This position also argues that humans evolved from pre-human ancestors, and over a period of time the Image of God and human sin were gradually and mysteriously manifested.[33]

Francis Collins (b. 1950), the leader of the Human Genome Project and director of the National Institutes of Health in the US until 2021, is probably the best-known scientist who is a proponent of evolutionary creationism.

The view of the intelligent design[34] movement may encompass everything from old Earth creationism to guided evolution. The Earth is typically billions of years old. Some doubt macroevolution, while others accept it to a limited extent. They argue that there is evidence of what they call irreducible or specified complexity in creation, and that science can be used to find traces of the designer. This is briefly discussed in chapter 6, under the heading "The Complex Complexity Argument."

Despite the differences, there is more that unites Christians than separates them. All believe in the existence of an intelligent Creator, as the Nicene Creed quoted above affirms. It is also impossible to be a Christian without believing that there is intelligence behind the universe and life. This belief in creation, which unites all Christians, is also the original meaning of the word *creationist*, but unfortunately in our time, the word is mainly associated with those who believe that humans were created a few thousand years ago.

It is not possible to make a direct connection between these seven approaches and the seven perspectives in chapter 1. An approximate connection is as follows: atheistic evolution conflicts with theology as it is the view that "science is always right." Deistic evolution can fit into the category of "science redefining theology," but some may also argue that it is based on "independence," where science and theology have nothing to do with each other. Young Earth creationism, old Earth creationism, and progressive creationism are, to a greater or lesser extent, about "theology is always right." Especially in guided evolution, and in many cases also planned evolution, are attempts to make science and theology complement each other, which is probably the dominant view among Christians.

---

33. Lamoureux, "Evolutionary Creation," 28.
34. As represented by, for instance, the Discovery Institute.

However, planned evolution can give rise to conflict if the Bible's account of a God who acts and performs miracles is devalued. The position can also be thought to fit into the category of "independence." It is important to keep in mind here that only a small fraction of Christians seem to find conflict between science and their faith, as the survey in chapter 1 shows. Most seem to align themselves with the categories of "guided evolution" or "planned evolution."

Some may become uncertain about whether they can praise God for creation if evolution is presented as a competing explanation for nature. In that case, it is important to remember that evolution only seeks to answer the question of how species came to be, it does not answer the question of why they are there. Evolution cannot speak to intentions, and it cannot explain itself—that is, why life evolves in the first place. If we can distinguish between these *how* and *why* questions, then Augustine's praise can become ours, regardless of which mechanism we believe God has used:

> Some people, in order to discover God, read books. But there is a great book: the very appearance of created things. Look above you! Look below you! Note it. Read it. God, whom you want to discover, never wrote that book with ink. Instead He set before your eyes the things that He had made. Can you ask for a louder voice than that? Why, heaven and Earth shout to you: "God made me!"[35]

THE BIBLE, SOUL, AND HUMAN NATURE

The Bible is not a textbook in either natural science or philosophy. What we primarily find support for there is that humans are something entirely unique, different from animals. The American theologian Francis Schaeffer (1912–1984) points out that "man is distinguished from both animals and machines on the basis of his creativity, his moral motions, his need for love, his fear of non-being, and his longings for beauty and for meaning. Only the biblical system has a way of explaining these factors which make man unique."[36]

---

35. From a sermon by Augustine, in Ortlund, *Retrieving Augustine's Doctrine of Creation*, 61.

36. From *Death in the City* in Schaeffer, *Complete Works*, 4:268.

In times of strong Greek influence, the Bible has been used to justify a dualistic view of man, but I think equally good support is found for a stronger connection between body and soul. The creation story tells us of man that "the Lord God formed a man from the dust of the ground and breathed into his nostrils the breath of life, and the man became a living being" (Gen 2:7). We started with a material body into which life was breathed. The term "living being" in earlier translations was rendered as "living soul." A similar term is used for sea creatures, birds, and land animals, all described as having "the breath of life" (Gen 7:22). Since the "breath of life" is a common trait in humans and animals, it seems the term describes consciousness in terms of sensory capacities. In the Old Testament book of Ecclesiastes, it is written: "Surely the fate of human beings is like that of the animals; the same fate awaits them both: As one dies, so dies the other. All have the same breath; humans have no advantage over animals" (Eccl 3:19). In this context, Linnaeus was right to place us in the same family as the great apes. It seems that "the breath of life" is the very principle of life. It is that which gives the body life, and it seems as if the breath of life is extinguished when we die. This is reminiscent of Aristotle's explanation, where the soul is the principle of life that permeates the body.

Nevertheless, man stands in a unique position, as he is the only one into whom God has breathed his breath or spirit. Thomas Aquinas quotes Augustine and says that "man's excellence consists in the fact that God made him to His own image by giving him an intellectual soul, which raises him above the beasts of the field."[37] This also points to the double affirmation that "God created mankind in his own image, in the image of God he created them" (Gen 1:27). In the following verses, it is clear that "the image of God" includes language. We reflect God's way of communicating. "The image of God" also encompasses a mission to fill the Earth and subdue it. Furthermore, it includes aesthetic and artistic abilities as it is about the garden of Eden, where the trees were "pleasing to the eye" (Gen 2:9). Intellectual properties that only man possesses are also part of the image of God within us, as well as the abilities we have to communicate with God, which have something of eternity about them.

In the New Testament, Jesus says that we should not be "afraid of those who kill the body but cannot kill the soul" (Matt 10:28). The story of the thief on the cross testifies that there is something that lives on after

---

37. Aquinas, *Summa Theologica*, pt. 6, question 93, art. 2, in Kreeft, *Shorter* Summa, 312.

the body is dead. Jesus's answer to the thief is clear in this respect: "Today you will be with me in paradise" (Luke 23:43). This may remind us of Greek and perhaps also Cartesian dualism. But viewed in conjunction with the creeds from the early church, which speak of the resurrection of the body, the body still plays a central role.

The Bible describes humans as a spirited and ensouled body, not an incarnated soul. It is our body that will rise again one day, not just the spirit or soul. This could be reconciled with dualism, but here it also fits well with two-aspect monism. Aristotle's form-matter model also harmonizes with the Biblical view of man, though none of these models necessarily covers everything. The Bible is clear that reductionist materialism alone is not sufficient. On the other hand, a pure idealism is also impossible to reconcile with Jesus Christ considering it worth the trouble to become human for our sake.

Evolution of Man

We can reconcile our knowledge of evolution of man with fidelity to the Biblical perspective in several different ways.

The Catholic Church has stated that the body may have evolved from other biological forms under God's guidance, but that our soul is created by God and not developed.[38] This highlights the uniqueness of mankind without necessarily elaborating on exactly how God did it. It is reasonable to think that a "created soul" means that consciousness and spirituality have been imparted to the body from the outside, as in a dualistic view. It might require a separate act of creation in which God, at some point in time, introduced what made humans special. Mathematician and apologist John Lennox advocates for this view.[39]

Another way to combine evolution and the Bible is to consider that self-awareness and awareness of God could have emerged from the material without full comprehension of how. If so, it would not be the first time in the history of the universe that something more complex has arisen from something simpler. This occurred at the big bang and when the first stars were formed. It also happened when the most important

---

38. Stated by John Paul II in October 1996, as Pius XII had said before him also.

39. Lennox, *God's Undertaker*. Lennox speaks of at least three instances where he believes God must have intervened directly, beyond the "ordinary" maintenance of creation and the laws of nature: the origin of the universe, the beginning of life, and the creation of humans.

elements for life, such as hydrogen, carbon, nitrogen, and oxygen, were formed; when our solar system, the planets, and the Earth were formed; when proteins were formed; and when life began (as explained in chapter 2). From this perspective, this did not happen at random but was the result of a willed evolution by the Creator. This leans more toward a monistic view of humanity—that we consist of only one "substance," but it manifests in two equivalent ways: body and soul, thus two-aspect monism. In one way, this perspective resembles materialism. The important difference is that in materialism, the mental is an unintended effect of the material. Here, however, it is a fully valid side of humanity and intended by God. God is the teleological explanation. Whereas reductionist materialists dismiss the grandeur of human consciousness and its free will, this view considers them valuable in their own right.

Norwegian authors Bjørn Are Davidsen and Atle Ottesen Søvik are closest to this latter view.[40] Theologian Ottesen Søvik also presents a theory of what consciousness could be. Just as there are invisible electric, magnetic, and gravitational fields, it is conceivable that a consciousness field exists that is even more fundamental than the physical fields and represents God's spiritual nature. This is the basis for both the physical and the conscious that has evolved through evolution. There is no denying that there is something deeply mysterious about how the complex can arise from the simpler, and especially how human consciousness and spirit have come into being. The idea of a consciousness field may articulate this mystery. Comparisons with physical fields give some insight, but they have their limitations. The concept of physical fields can be used to calculate the effect of gravity and how radio waves spread even in a vacuum, but so far, little insight like this has come from the idea of a consciousness field.

Moreover, it is characteristic that the study of consciousness lacks a unified theory.[41] The theory of a consciousness field competes with several other theories, among them integrated information theory, which implies that consciousness is everywhere. This is a form of panpsychism that seems to be growing in popularity as the shortcomings of a materialistic view of consciousness become clearer.

---

40. Davidsen and Søvik, *Evolusjon eller kristen tro?* [Evolution or Christian faith?], 133. This is elaborated in Søvik, *Basic Theory of Everything*, where it is called a qualia field, from *qualia* which denotes instances of subjective, conscious experience.

41. Cobb, *Idea of the Brain*, ch. 15.

I find both the view of the Catholic Church and of Lennox, which is reminiscent of what was called "guided evolution" earlier in this appendix, and Davidsen and Søvik's view, which is closer to "planned evolution," to have their merits. Personally, I lean toward the "guided evolution" view, but there is so much uncertainty and mystique surrounding both viewpoints that there are no convincing arguments compelling a choice between the two.

In the past it was possible for natural philosophers and scientists to use the term *God* or *the Creator* in scientific literature, as Darwin did. He did not use it to label the gaps we still have in science, but about things outside of science, like when he said that life originally was breathed by the Creator. It's more problematic to say such things today. The closest we can come is to admit that "how intelligence evolved still remains one of science's greatest mysteries."[42] I have collected scientific papers that are concerned with "mystery," "enigma," or "conundrum" and there are quite of few of them in the field of consciousness in particular. On the one hand, it expresses a hope that the mystery will one day be solved. On the other hand, it probably also implies an openness to the question of consciousness lying outside of what science will ever figure out. That is a stance for which I have a great understanding.

The status in science today is that we agree neither on what consciousness is nor how it relates to the body, and we also know little about how its foremost feature, language, originated. But when we complement the image that nature gives us with God's other book, we see clearer. The Bible fills in some of the most mysterious sides.

Adam and Eve

Some parts of the Bible may be more difficult to reconcile with an evolutionary perspective on humanity than others, and the account of Adam and Eve and how we began to hide from God is one of them. It's worth learning from Augustine, who is perhaps the theologian who has been most concerned with creation. He wrote several comments on it and spent fifteen years on his book *The Literal Meaning of Genesis*. It's interesting that even after his long studies, Augustine is still so wide-ranging in his interpretation that today he is quoted and used by everyone from young Earth creationists to theistic evolutionists.

42. Pika et al., "Ravens Parallel Great Apes."

Theologians tell me that the word *adam* has three meanings: (1) humanity in general, (2) man or individual, and (3) the name of a person. In Gen 1 "adam" is used for humanity and encompasses both man and woman. In Gen 2, attention is directed to an individual human. In addition, there is a play on the relationship to the earth, as the feminine form of "adam," which is "adamah," means earth. We come from the earth, we are to cultivate the earth, and we return to the earth when we die. In the text, we thus move from the general—"humanity"—to the more specific—"human"—and later, as in Gen 4:25, to the personal name of Adam. There is thus a spectrum in the text with room for both metaphorical reading and reference to a specific individual. Similarly, Eve ("Hawwah") means "life-giver." The word also has something to do with "breath." The relation is apparent in many languages—as in English where "spirit" and "breath" are related. This shows how we are formed from matter that has been given life and spirit.

Adam is only found in the first five chapters of Genesis in the Old Testament. Many elements in the creation and fall stories have strong symbolic meaning, and if the stories stood by themselves, we could have thought they were meant purely symbolically. But both the rest of the story in Genesis and Paul's discussion in the New Testament indicate that Adam and Eve were real people. If so, the question is how and when this can fit into humanity's history. Here, there seems to be basically three possible scenarios.

Bottleneck Theory

The starting point here is that at some point in human history there were only two people, Adam and Eve. This was a so-called bottleneck in human development. All people stem 100 percent from this pair that God created in his image, and who then went through the fall. There were some geneticists who held such a view in the 1970s and 1980s. Then objections arose in the 1990s. What I find most problematic with this hypothesis is that the bottleneck seems to lie very far back in history. I have seen estimates suggesting five hundred thousand years. That places the bottleneck long before the supposed interbreeding with Neanderthals forty thousand to fifty thousand years ago. Then a consequence is that Neanderthals must also be considered as fully human, which of course is possible. However, the objections from the 1990s now seem to be partially answered, opening the possibility that the bottleneck could have been after this interbreeding as well.[43]

Representation Model

It is possible to view Adam and Eve as a historical couple that God specifically chose, just like Abraham, Moses, and others were chosen later. Adam and Eve become the first to have fellowship with God—*Homo divinus*, as the English theologian John Stott (1921–2011) called them. He puts it like this:

> My acceptance of Adam and Eve as historical is not incompatible with my belief that several forms of pre-Adamic "hominid" may have existed for thousands of years previously. These hominids began to advance culturally. They made their cave drawings and buried their dead. It is conceivable that God created Adam out of one of them. You may call them *homo erectus*. I think you may even call some of them *homo sapiens*, for these are arbitrary scientific names.[44] But Adam was the first *homo divinus*,[45] if I may coin a phrase, the first man to whom may be given the Biblical designation "made in the image of God."[46]

Adam and Eve thus became representatives or proxies for all other people, without any direct genetic connection to the entire human race. There will also be other humans, *Homo sapiens*, existing simultaneously with them. From this first couple, God then began to reveal himself to mankind. The next theory is related, but a bit more concrete.

Genealogical Model

I am among those who can boast of being related to the first king of Norway, Harald Fairhair (ca. 850–ca. 932). Many in Norway say that. The surprising thing is that it actually is true. It is quite certain that all who have their roots in Europe can trace their ancestors back to Harald Fairhair, Charlemagne, or any well-known European who lived at least six hundred years ago.

---

43. For scientific references about the bottleneck theory, consult Buggs, "Adam and Eve."

44. The "upright man" and "knowledgeable man" respectively.

45. *Homo divinus*—not to be confused with Harari's transhuman *Homo deus*, which he believes will come after humans.

46. Ortlund, *Retrieving Augustine's Doctrine of Creation*, 228.

The aforementioned bottleneck theory argues that all humans descend from a single common pair. This is about genetic kinship. A genealogical approach gives a different result. I have only half of my genes from my father, a quarter from my grandfather, and it thins out for each generation going backward. But in many theories about Adam and Eve in recent decades, we have been so focused on genetic ancestry that we have forgotten how we think about ordinary ancestry. For why should the Bible deal with the modern concept of "genetic ancestry" and not the traditional view of kinship? After all, genetics did not become important until neo-Darwinism appeared in the first half of the twentieth century.

I have two parents, four grandparents, eight great-grandparents, and sixteen great-great-grandparents. Assuming 30 years per generation, I have sixteen ancestors 120 years ago. The number grows to 1 million at twenty generations, which was about 600 years ago, and 8 billion at thirty-three generations, which is 1,000 years ago. But then we're talking about as many as the world's population today, and far more than the population at the time. This can't be right, and the reason is, of course, that there is a significant overlap when I go far enough back in time. My family history is not like a tree with branches spreading out; it's more like a web where everything is intertwined with everyone else living now.

It's possible to create simple statistical theories where all people live in the same place and randomly pair up with each other. But more interesting are computer simulations that consider natural barriers, like the one between Australia and Indonesia and the one across the Bering Strait to North America. Even then, the conclusion is that all people living today have the same common ancestors, and that these lived sometime between four thousand and seven thousand years ago. Those who lived before that will either be related to everyone living today or have no descendants at all. None of this is exact, because we simply do not know enough to ever find out the details. But the interesting thing is that the time estimates here are much closer to our time than the theory of a genetic bottleneck. The surprising conclusion is that,

> no matter the languages we speak or the color of our skin, we share ancestors who planted rice on the banks of the Yangtze, who first domesticated horses on the steppes of the Ukraine, who hunted giant sloths in the forests of North and South America, and who labored to build the Great Pyramid of Khufu.[47]

47. Concluding section from Rohde et al., "Modelling the Recent Common Ancestry," which this section builds on.

Theologically, therefore, one of these pairs of our common predecessors could be Adam and Eve. To ensure that even ancient humans stem from them, we can, for example, place Adam and Eve at the start of agriculture almost ten thousand years ago. Either they were chosen among those living then, or they could have been created in a special act of creation, which is untraceable. These are the ones who received the image of God and who rebelled against God. All people in the last millennia would be related to them. This is the theory that American biologist Joshua Swamidass launched a few years ago and which has stimulated new dialogue around this question.[48] I favor this model, as it requires no scientific leaps, and because it is consistent with everything stated about Adam and Eve in the book of Genesis, including the statement that other humans lived simultaneously with them.

Good and Evil

The reason the story of Adam and Eve is so important is that this is where the Bible both tells us that we were created in the image of God and provides an explanation for evil. Russian author Aleksandr Solzhenitsyn (1918–2008) put it this way, based on his experience with the Gulag, the Soviet prison camps, in the 1940s:

> The line separating good and evil passes not through states, nor between classes, nor between political parties either—but right through every human heart—and through all human hearts.... And even within hearts overwhelmed with evil, one small bridgehead of good is retained. And even in the best of all hearts, there remains ... an un-uprooted small corner of evil.[49]

Many who have lived under better conditions than Solzhenitsyn agree with these words. We have this rebellion in us against God, as the account of Adam and Eve's fall so clearly portrays. We also have our egoism, our potential for evil, and our strong tendency toward revenge, as the story of Cain, who killed his brother Abel, attests. As noted in chapter 1, this realistic portrayal of the negative side of humans was important for me in the process of becoming convinced that the Bible is credible; it so accurately described my experience and my observations of people around me. The Bible's sober realism contrasts sharply with humanistic

---

48. Swamidass, "Overlooked Science of Genealogical Ancestry."
49. Solzhenitsyn, *Gulag Archipelago*, pt. 4, ch. 1.

naïve depictions of humanity as largely good and noble. The Bible's point is not that such good traits are foreign to humanity, but that this is only one side of the truth about us. Human sinful nature is also central to understanding that we need salvation from evil.

The duality of humans is unique to the biblical narrative. We also possess this goodness within us as part of God's good creation. In fact, the Creator has given us an exalted position as he "made them a little lower than the angels and crowned them with glory and honor" (Ps 8:5). Over time, different denominations have emphasized the good and the evil in humans in varying proportions, but there is consensus that we all possess both aspects.

The theory of evolution has problems in offering a satisfactory explanation for human evil and human greatness. Evil is explained as a side effect of natural selection, and thus it's part of nature. This is in contrast to the Bible, which does not hold God responsible for evil, or "sin," which is the biblical term. Instead, we ourselves are responsible for our lives. Augustine puts it this way: "Remember that there is absolutely no nature that he did not create. And that's why He punishes sin, which he didn't make, because it fouls the nature, which he did create."[50]

Many materialists also struggle to accept human greatness. The vastness of space and the smallness of Earth tell them instead how small and insignificant we are. In contrast, the creation narrative says that creation is good. This is stated seven times in Gen 1 and applies to light, land and sea, plants, Moon and Sun, sea creatures and birds, and land animals. Finally, it is said that the entire creation, including humans, is very good. God created humans in his image, and human greatness is not justified by physical size, but by God himself, who is the origin of the entire universe.

Some believe, based on these statements, that the created world was "perfect" before sin entered. But humans were called to fill the Earth and subdue it, which can be interpreted to mean to cultivate the Earth and make it even better, and this doesn't make sense if the world was already perfect. Augustine also differentiates between "good" and "perfect," for only the latter means that there is no need for change. Only God does not need to change, Augustine emphasizes: "He alone is immutable, while all the things that he has made are mutable because he made them from

---

50. From one of Augustine's sermons, Ortlund, *Retrieving Augustine's Doctrine of Creation*, 51.

nothing"[51] and "If the first man was created wise, then why did he allow himself to be seduced?"[52] Even before the fall, we were not perfect.

Some also believe that animals did not die before the fall, but no statements in the Bible confirm that view. Again, it might be an interpretation based on the understanding that "good" is the same as "perfect." Animals were to "be fruitful and increase in number and fill the water in the seas, and let the birds increase on the earth" (Gen 1:22). It is almost impossible to imagine an Earth that is filled up without death; it would soon be overcrowded. Moreover, humans were to "rule over the fish in the sea and the birds in the sky and over every living creature that moves on the ground" (Gen 1:28). In verse 26, "to rule over . . . the livestock" is also mentioned. It seems logical to think that the task given to humans would involve having to take the lives of animals, whether wild or domesticated, use their skins, and eat their meat. Augustine limits himself to saying that animals died, and that humans shared in the same death through the fall.[53]

Paul writes that "sin entered the world through one man, and death through sin, and in this way, death came to all people, because all sinned" (Rom 5:12). I am told that traditionally, the last words of this verse have been translated "in whom all have sinned" with a history going back to Jerome's (347–420) Latin translation, the Vulgate. Jerome's version has been used to justify the belief that sin affected all people through Adam and Eve. This is part of the background for the doctrine of original sin, which has its roots going back to Augustine. Although this doctrine was toned down during the Middle Ages, it was carried forward by Luther. Some claim that this doctrine may have been built on an inaccuracy in Jerome's translation from Greek to Latin. In the Greek original, the last phrase is closer to "because all sinned," as just quoted and not "in whom all have sinned." Jerome's choice of words may have overemphasized Adam's role in the fall at the expense of individual responsibility. Nonetheless, we cannot get around the fact that Paul places great emphasis on Adam when he compares Adam with Christ, saying that just as the first brought sin into the world, so the second brought grace.

Many also read this as if physical death for humans was introduced into the world in the fall. But here I think the American philosopher and

---

51. Ortlund, *Retrieving Augustine's Doctrine of Creation*, 38.
52. Ortlund, *Retrieving Augustine's Doctrine of Creation*, 210.
53. Ortlund, *Retrieving Augustine's Doctrine of Creation*, 154.

apologist William Lane Craig (b. 1949) shows that other interpretations are possible. He brings up a point from Paul's First Letter to the Corinthians.[54] Chapter 15 deals with the resurrection, and it says, "For as in Adam all die, so in Christ all will be made alive" (1 Cor 15:22). What does this mean—that death only entered the world through Adam and Eve's sin? The explanation comes later in the chapter:

> So it is written: "The first man Adam became a living being"; the last Adam, a life-giving spirit. The spiritual did not come first, but the natural, and after that the spiritual. The first man was of the dust of the earth; the second man is of heaven. (1 Cor 15:45–47)

This is a reference back to the creation narrative, where Adam was formed from dust and God breathed life into him. Thus, it is the creation of Adam that is linked to death, not Adam's fall. Adam must have been created as a mortal being. It is only in this way that the story of the "tree of life" makes sense, because why would you need such a tree if you were born immortal? (Gen 3:22). Paul's discussion of sin and death in the Letter to the Romans, chapter 5, in light of this would be about spiritual death, not physical death.

The fall concerns humans wanting to be like God and rejecting God's absolute authority. The story also implies that there will never be a sin-free human being. As a result, we humans feel shame and guilt and perceive ourselves as naked. We hide from God and each other, and we have become the only creatures that feel the need for clothing. It seems to me that the explanation for sin and the fall must be associated with the explanation of consciousness. Without an awareness of the difference between good and evil, no one can be held responsible for a wrong choice. Therefore, the possible explanations of how we gained consciousness discussed in chapter 7 may say something about how sin entered the world also.

One question is whether this sin also has consequences for other parts of creation. The verses in Rom 8:19–22 say that "creation waits in eager expectation . . . [to] be liberated from its bondage to decay." This could give the impression that it is the whole of creation—humans, animals, and plants—that is subject to decay as a result of the fall.

However, I am told that the Greek word for "creation" in these verses can have several meanings. Elsewhere in the New Testament, it is used in

---

54. Craig, "Relation Between Adam's Sin and Death."

a more limited sense about humanity.[55] The context in Rom 8 may not concern all of creation, but rather humanity, and therefore it is possible to interpret these verses as indicating that it is only humanity that longs to be freed from decay, not the entire creation.

In ending this discussion, it is appropriate to mention that the fall and its consequences have been, from the infancy of modern science, a motivation to explore nature, engage in science, and particularly in the form of useful technology. Francis Bacon said,

> Man by the Fall fell at the same time from the state of innocence and from his dominion over creation. Both of these losses, however, can even in this life be in some part repaired; the former by religion and faith, the latter by arts and sciences. For creation was not by the curse made altogether and forever a rebel, but in virtue of that covenant "In the sweat of thy face thou shalt eat bread" it is now by various labours at length, and in some measure subdued to the supplying of man with bread; that is to the uses of human life.[56]

---

55. The word for the created, Greek "ktisis," can be found in the Great Commission in Mark 16:15, in the statement that no creature is hidden from God in Heb 4:13, and about man as a new creation in 2 Cor 5:17 and Gal 5:15. Robert, "Church of England Gone Creationist?"

56. Bacon, "New Organon," concluding lines.

Afterword

THE MAIN DIFFERENCE BETWEEN this English version and the Norwegian original from 2021 is that the appendix consists of material which was previously at the end of chapters 3, 4, 6, and 7. The section titled "The Complex Complexity Argument" in chapter 6 has been completely rewritten and shortened. The section on "What Is Science?" at the end of chapter 5, the section "The Inexplicability of Evolutionary Transitions" in chapter 6, and "The Mystery of Language Evolution" in chapter 7 are all new, as is chapter 8, which has been completely rewritten. There are, in addition, minor differences from the original in most chapters.

References

Abbott, Alison. "Discovery of Galileo's Long-Lost Letter Shows He Edited His Heretical Ideas to Fool the Inquisition." *Nature* 561 (2018) 441–42. https://doi.org/10.1038/d41586-018-06769-4.

Abernethy, Bob. "Dr. Francis S. Collins Interview." PBS, July 21, 2006. https://www.pbs.org/wnet/religionandethics/2006/07/21/july-21-2006-dr-francis-s-collins-interview/3676/.

Aikman, Duncan. "Lemaître Follows Two Paths to Truth." *New York Times*, February 19, 1933. https://www.nytimes.com/1933/02/19/archives/lemaitre-follows-two-paths-to-truth-the-famous-physicist-who-is.html.

Anderson, John Edmund. *The Heresy of Ham: What Every Evangelical Needs to Know About the Creation-Evolution Controversy*. Birminghan, AL: Archdeacon, 2016.

Anglican Communion Office. "Nicene Creed." https://www.anglicancommunion.org/media/109020/Nicene-Creed.pdf.

Appolloni, Simon. "'Repugnant,' 'Not Repugnant at All': How the Respective Epistemic Attitudes of Georges Lemaître and Sir Arthur Eddington Influenced How Each Approached the Idea of a Beginning of the Universe." *IBSU Scientific Journal* 5 (2011) 19–44.

Aquinas, Thomas. *Exposition of Aristotle's Treatise on the Heavens*. Translated by Fabian R. Larcher and Pierre H. Conway. Columbus, OH: College of St. Mary of the Springs, 1964.

Ariew, Roger. "Pierre Duhem." Stanford Encyclopedia of Philosophy (Fall 2020 ed.), last revised July 26, 2018. https://plato.stanford.edu/archives/fall2020/entries/duhem/.

Aristotle. *De anima [On the Soul]*. Translated by J. A. Smith. In vol. 3 of *The Works of Aristotle*. Oxford: Clarendon, 1931. https://classics.mit.edu/Aristotle/soul.html

Armstrong, John R. "William Buckland in Retrospect." *Perspectives on Science and Christian Faith* 42 (1990) 34–38.

Atkinson, Quentin D. "Phonemic Diversity Supports a Serial Founder Effect Model of Language Expansion from Africa." *Science* 332 (2011) 346–49.

Augustine. *The Confessions*. Translated by Maria Boulding, edited by John E. Rotelle. New York: New City, 2010.

———. *The Literal Meaning of Genesis*. Vol. 1, bks. 1–6. Translated and annotated by John Hammond Taylor. New York: Newman, 1982.

———. *On Christian Doctrine, in Four Books.* Christian Classics Ethereal Library. https://ccel.org/ccel/augustine/doctrine/doctrine.xix_1.html.

Bacon, Francis. *The Advancement of Learning.* Edited by Henry Morley. London: Cassell, 1893. Transcribed by David Price and Richard Tonsing, Project Gutenberg, 2004. Last revised April 12, 2021. https://www.gutenberg.org/cache/epub/5500/pg5500-images.html.

———. "The New Organon: Or True Directions Concerning the Interpretation of Nature." 1620. https://constitution.org/2-Authors/bacon/nov_org.htm.

———. "XVI. Of Atheism." In *Essays.* Vol. 1 of *The Works of Francis Bacon.* 1884. https://en.wikisource.org/wiki/The_Works_of_Francis_Bacon/Volume_1/Essays/Of_Atheism.

Badash, Lawrence. "The Age-of-the-Earth Debate." *Scientific American* 261 (1989) 90–97.

Bagge, Sverre. Introduction to *Kongespeilet* [*The King's Mirror*], translated by Anton Wilhelm Brøgger, vii–lxxxi. [In Norwegian.] Oslo: Bokklubben, 2000.

Bailey, Solon I. "Henrietta Swan Leavitt." *Popular Astronomy* 30 (1922) 197–99.

Baker, Lynne Rudder. "Christians Should Reject Mind-Body Dualism." In *Contemporary Debates in Philosophy of Religion,* edited by Michael L. Peterson and Raymond J. VanArragon, 327–38. Malden, MA: Blackwell, 2004.

Ball, Philip. *How Life Works: A User's Guide to the New Biology.* Chicago: University of Chicago Press, 2023.

Barbour, Ian G. *Religion and Science: Historical and Contemporary Issues.* London: SCM, 1997.

Barr, James. "Pre-Scientific Chronology: The Bible and the Origin of the World." *Proceedings of the American Philosophical Society* 143 (1999) 379–87.

———. "Why the World Was Created in 4004 BC: Archbishop Ussher and Biblical Chronology." *Bulletin of the John Rylands Library* 67 (1985) 575–608.

Barrow, John, and Frank Tipler. *The Cosmological Anthropic Principle.* Oxford: Oxford University Press, 1986.

Bartholomew, David J. "Probability, Statistics and Theology." *Journal of the Royal Statistical Society: Series A (Statistics in Society)* 151 (1988) 137–59.

Baumgardt, Carola. *Johannes Kepler: Life and Letters.* London: Gollanz, 1952.

Bede. *The Reckoning of Time.* Translated by Faith Wallis. 2nd ed. Translated Texts for Historians 29. Liverpool: Liverpool University Press, 1999.

Behe, Michael J. *Darwin's Black Box: The Biochemical Challenge to Evolution.* New York: Free Press, 1996.

———. *Darwin Devolves: The New Science About DNA That Challenges Evolution.* New York: HarperCollins, 2019.

Berry, Robert James. *Real Science, Real Faith: Sixteen Leading British Scientists Discuss Their Science and Their Personal Faith.* Eastbourne, UK: Monarch, 1991.

Biagioli, Mario. *Galileo, Courtier: The Practice of Science in the Culture of Absolutism.* Chicago: University of Chicago Press, 1993.

Bishop, Morris. *Pascal: The Life of Genius.* New York: Reynal & Hitchcock, 1936.

Blackmore, Susan. *Consciousness: A Very Short Introduction.* Oxford: Oxford University Press, 2017.

Boethius. *The Consolation of Philosophy.* Translated by Victor Watts. London: Penguin Classics, 1999.

Boyle, Robert. *The Christian Virtuoso Shewing That by Being Addicted to Experimental Philosophy, a Man Is Rather Assisted Than Indisposed to Be a Good Christian (1690)*. Hungerford, UK: Legare Street, 2022.
Brooke, John Hedley. *Science and Religion: Some Historical Perspectives*. Cambridge History of Science. Cambridge: Cambridge University Press, 1991.
Bube, Richard H. *Putting It All Together: Seven Patterns for Relating Science and the Christian Faith*. Lanham, MA: University Press of America, 1995.
Buckland, William. *Geology and Mineralogy Considered with Reference to Natural Theology*. Vol. 1. Philadelphia: Lea & Blanchard, 1841.
———. *Reliquiae Diluvianae; Or, Observations on the Organic Remains Contained in Caves, Fissures, and Diluvial Gravel* [. . .].London: Murray, 1823.
Buggs, Richard. "Adam and Eve: Lessons Learned." Richard Buggs, April 18, 2018. https://richardbuggs.com/2018/04/18/adam-and-eve-lessons-learned/.
———. "The Deepening of Darwin's Abominable Mystery." *Nature Ecology & Evolution* 1 (2017) 1–2.
Busterud, Guro. "Den fødte pratmaker" [The natural born speaker]. *A-Magasinet* 16 (Mai 2008) 62. https://elearning.kompetansenorge.no/norsk1/assets/66C78F00-5056-9CB2-9B2A-C75165D54E9D.pdf.
Butterfield, Herbert. *The Origins of Modern Science: 1300–1800*. New York: Macmillan, 1951.
———. *The Whig Interpretation of History*. London: Bell, 1931.
Camerota, Michele, et al. "The Reappearance of Galileo's Original Letter to Benedetto Castelli." *Notes and Records: The Royal Society Journal of the History of Science* 73 (2019) 11–28.
Capanna, Ernesto. "Lazzaro Spallanzani: At the Roots of Modern Biology." *Journal of Experimental Zoology* 285 (1999) 178–96.
Capra, Frifjof. *The Tao of Physics: An Exploration of the Parallels Between Modern Physics and Eastern Mysticism*. Boulder, CO: Shambhala, 1975.
Cartwright, Nancy. "Is Natural Science 'Natural' Enough?: A Reply to Philip Allport." *Synthese* (1993) 291–301.
———. "No God, No Laws." Working paper, School of Advanced Study, University of London, 2008. https://sas-space.sas.ac.uk/963/1/N_Cartwright_God.pdf.
Chaisson, Eric J. "Cosmic Evolution: A Synthesis of Matter and Life." *Zygon* 14 (1979) 23–39.
———. "Cosmic Evolution—More Than Big History by Another Name." *Evolution: A Big History Perspective* (2012) 37–48.
Chalmers, David J. "Facing up to the Problem of Consciousness." *Journal of Consciousness Studies* 2 (1995) 200–219.
———. "Strong and Weak Emergence." In *The Re-Emergence of Emergence: The Emergentist Hypothesis from Science to Religion*, edited by Philip Clayton and Paul Davies, 244–56. Oxford: Oxford University Press, 2006.
Chapman, Allan. *Caves, Coprolites and Catastrophes: The Story of Pioneering Geologist and Fossil-Hunter William Buckland*. London: SPCK, 2020.
Charlesworth, Brian, and Deborah Charlesworth. *Evolution: A Very Short Introduction*. Oxford: Oxford University Press, 2017.
Chesterton, G. K. *The Everlasting Man*. London: Hodder & Stoughton, 1925.
———. "The Revival of Philosophy—Why?" In *The Common Man*, 173–80. London: Sheed and Ward, 1950.

———. "The Separation of Science and Popular Science." In *The Illustrated London News 1920–1922*, edited by George J. Marlin et al., 351–55. Vol. 32 of *The Collected Works of G. K. Chesterton*. San Francisco: Ignatius, 1989.
Christian, David. "The Case for 'Big History.'" *Journal of World History* 2 (1991) 223–38.
———. *Maps of Time: An Introduction to Big History*. Berkeley: University of California Press, 2004.
Christie, Thony. "The Emergence of Modern Astronomy—A Complex Mosaic: Part XXXVII." Renaissance Mathematicus, June 3, 2020. https://thonyc.wordpress.com/2020/06/03/the-emergence-of-modern-astronomy-a-complex-mosaic-part-xxxvii/.
———. "Galileo's Reputation Is More Hyperbole than Truth." Aeon, March 31, 2016. https://aeon.co/ideas/galileo-s-reputation-is-more-hyperbole-than-truth.
———. "How to Create Your Own Galileo." Renaissance Mathematicus, May 27, 2020. https://thonyc.wordpress.com/2020/05/27/how-to-create-your-own-galileo/.
———. "In Defence of the Indefensible." Renaissance Mathematicus, October 25, 2009. https://thonyc.wordpress.com/2009/10/25/in-defence-of-the-indefensible/.
Cobb, Matthew. *The Idea of the Brain: The Past and Future of Neuroscience*. London: Profile, 2020.
Comfort, Ray. *Scientific Facts in the Bible: 100 Reasons to Believe the Bible Is Supernatural in Origin*. Newberry, FL: Bridge Logos, 2001.
Condorcet, Nicolas de. *Sketch for an Historical Picture of the Advances of the Human Mind*. 1795. Prepared by Jonathan Bennett, Early Modern Texts, 2017. https://www.earlymoderntexts.com/assets/pdfs/condorcet1795.pdf.
Connor, James A. *Kepler's Witch: An Astronomer's Discovery of Cosmic Order amid Religious War, Political Intrigue, and the Heresy Trial of His Mother*. San Francisco: HarperSanFrancisco, 2004.
Copernicus, Nicolaus. *On the Revolution of Heavenly Spheres*. In *On the Shoulders of Giants: The Great Works of Physics and Astronomy*, edited by Stephen Hawking, 1–388. New York: Penguin, 2002.
Cormack, Lesley B. "Flat Earth or Round Sphere: Misconceptions of the Shape of the Earth and the Fifteenth-Century Transformation of the World." *Ecumene* 1 (1994) 363–85.
Coyne, Jerry A. *Why Evolution Is True*. Oxford: Oxford University Press, 2010.
Craig, William L. "The Relation Between Adam's Sin and Death." Reasonable Faith, May 24, 2020. https://www.reasonablefaith.org/writings/question-answer/the-relation-between-adams-sin-and-death.
Crick, Francis. *The Astonishing Hypothesis: The Scientific Search for the Soul*. New York: Scribner, 1994.
———. *What Mad Pursuit: A Personal View of Scientific Discovery*. New York: Basic, 1988.
Danielson, Dennis R. "The Great Copernican Cliché." *American Journal of Physics* 69 (2001) 1029–35.
Danielson, Dennis R., and Christopher M. Graney. "The Case Against Copernicus." *Scientific American* 310 (2014) 72–77.
Darwin, Charles. *The Autobiography of Charles Darwin, 1809–1882*. Edited by Nora Barlow. London: Collins, 1958.
———. *The Descent of Man*. London: John Murray, 1871.

———. "Letter to Joseph Dalton Hooker, February 1, 1871." Darwin Correspondence Project. https://www.darwinproject.ac.uk/letter/?docId=letters/DCP-LETT-7471.xml.

———. *The Origin of Species.* 1859. New York: Penguin, 1958.

Davidsen, Bjørn Are, and Atle Ottesen Søvik. *Evolusjon eller kristen tro? Ja takk, begge deler!* [Evolution or Christian faith? Yes please, both of them!]. Follese, Norway: Efrem, 2016.

Dawkins, Richard. *The Blind Watchmaker: Why the Evidence of Evolution Reveals a Universe Without Design.* New York: Norton, 1996.

———. *River Out of Eden: A Darwinian View of Life.* New York: Basic, 2008.

Dickson, John. *Bullies and Saints: An Honest Look at the Good and Evil of Christian History.* Grand Rapids: Zondervan, 2021.

Dobzhansky, Theodosius. "Nothing in Biology Makes Sense Except in the Light of Evolution." *American Biology Teacher* 35 (1973) 125–29.

Drake, Stillman, trans. *Discoveries and Opinions of Galileo.* New York: Anchor, 1957.

Drosnin, Michael. *The Bible Code.* New York: Simon & Schuster, 1977.

Druyan, Ann, and Steven Soter, creators. *Cosmos: A Spacetime Odyssey.* Cosmos Studios, Fuzzy Door Productions, and Santa Fe Studios, 2014.

Dry, Sarah. *The Newton Papers: The Strange and True Odyssey of Isaac Newton's Manuscripts.* Oxford: Oxford University Press, 2014.

Duhem, Pierre. "Research on the History of Physical Theories." *Synthese* 83 (1990) 189–200.

Dunn, Jacob C., and Jeroen B. Smaers. "Neural Correlates of Vocal Repertoire in Primates." *Frontiers in Neuroscience* 12 (2018) 1–7.

Ecklund, Elaine Howard, et al. "Religion Among Scientists in International Context: A New Study of Scientists in Eight Regions." *Socius* 2 (2016) 1–9.

Egnor, Michael. "Why Consciousness Shows That Materialism Is False." Mind Matters, December 7, 2020. https://mindmatters.ai/2020/12/why-consciousness-shows-that-materialism-is-false/.

Einstein, Albert. *Ideas and Opinions.* New York: Crown, 1954.

Elgvin, Torleif. "Hvordan lese gammeltestamentlige tekster" [How to read Old Testament texts]. *Theofilos* 7 (2015) 76–87.

Ellis, George, and Joe Silk. "Scientific Method: Defend the Integrity of Physics." *Nature News* 516 (2014) 321–23.

Elsdon-Baker, Fern. "Questioning Evolution Is Neither Science Denial nor the Preserve of Creationists." *Guardian*, September 5, 2017. https://amp.theguardian.com/science/political-science/2017/sep/05/questioning-evolution-is-neither-science-denial-nor-the-preserve-of-creationists.

Ewart, Paul. "The Necessity of Chance: Randomness, Purpose and the Sovereignty of God." *Science & Christian Belief* 21 (2009) 111–31.

Falk, Seb. *The Light Ages: A Medieval Journey of Discovery.* London: Penguin, 2020.

Farrell, John. *The Day Without Yesterday: Lemaître, Einstein, and the Birth of Modern Cosmology.* New York: Basic, 2005.

Felipe, Pablo de, et al. "Georges Lemaître's 1936 Lecture on Science and Faith." *Science & Christian Belief* 27 (2015) 154–79.

Ferguson, Duncan S. "Historical Understanding and the Enlightenment: Edward Gibbon on Christianity." *Historical Magazine of the Protestant Episcopal Church* 52 (1983) 391–403.

Ferngren, Gary, and R. Numbers. "C. S. Lewis on Creation and Evolution: The Acworth Letters, 1944–1960." *Perspectives on Science and Christian Faith* 48 (1996) 28–33.

Feser, Edward. "The Road from Atheism." Edward Feser, July 17, 2012. https://edwardfeser.blogspot.com/2012/07/road-from-atheism.html.

———. "Teleology: A Shopper's Guide." *Philosophia Christi* 12 (2010) 142–59.

Feynman, Richard Phillips, and Ralph Leighton. *"Surely You're Joking, Mr. Feynman!": Adventures of a Curious Character*. New York: Random House, 1992.

Fitch, W. Tecumseh. "Empirical Approaches to the Study of Language Evolution." *Psychonomic Bulletin & Review* 24 (2017) 3–33.

Frege, Gottlob. "The Thought: A Logical Inquiry." *Mind* 65 (1956) 289–311.

Futuyma, Douglas J. *Evolutionary Biology*. 3rd ed. Sunderland, MA: Sinauer, 1998.

———. "Evolutionary Biology Today and the Call for an Extended Synthesis." *Interface Focus* 7 (2017) 1–13.

Galilei, Galileo. *Dialogue Concerning the Two Chief World Systems—Ptolemaic & Copernican*. Translated by Stillman Drake. Berkeley: University of California Press, 1967.

———. "Galileo's Discourse on the Tides." In *The Galileo Affair: A Documentary History*, edited and translated by Maurice Finocchiaro, 119–33. Berkeley: University of California Press, 1989.

———. *Two New Sciences, Including Centers of Gravity and Forces of Percussion*. Translated by Stillman Drake. Madison: University of Wisconsin Press, 1974.

Garnett, William, and Lewis Campbell. *The Life of James Clerk Maxwell, with a Selection from His Correspondence and Occasional Writings and a Sketch of His Contributions to Science*. London: Macmillan, 1882.

Gendle, Mathew H. "Discussing Philosophy of Mind in Introductory Neuroscience Classes." *Journal of Undergraduate Neuroscience Education* 9 (2011) E5–E7.

Gingerich, Owen. *The Book Nobody Read: Chasing the Revolutions of Nicolaus Copernicus*. New York: Walker, 2004.

Gingerich, Owen, and Robert S. Westman. "The Wittich Connection: Conflict and Priority in Late Sixteenth-Century Cosmology." *Transactions of the American Philosophical Society* 78 (1988) 1–148.

Gleick, James. *Isaac Newton*. London: Harper Perennial, 2003.

Goodrum, Matthew R. "Atomism, Atheism, and the Spontaneous Generation of Human Beings: The Debate over a Natural Origin of the First Humans in Seventeenth-Century Britain." *Journal of the History of Ideas* 63 (2002) 207–24.

Gosse, Philip. *Omphalos: An Attempt to Untie the Geological Knot*. 1857. Repr., London: Routledge, 2004.

Graney, Christopher M. "But Still, It Moves: Tides, Stellar Parallax, and Galileo's Commitment to the Copernican Theory." *Physics in Perspective* 10 (2008) 258–68.

———. "Coriolis Effect, Two Centuries Before Coriolis." *Physics Today* 64 (2011) 8–9.

———. "Objects in Telescope Are Farther than They Appear: How Diffraction Tricked Galileo into Mismeasuring Distances to the Stars." *Physics Teacher* 47 (2009) 362–65.

———. *Setting Aside All Authority: Giovanni Battista Riccioli and the Science Against Copernicus in the Age of Galileo*. Notre Dame: University of Notre Dame Press, 2015.

———. "Teaching Galileo? Get to Know Riccioli! What a Forgotten Italian Astronomer Can Teach Students About How Science Works." *Physics Teacher* 50 (2012) 18–21.

———. "The Telescope Against Copernicus: Star Observations by Riccioli Supporting a Geocentric Universe." *Journal for the History of Astronomy* 41 (2010) 453–67.

Graney, Christopher M., and Timothy P. Grayson. "On the Telescopic Disks of Stars: A Review and Analysis of Stellar Observations from the Early Seventeenth Through the Middle Nineteenth Centuries." *Annals of Science* 68 (2011) 351–73.

Grant, Edward. *The Foundations of Modern Science in the Middle Ages: Their Religious, Institutional and Intellectual Contexts*. Cambridge: Cambridge University Press, 1996.

Gribbin, John. *The Fellowship: Gilbert, Bacon, Harvey, Wren, Newton, and the Story of a Scientific Revolution*. New York: Overlook, 2007.

Gundersen, Trygve Riiser. "Forandringens fellesskap" [The community of change]. *Morgenbladet*, May 16, 2019. Updated April 29, 2021. https://www.morgenbladet.no/ideer/forandringens-fellesskap/9106846.

Gwatkin, Henry Melvill. *Selections from Early Writers Illustrative of Church History to the Time of Constantine*. London: Macmillan, 1902.

Halldorf, Peter. *21 kirkefedre: Historien om hvordan kristendommen ble utformet* [21 church fathers: The story of how Christianity was formed]. Translated by Randi Steen Hilmersen. Oslo: Luther, 2012.

Hannam, James. "Church Discipline of Natural Philosophers in the Middle Ages: The Case of Cecco D'ascoli." MA diss., University of London, 2003. https://jameshannam.com/Church%20Discipline%20of%20Natural%20Philosophers%20in%20the%20Middle%20Ages.pdf.

———. *The Genesis of Science: How the Christian Middle Ages Launched the Scientific Revolution*. Washington, DC: Regnery, 2011.

Harrison, Peter. *The Territories of Science and Religion*. Chicago: University of Chicago Press, 2015.

Hart, David Bentley. *The Experience of God: Being, Consciousness, Bliss*. New Haven: Yale University Press, 2013.

Hartmann, William M. "How We Localize Sound." *Physics Today* 52 (1999) 24–29.

Hauser, Marc D., et al. "The Mystery of Language Evolution." *Frontiers in Psychology* 5 (2014) 1–12.

Hawking, Stephen. *Brief Answers to the Big Questions*. New York: Bantam, 2018.

———. *A Brief History of Time*. New York: Bantam, 1988.

Hawking, Stephen, and Leonard Mlodinow. *The Grand Design*. New York: Random House Digital, 2010.

Heffner, Henry E., and Rickye S. Heffner. "The Evolution of Mammalian Sound Localization." *Acoustics Today* 12 (2016) 20–27.

Heilbron, John L. *Galileo*. Oxford: Oxford University Press, 2012.

———. *The Sun in the Church: Cathedrals as Solar Observatories*. Cambridge: Harvard University Press, 1999.

Heine, Heinrich. "Neunter Brief." May 1837. From "Über die Französische Bühne: Vertraute Briefe an August Lewald; Geschrieben im Mai 1837, auf einem Dorfe bei Paris," in *Allgemeinen Theaterrevue*. http://www.heinrich-heine-denkmal.de/heine-texte/fr-buehne09.shtml.

———. *The Salon*. Translated by Charles Godfrey Leland. Vol. 4 of *The Works of Heinrich Heine*. London: Heinemann, 1893.

Hendrix, Jimi. "Voodoo Chile." Track 4 on *Electric Ladyland*. New York: Record Plant, 1968.

Henry, John. "Metaphysics and the Origins of Modern Science: Descartes and the Importance of Laws of Nature." *Early Science and Medicine* 9 (2004) 73–114.
Henshilwood, Christopher S., et al. "An Abstract Drawing from the 73,000-Year-Old Levels at Blombos Cave, South Africa." *Nature* 562 (2018) 115–18.
Herculano-Houzel, Suzana. "The Remarkable, Yet Not Extraordinary, Human Brain as a Scaled-Up Primate Brain and Its Associated Cost." Edited by Francisco J. Ayala. *Proceedings of the National Academy of Sciences* 109, supplement 1 (2012) 10661–68.
Hestmark, Geir. "Jens Esmark's Mountain Glacier Traverse 1823—The Key to His Discovery of Ice Ages." *Boreas* 47 (2018) 1–10.
Hocutt, Max. "Aristotle's Four Becauses." *Philosophy* 49 (1974) 385–99.
Holland, Tom. *Dominion: The Making of the Western Mind*. London: Little, Brown, 2019.
Holm, Sverre. *Den innbilte konflikten: Om naturvitenskap og Gud*. Oslo: Veritas, 2021.
———. "Learning from C. S. Lewis's View on Evolution." To appear in Theofilos (Nordic journal in the fields of Theology, Philosophy, and Culture).
———. "On the Alleged Coherence Between the Global Temperature and the Sun's Movement." *Journal of Atmospheric and Solar-Terrestrial Physics* 110 (2014) 23–27.
———. "Prudence in Estimating Coherence Between Planetary, Solar and Climate Oscillations." *Astrophysics and Space Science* 357 (2015) 1–8.
———. *Waves with Power-Law Attenuation*. Switzerland: Springer, 2019.
Holm, Sverre, and Martin Blomhoff Holm. "Restrictions on Wave Equations for Passive Media." *Journal of the Acoustical Society of America* 142 (2017) 1888–96.
Horgan, John. *The End of Science: Facing the Limits of Knowledge in the Twilight of the Scientific Age*. New York: Broadway, 1997.
———. "Pssst! Don't Tell the Creationists, but Scientists Don't Have a Clue How Life Began." Scientific American, February 28, 2011. https://www.scientificamerican.com/blog/cross-check/pssst-dont-tell-the-creationists-but-scientists-dont-have-a-clue-how-life-began/.
Hossenfelder, Sabine. *Lost in Math: How Beauty Leads Physics Astray*. New York: Basic, 2018.
Humanists UK. "John Maynard Smith." Humanist News, 2001. https://humanists.uk/humanism/the-humanist-tradition/20th-century-humanism/john-maynard-smith/.
Hummel, Charles E. *The Galileo Connection*. Downers Grove, IL: InterVarsity, 1986.
Humphreys, Colin, and Graeme Waddington. "Solar Eclipse of 1207 BC Helps to Date Pharaohs." *Astronomy & Geophysics* 58 (2017) 5.39–35.42.
Jacob, Margaret C. Introduction to *Newton and Newtonianism: New Studies*, edited by James E. Force and Sarah Hutton, ix–xvii. New York: Kluwer Academic, 2004.
Jaki, Stanley L. "The Biblical Basis of Western Science." Crisis Magazine, October 1, 1997. https://www.crisismagazine.com/vault/the-biblical-basis-of-western-science-2.
———. "The Power and Poverty of Science." *Asbury Journal* 57 (2002) 49–65.
———. *Science and Creation: From Eternal Cycles to an Oscillating Universe*. Edinburgh: Scottish Academic, 1986.
Janin, Joseph. "La vie passionnée d'André-Marie Ampère" [The passionate life of André-Marie Ampère]. *Bulletin de la Sabix* 37 (2004) 10–20. https://doi.org/10.4000/sabix.464.

Jeynes, Christopher, abr. "Science and Creation." University of Surrey, 2002. https://openresearch.surrey.ac.uk/esploro/outputs/99512353802346.

Jonas, Eric, and Konrad Paul Kording. "Could a Neuroscientist Understand a Microprocessor?" *PLOS Computational Biology* 13 (2017) 1–24.

Kacki, Sacha, et al. "Rich Table but Short Life: Diffuse Idiopathic Skeletal Hyperostosis in Danish Astronomer Tycho Brahe (1546–1601) and Its Possible Consequences." *PLOS One* 13 (2018) 1–31.

Kaneda, Toshiko, and Carl Haub. "How Many People Have Ever Lived on Earth?" PRB, November 15, 2022. https://www.prb.org/articles/how-many-people-have-ever-lived-on-earth/.

Kastrup, Bernardo. *The Idea of the World: A Multi-Disciplinary Argument for the Mental Nature of Reality*. Winchester, UK: Iff, 2019.

Kepler, Johannes. *Epitome of Copernican Astronomy & Harmonies of the World*. Translated by Charles Glenn Wallis. Amherst, NY: Prometheus, 1995.

———. *The Harmony of the World*. Translated by E. J. Aiton et al. Memoirs of the American Philosophical Society 209. Philadelphia: American Philosophical Society, 1997.

———. *Kepler's Conversation with Galileo's Sidereal Messenger*. Translated by Edward Rosen. New York: Johnson Reprint, 1965.

———. *New Astronomy*. Translated by William H. Donahue. Cambridge: Cambridge University Press, 1992.

———.*Tabulae Rudolphinae*. Edited by Franz Hammer. Vol. 10 of *Gesammelte Werke*. Munich: Beck, 1969.

Kirshner, Robert P. "Hubble's Diagram and Cosmic Expansion." *Proceedings of the National Academy of Sciences* 101 (2004) 8–13.

Kjeldstadli, Knut. *Fortida er ikke hva den en gang var: En innføring i historiefaget* [The past is not what it once was: An introduction to the subject of history]. Oslo: Universitetsforlaget, 1999.

Kneller, Karl Alois. *Christianity and the Leaders of Modern Science: A Contribution to the History of Culture in the Nineteenth Century*. Translated by T. M. Kettle. London: Herder, 1911.

Knudsen, Børre. *Grunnsøylene* [The foundational pillars]. Oslo: Credo, 1995.

Kojonen, Erkki Vesa Rope. *The Compatibility of Evolution and Design*. Cham, Switzerland: Palgrave Macmillan, 2021.

Kolbert, Elizabeth. *The Sixth Extinction: An Unnatural History*. New York: Holt, 2014.

Koperski, Jeffrey. *Divine Action, Determinism, and the Laws of Nature*. New York: Routledge, 2020.

Kragh, Helge. *Entropic Creation: Religious Contexts of Thermodynamics and Cosmology*. Science, Technology and Culture, 1700–1945. London: Routledge, 2016.

———. "Georges Lemaître, Pioneer of Modern Theoretical Cosmology." *Foundations of Physics* 48 (2018) 1333–48.

———. "The Origin and Earliest Reception of Big-Bang Cosmology." *Publications de l'Observatoire Astronomique de Belgrade* 85 (2008) 7–16.

———. "Pierre Duhem, Entropy, and Christian Faith." *Physics in Perspective* 10 (2008) 379–95.

Kreeft, Peter. *A Shorter Summa: The Essential Philosophical Passages of St. Thomas Aquinas' Summa Theologica, Edited and Explained for Beginners*. San Francisco: Ignatius, 2010.

Kretschmer, Konrad. *Einleitung in die Geschichte der physischen Erdkunde im christlichen Mittelalter* [Introduction to the history of physical geography in the Christian Middle Ages]. Vienna: Eduard Hölzel, 1889.

Krukonis, Greg, and Tracy Barr. *Evolution for Dummies.* Hoboken, NJ: Wiley & Sons, 2011.

Kwan, Alistair, et al. "Who Really Discovered Snell's Law?" *Physics World* 15 (2002) 64.

Laland, Kevin, et al. "Does Evolutionary Theory Need a Rethink? Point Yes, Urgently." *Nature News* 514 (2014) 161–64.

Lambert, Simon A., et al. "Bridging Three Orders of Magnitude: Multiple Scattered Waves Sense Fractal Microscopic Structures Via Dispersion." *Physical Review Letters* 115 (2015) 1–6.

Lamoureux, Denis O. "Do the Heavens Declare the Glory of God? Toward a Biblical Model of Intelligent Design." *Faith & Thought* 59 (2015) 18–38.

———. "Evolutionary Creation: Moving Beyond the Evolution Versus Creation Debate." *Christian Higher Education* 9 (2009) 28–48.

Larson, Laurence Marcellus, trans. *The King's Mirror (Speculum regale—Konungs skuggsjá).* Library of Scandinavian Literature 15. New York: American-Scandinavian Foundation, 1917.

Lausanne Movement. "The Lausanne Covenant." 1974. https://lausanne.org/statement/lausanne-covenant.

Leibniz, Gottfried Wilhelm. *Principles of Nature and Grace, Based on Reason.* Prepared by Jonathan Bennett. Early Modern Texts, 2004. https://www.earlymoderntexts.com/assets/pdfs/leibniz1714a.pdf.

Lennox, John C. *God's Undertaker: Has Science Buried God?* Worcestershire, UK: Lion, 2009.

———. *Seven Days That Divide the World: The Beginning According to Genesis and Science.* Grand Rapids: Zondervan, 2011.

Levere, Trevor H. "Faraday, Matter, and Natural Theology—Reflections on an Unpublished Manuscript." *British Journal for the History of Science* 4 (1968) 95–107.

Lewis, C. S. *The Abolition of Man.* In *The Complete C. S. Lewis Signature Classics*, 689–738. New York: HarperOne, 2007.

———. "The Funeral of a Great Myth." In *Christian Reflections*, edited by Walter Hooper, 82–93. Grand Rapids: Eerdmans, 1967.

Lewis, Geraint F., and Luke A. Barnes. *A Fortunate Universe: Life in a Finely Tuned Cosmos.* Cambridge: Cambridge University Press, 2016.

Lindberg, David C. *The Beginnings of Western Science: The European Scientific Tradition in Philosophical, Religious, and Institutional Context, Prehistory to AD 1450.* Chicago: University of Chicago Press, 2010.

Lindberg, David C., and Ronald L. Numbers. "Beyond War and Peace: A Reappraisal of the Encounter Between Christianity and Science." *Church History* 55 (1986) 338–54.

———. *When Science and Christianity Meet.* Chicago: University of Chicago Press, 2003.

Linnebo, Øystein. "Platonism in the Philosophy of Mathematics." Stanford Encyclopedia of Philosophy (Summer 2024 ed.), last revised March 28, 2023. https://plato.stanford.edu/archives/sum2024/entries/platonism-mathematics/.

Livio, Mario. *Galileo and the Science Deniers.* New York: Simon and Schuster, 2020.

Logothetis, Nikos K. "What We Can Do and What We Cannot Do with fMRI." *Nature* 453 (2008) 869–78.
Loke, Andrew. "A New Fourfold Taxonomy of Science-Religion Relations." *Theology and Science* 21 (2023) 29–43.
Lyell, Charles. *Principles of Geology: Being an Attempt to Explain the Former Changes of the Earth's Surface, by Reference to Causes Now in Operation.* 3 vols. London: Murray, 1830–1833.
Macdougall, Doug. *Nature's Clocks: How Scientists Measure the Age of Almost Everything.* Berkeley: University of California Press, 2009.
MacKay, Donald MacCrimmon. *The Clockwork Image: A Christian Perspective on Science.* London: Inter-Varsity, 1974.
Maienschein, Jane. "Epigenesis and Preformationism." Stanford Encyclopedia of Philosophy (Spring 2017 ed.), last revised December 22, 2016. https://plato.stanford.edu/archives/spr2017/entries/epigenesis/.
Manolio, Teri A., et al. "Finding the Missing Heritability of Complex Diseases." *Nature* 461 (2009) 747–53.
Martin, R. Niall D. "The Genesis of a Mediaeval Historian: Pierre Duhem and the Origins of Statics." *Annals of Science* 33 (1976) 119–29.
McGrath, Alister E. *Science & Religion: A New Introduction.* 3rd ed. Hoboken, NJ: Wiley & Sons, 2020.
Miller, David Marshall. "The Thirty Years War and the Galileo Affair." *History of Science* 46 (2008) 49–74.
Miller, Hugh. *The Testimony of the Rocks: Or, Geology in Its Bearings on the Two Theologies, Natural and Revealed.* Boston: Gould and Lincoln, 1859.
Moreland, J. P. "Philosophical Apologetics, the Church, and Contemporary Culture." *Journal of the Evangelical Theological Society* 39 (1996) 123–40.
Morris, Simon Conway. *Life's Solution: Inevitable Humans in a Lonely Universe.* Cambridge: Cambridge University Press, 2003.
Morris, Henry M. *Scientific Creationism.* Green Forest, AR: New Leaf, 1974.
Munroe, Randall. "Fields Arranged by Purity." XKCD, June 11, 2008. https://xkcd.com/435/.
Nagel, Thomas. *Mind and Cosmos: Why the Materialist Neo-Darwinian Conception of Nature Is Almost Certainly False.* Oxford: Oxford University Press, 2012.
———. "What Is It Like to Be a Bat?" *Philosophical Review* 83 (1974) 435–50.
Naturhistorisk Museum. "Evolusjon" [Evolution]. University of Oslo, December 14, 2011. https://www.nhm.uio.no/forskning/temaer/evolusjon/erklaring-om-evolusjon.html.
Naylor, Ron. "Galileo's Tidal Theory." *Isis* 98 (2007) 1–22.
Newton, Isaac. *The Principia: Mathematical Principles of Natural Philosophy.* Translated by I. Bernard Cohen and Anne Whitman, assisted by Julia Budenz. Authoritative Ed. Oakland: University of California Press, 1999.
Nicholson, Daniel J. "Organisms ≠ Machines." *Studies in History and Philosophy of Science Part C: Studies in History and Philosophy of Biological and Biomedical Sciences* 44 (2013) 669–78.
Noble, Denis. *Dance to the Tune of Life: Biological Relativity.* Cambridge: Cambridge University Press, 2016.
Numbers, Ronald L. *The Creationists: From Scientific Creationism to Intelligent Design.* Cambridge: Harvard University Press, 2006.

Ogawa, Seiji, et al. "Brain Magnetic Resonance Imaging with Contrast Dependent on Blood Oxygenation." *Proceedings of the National Academy of Sciences* 87 (1990) 9868–72.

Olson, Carl. "Galileo Was Right—But So Were His Critics." Strange Notions, May 30, 2015. https://strangenotions.com/galileo-was-right-but-so-were-his-critics/.

O'Raifeartaigh, Cormac, and Simon Mitton. "Interrogating the Legend of Einstein's 'Biggest Blunder.'" *Physics in Perspective* 20 (2018) 318–41.

Ortlund, Gavin. *Retrieving Augustine's Doctrine of Creation: Ancient Wisdom for Current Controversy*. Downers Grove, IL: InterVarsity Academic, 2020.

Osler, Margaret J. "The New Newtonian Scholarship and the Fate of the Scientific Revolution." In *Newton and Newtonianism: New Studies*, edited by James E. Force and Sarah Hutton, 1–13. New York: Kluwer Academic, 2004.

Pannekoek, Anton. *A History of Astronomy*. London: Allen & Unwin, 1961.

Parfit, Derek. "Why Anything? Why This?" *London Review of Books* 20 (1998) 1–27.

Pascal, Blaise. *Pascal's Pensées*. Translated by W. F. Trotter. New York: Dutton, 1958.

Patapievici, Horia-Roman. "The 'Pierre Duhem Thesis.' A Reappraisal of Duhem's Discovery of the Physics of the Middle Ages." *Logos & Episteme* 6 (2015) 201–18.

Patz, Samuel, et al. "Imaging Localized Neuronal Activity at Fast Time Scales Through Biomechanics." *Science Advances* 5 (2019) 1–12.

Peacocke, Arthur R. "Chance and the Life Game." *Zygon* 14 (1979) 301–22.

Pearce, Daniel J. G., et al. "Role of Projection in the Control of Bird Flocks." *Proceedings of the National Academy of Sciences* 111 (2014) 10422–26.

Pennisi, Elizabeth. "Bats and Dolphins Evolved Echolocation in Same Way." Science, September 4, 2013. https://www.sciencemag.org/news/2013/09/bats-and-dolphins-evolved-echolocation-same-way.

———. "Hear That? Bats and Whales Share Sonar Protein." Science, January 25, 2010. https://www.sciencemag.org/news/2010/01/hear-bats-and-whales-share-sonar-protein.

Peters, Ted, and Martin Hewlett. *Evolution from Creation to New Creation: Conflict, Conversation, and Convergence*. Nashville: Abingdon, 2003.

Pew Research Center. *Being Christian in Western Europe*. May 29, 2018. https://www.pewresearch.org/religion/2018/05/29/being-christian-in-western-europe/.

Pika, Simone, et al. "Ravens Parallel Great Apes in Physical and Social Cognitive Skills." *Scientific Reports* 10 (2020) 1–19.

Pius XII, Pope. "The Proofs for the Existence of God in the Light of Modern Natural Science." Papal Encyclicals Online, 1951. https://www.papalencyclicals.net/pius12/p12exist.htm.

Plantinga, Alvin. *Where the Conflict Really Lies: Science, Religion, and Naturalism*. Oxford: Oxford University Press, 2011.

Polkinghorne, John. *Belief in God in an Age of Science*. New Haven: Yale University Press, 1998.

Pontifical Academy of Sciences. *Papal Addresses to the Pontifical Academy of Sciences 1917–2002 and to the Pontifical Academy of Social Sciences 1994–2002*. Scripta Varia 100. Vatican City: Pontifical Academy of Sciences, 2003.

Popkin, Richard H. "Plans for Publishing Newton's Religious and Alchemical Manuscripts, 1982–1998." In *Newton and Newtonianism: New Studies*, edited by James E. Force and Sarah Hutton, 15–22. New York: Kluwer Academic, 2004.

Pratt, John P. "Newton's Date for the Crucifixion." *Quarterly Journal of the Royal Astronomical Society* 32 (1991) 301–4.

Premack, David, and Ann James Premack. *The Mind of an Ape*. New York: Norton, 1983.

Priest, Greg. "Thierry Hoquet, Revisiting the Origin of Species: The Other Darwins." *History and Philosophy of the Life Sciences* 42 (2020) 1–4.

Pross, Addy, and Robert Pascal. "The Origin of Life: What We Know, What We Can Know and What We Will Never Know." *Open Biology* 3 (2013) 1–5.

Rees, Martin. *Just Six Numbers: The Deep Forces That Shape the Universe*. London: Weidenfeld & Nicolson, 1999.

Roberts, Michael B. *Evangelicals and Science*. Greenwood Guides to Science and Religion. Westport, CT: Greenwood, 2008.

———. "Genesis Chapter 1 and Geological Time from Hugo Grotius and Marin Mersenne to William Conybeare and Thomas Chalmers (1620–825)." *Geological Society, London, Special Publications* 273 (2007) 39–49.

———. "The Genesis of John Ray and His Successors." *Evangelical Quarterly* 74 (2002) 143–63.

———. "Has the Church of England Gone Creationist in Live Lent?" Peddling and Scaling God and Darwin, March 25, 2021. https://michaelroberts4004.wordpress.com/2021/03/25/has-the-church-of-england-gone-creationist-in-live-lent/.

Roberts, Noel Keith. "Newman on the Argument from Design." *New Blackfriars* 88 (2007) 56–66.

Rocha, Gustavo Rodrigues, and Helge Kragh. "Interview: Helge Kragh." *Transversal: International Journal for the Historiography of Science* 2 (2017) 233.

Rohde, Douglas L. T., et al. "Modelling the Recent Common Ancestry of All Living Humans." *Nature* 431 (2004) 562–66.

Rovelli, Carlo. "Aristotle's Physics: A Physicist's Look." *Journal of the American Philosophical Association* 1 (2015) 23–40.

Ruby, Jane E. "The Origins of Scientific 'Law.'" *Journal of the History of Ideas* 47 (1986) 341–59.

Ryan, William B. F., et al. "An Abrupt Drowning of the Black Sea Shelf." *Marine Geology* 138 (1997) 119–26.

Sagan, Carl, et al., creators. *Cosmos: A Personal Voyage*. PBS, 1980–1981.

Schaechter, Moselio. "Lynn Margulis (1938–2011)." *Science* 335 (2012) 302.

Schaeffer, Francis A. *The Complete Works of Francis A. Schaeffer: A Christian Worldview*. 5 vols. 2nd ed. Wheaton, IL: Crossway, 1982.

———. *The Francis A. Schaeffer Trilogy: The Three Essential Books in One Volume*. Wheaton, IL: Crossway, 1990.

Schrödinger, Erwin. *What Is Life? The Physical Aspect of the Living Cell and Mind*. Cambridge: Cambridge University Press, 1944.

Simpson, George Gaylord. *The Meaning of Evolution: A Study of the History of Life and of Its Significance for Man*. New Haven: Yale University Press, 1949.

Singham, Mano. "The Copernican Myths." *Physics Today* 60 (2007) 48–52.

Smeaton, William A. "French Scientists in the Shadow of the Guillotine: The Death Roll of 1792–1794." *Endeavour* 17 (1993) 60–63.

Smith, John Maynard, and Eors Szathmáry. *The Origins of Life: From the Birth of Life to the Origin of Language*. Oxford: Oxford University Press, 2000.

Snobelen, Stephen D. "Isaac Newton: His Science and Religion." In *Science, Religion and Society*, edited by Arri Eisen and Gary Laderman, 375–89. Armonk, NY: Sharpe, 2007.

Solzhenitsyn, Aleksandr. *The Gulag Archipelago*. 1973. Wikiquotes, last edited June 21, 2025. https://en.wikiquote.org/wiki/The_Gulag_Archipelago.

Søvik, Atle Ottesen. *A Basic Theory of Everything: A Fundamental Theoretical Framework for Science and Philosophy*. Berlin: De Gruyter, 2022.

Spencer, Nick. *Darwin and God*. London: SPCK, 2009.

Stanley, Matthew. "By Design: James Clerk Maxwell and the Evangelical Unification of Science." *British Journal for the History of Science* 45 (2012) 57–73.

———. "Why Study History." *Physics Today* 69 (2016) 38–44.

Stephenson, Bruce. *The Music of the Heavens: Kepler's Harmonic Astronomy*. Princeton: Princeton University Press, 1994.

Stewart, Balfour, and Peter Guthrie Tait. *The Unseen Universe: Or Physical Speculations on a Future State*. 3rd ed. New York: Macmillan, 1875.

Stinner, Arthur. "Calculating the Age of the Earth and the Sun." *Physics Education* 37 (2002) 296–305.

Swamidass, S. Joshua. "The Overlooked Science of Genealogical Ancestry." *Perspectives on Science and Christian Faith* 70 (2018) 19–20.

Swanson, Larry W. "Quest for the Basic Plan of Nervous System Circuitry." *Brain Research Reviews* 55 (2007) 356–72.

Szathmáry, Eörs. "Toward Major Evolutionary Transitions Theory 2.0." *Proceedings of the National Academy of Sciences* 112 (2015) 10104–11.

Szathmáry, Eörs, and John Maynard Smith. "The Major Evolutionary Transitions." *Nature* 374 (1995) 227–32.

Taleb, Nassim Nicholas. *The Black Swan: The Impact of the Highly Improbable*. London: Penguin, 2008.

Tanzella-Nitti, Giuseppe. "The Two Books Prior to the Scientific Revolution." *Perspectives on Science and Christian Faith* 57 (2005) 235–48.

Tattersall, Ian. *Masters of the Planet: The Search for Our Human Origins*. New York: St. Martin's, 2012.

The Third Way. "Rationale." May 30, 2014. https://www.thethirdwayofevolution.com/.

Thompson, Silvanus Phillips. *The Life of William Thomson, Baron Kelvin of Largs*. Vol. 2. London: Macmillan, 1910.

Thorvaldsen, Steinar. "From Keplerian Orbits to Precise Planetary Predictions: The Transits of the 1630s." *Journal of Astronomical Data* 19 (2013) 97–108.

Thorvaldsen, Steinar, and Ola Hössjer. "Using Statistical Methods to Model the Fine-Tuning of Molecular Machines and Systems." *Journal of Theoretical Biology* 501 (2020) 1–14.

Tour, James. "The Controversial Views of Isaac Newton with James Tour & Kees Roos." Dr. James Tour, YouTube, February 16, 2024. https://www.youtube.com/watch?v=-IJxB3S2OVo.

Townes, Charles H. "The Convergence of Science and Religion." *Zygon* 1 (1966) 301–11.

Trasancos, Stacy. *Science Was Born of Christianity: The Teaching of Fr. Stanley L. Jaki*. Titusville, FL: Habitation of Chimham, 2014.

Tunstad, Erik. *Darwins teori—Evolusjon gjennom 400 år* [Darwin's theory—Evolution through 400 years]. Oslo: Humanist, 2009.

Van der Waerden, Bartel Leendert. "The Great Year in Greek, Persian and Hindu Astronomy." *Archive for History of Exact Sciences* 18 (1978) 359–83.

Victora, Cesar G., et al. "Breastfeeding in the 21st Century: Epidemiology, Mechanisms, and Lifelong Effect." *Lancet* 387 (2016) 475–90.

Vogt, Carl. *Physiologische Briefe für Gebildete aller Stände* [Physiological letters for educated people of all classes]. 4 aufl. Giessen, Ger.: Ricker, 1874.

Voit, Eberhard O., et al. "150 Years of the Mass Action Law." *PLOS Computational Biology* 11 (2015) 1–7.

Voltaire. "Lettre XIV: Sur Descartes et Newton" [Letter XIV: On Descartes and Newton]. In *Lettres philosophiques*, 127–32. Vol. 22 of *Oeuvres complètes de Voltaire*. Paris: Garnier Frères, 1879. https://fr.wikisource.org/wiki/Lettres_philosophiques/Lettre_14.

Von Glasersfeld, Ernst. "Teleology and the Concepts of Causation." *Philosophica* 46 (1990) 17–43.

Waage, Peter. *Det daglige livs kjemi: Belyst ved forsøk* [The chemistry of daily life, illuminated by experiments]. Oslo: Aschehoug, 1897.

Walsh, Fernando José. *Quotes from Believer Scientists. Men of Science Speak of God*. Buenos Aires: Independent, 2021.

Walton, John H. *The Lost World of Genesis One: Ancient Cosmology and the Origins Debate*. Downers Grove, IL: InterVarsity, 2010.

Weinberg, Steven. *The First Three Minutes: A Modern View of the Origin of the Universe*. New York: Basic, 2022.

Whitcomb, John C., and Henry M. Morris. *The Genesis Flood: The Biblical Record and Its Scientific Implications*. Philadelphia: Presbyterian and Reformed, 1964.

White, Andrew Dickson. *A History of the Warfare of Science with Theology*. New York: Appleton, 1896.

Wigner, Eugene. "The Unreasonable Effectiveness of Mathematics in the Natural Sciences." In *Mathematics and Science*, edited by Ronald E. Mickens, 291–306. Singapore: World Scientific, 1990.

Wikipedia. "Apostles' Creed." Last edited September 17, 2025. https://en.wikipedia.org/wiki/Apostles%27_Creed.

———. "Athanasian Creed." Last edited September 10, 2025. https://en.wikipedia.org/wiki/Athanasian_Creed.

———. "Fred Hoyle." Last edited September 15, 2025. https://en.wikipedia.org/wiki/Fred_Hoyle.

———. "Scientisme" [Scientism]. Last edited June 9, 2025. https://fr.wikipedia.org/wiki/Scientisme.

———."Voltaire." Last edited September 23, 2025. https://en.wikipedia.org/wiki/Voltaire.

Wilkinson, Paul. "Darwin's Theory of Evolution Found Lacking by Non-Religious People in the UK and Canada." Church Times, September 8, 2017. https://www.churchtimes.co.uk/articles/2017/8-september/news/uk/darwin-theory-found-lacking-by-non-religious-people-in-the-uk-and-canada.

Worsley, Peter. "Jens Esmark, Vassryggen and Early Glacial Theory in Britain." *Mercian Geologist* 16 (2006) 161–72.

Wray, Gregory A., et al. "Does Evolutionary Theory Need a Rethink? Counterpoint No, All Is Well." *Nature News* 514 (2014) 161–64.

Index

accommodation, 132, 239, 245–46
agnostic, 166, 185, 221
animism, 106, 142, 151, 156, 220
Anning, Mary, 122
anthropic principle, 50
Aquinas, Thomas
    consciousness, 205-7, 251
    epigenesis, 115
    eternal world, 107, 133
    philosophy, 141, 147
    primary, secondary causes, 145
    teleology, 49, 183–84
Aristotle
    eternal world, 104, 107, 125, 133, 138
    Great Year, 106
    mechanics, 54–56
    philosophy, 107, 143, 147–54, 181, 205, 212
    spherical earth, 70
    spontaneous life, 114–15
artificial intelligence, 208, 231
astrology, 6, 65, 106–8, 214
atheism, 114, 154, 182, 193, 248–49
Augustine,
    science, 109, 113, 125, 134
    theology, 14, 240, 241–44, 250–51, 254, 259–60

Bacon, Francis, 16, 152–54, 182, 262
Bacon, Roger, 154
Ball, Philip, 188–89
Bellarmine, cardinal, 87–88

big bang,
    Lemaître, Georges, 129, 135–36, 138–40
    limitations, 134, 145, 157, 170, 195
    theology, 25, 50, 128, 131, 246, 252
    science, 11, 44, 47–48
Black Death, 58
blind chance, 164, 173, 181, 231
blind faith, 23, 215
Boethius, Anicius, 42, 71
Boyle, Robert, 31, 155, 194
Brahe, Tycho,
    astronomy, 60–61, 65, 72
    distance to stars, 99–100, 104
    geoheliocentric model, 53, 86–87, 96, 100–102
Brooke, John H., 16, 28, 87, 114, 228
Buckland, William, 116–19, 122–27, 243
Buridan, Jean, 57–58, 60, 74
Butterfield, Herbert, 1, 4

carbon 14 dating, 127
Cartwright, Nancy, 159–60
catastrophism, 121–23
Catholic Church, 83, 87, 91–93, 115, 228, 252
Cepheids, 135
Chalmers, David, 202, 207, 217
Chesterton, G. K., 141, 182, 198
communism, 138, 230
Comte, Auguste, 229–30
Conches, de, 145–47, 154

concordism, 95, 125, 243,
Condorcet, Nicolas de, 92, 229
Cotes, Roger, 153, 155–57, 159, 225
Copernican cliché, 43
Copernicus, Nikolaus,
  heliocentric model, 53, 64, 73, 82, 91, 100–102
  gigantic stars, 100, 244
  proof, lack of, 5, 66, 72, 75–76, 86–88, 97–98
  proof, 100–101
creationism. See young-earth or evolutionary creationism
creativity, 8, 236, 250
creed,
  Apostles', 185, 219
  Athanasian, 133–34
  Nicene, 246, 249
Crick, Francis, 171, 181, 188, 215
Cuvier, George, 121, 123

Darwinism, 165–68, 170
Davidsen, Bjørn Are, 253–54
Dawkins, Richard, 22, 168, 181–82, 188
deism, 23, 145, 158, 229, 248
determinism, 145, 180, 194
dinosaur, 103, 116, 121–23, 197
Dobzhansky, Theodosius, 182
dualism, 212–15, 220–22, 252
Duhem, Pierre, 54–60, 108,

Earth's age, 45, 112, 125–26, 128
Eddington, Arthur, 130–31, 136,
Einstein, Albert,
  philosophy, 7, 9, 25, 84, 137
  religion, 23, 158–59, 212
  science, 29, 43, 105, 131, 144
emergence, 175, 190, 192, 215–17
entropy, 47–48
epistemology, 13, 153, 180
evolution, guided or planned, 248–50, 254
evolutionary creationism, 248–49
evolutionism, 11, 182, 231
evolutionary transitions, 174–78, 184, 186–87, 263
extended evolutionary synthesis, 116, 185, 191–94

fall of man, 255, 258–62
Feser, Edward, 148, 183, 212
fine tuning, 43–46, 50–51
flat earth, 70, 228, 240
flood, Noah's, 25, 106, 116–18, 120–21, 124, 244–45
Frege, Gottlieb, 211–12
French revolution, 92, 229, 233
Futuyma, Douglas J., 169–70, 173–74, 181, 191, 193

Galilei, Galileo,
  edited letter, 94
  myth, 5, 52–53, 56, 63
  theology, 12, 83, 93–95
  tidal evidence, 65, 88–91
  science, 74, 80, 85–88, 97–98
geocentric model, 53, 69, 96, 100
geoheliocentric model, 53, 64, 76, 78, 100,
God of the gaps, 26, 254
Graney, Christopher, 53, 66, 74–75, 97–98, 100

Hawking, Stephen, 8, 19, 60, 79, 138–40, 230–31
heliocentric model. See Copernicus
Hipparchus, 70, 105
Holland, Tom, 17–18, 103, 143
Horgan, John, 157, 169
Hubble, Edward, 129, 135–37
hydrogen, 37–38, 41, 135, 137, 253

Ibn Sahl, 3, 79
idealism, 217–20, 252
image of God,
  in Genesis, 51, 143, 246, 249, 251, 258
  meaning of, 17, 37, 84, 231–32, 236, 256
Intelligent Design, 185–87, 190, 249
intervention, divine, 139, 158, 190
irreducible complexity, 185–86, 249
Islam, 15, 108, 145

Jaki, Stanley, 106, 162–63
Jesus, 12–13, 15, 20–21, 108, 111, 180

INDEX

Kastrup, Bernardo, 217–18
Kelvin, Lord, 45–47, 125–26, 235
Kepler, Johannes,
    Galileo's relation to, 80, 85–86, 89, 96–97
    laws, 65, 77–82, 85, 97, 101
    philosophy, 143, 154, 156–57, 212
    science, 79–82, 100–101
    theology, 82–85, 109
King's Mirror, 5–6, 70, 89, 147–48, 150
Kragh, Helge, 20, 59, 106–8, 129, 138

Lamarckism, 171, 193
language, human, 32–35, 175–76, 197–98, 208–9, 211, 251
Laplace, Pierre-Simon, 161, 194
law of nature,
    as cause, 139, 160–61, 230
    instead of form, 153–60
    lawgiver, 38, 142, 159–60
    origin, 8–10, 84
    trust, 12, 25, 137
Leavitt, Henrietta, 135–36
Leibniz, Gottfried, 10, 131, 158–59
Lemaître, Georges, 104, 128–38
Lennox, John, 50, 243, 248, 252, 254
Lewis, C. S., 103, 165, 174, 177, 182

materialism,
    eliminative, 214
    promissory, 215
    reductionism, 215–17, 220, 236, 252–53
mathematics,
    abstract, 206, 209–12
    proof, 45, 133
    elegance 144, 196, 236
    language of, 85–86, 110
    solution, 83, 129
    unreasonable effectiveness of, 9, 212
Maxwell, James Clerk, 38–39, 234, 241
Mendel, Gregor, 171–72
monism, 213–14, 219–21, 252–53
moon,
    Earth's, 39–40, 62, 70, 89, 99, 243
    planets, 39, 63, 82, 86
multiverse, 157
mysterian, 220–21

Nagel, Thomas, 207, 220
natural theology, 23, 27, 118, 124
neo-Darwinism, 115, 167, 171–74, 185, 187, 192–93
Newton, Isaac,
    age of the Earth, 125
    Newtonianism, 161, 194–95, 224–25
    philosophy, 8, 153–56, 185
    Principia, 74, 101, 153, 155–56, 161, 225
Nilakantha Somayaji, 3, 76
Noble, Dennis, 188–89, 193

occasionalism, 145
ontology, 13, 153, 180, 188
Oresme, Nicole, 57, 74
Origen, 109–10

pantheism, 18, 27, 107, 248
parallax, 72, 76, 97, 101, 135–36
Pascal, Blaise, 23–25, 41, 59, 83, 132
phenomenological description, 239–40
Philoponus, Johannes, 57, 107
phoneme, 32–33
Plantinga, Alvin, 232
Plato, 105–6, 148, 153, 183, 212
Platonic solids, 79, 156–57
Platonism, 210
pope,
    John Paul II, 92–93, 252
    Pius IX, 115,
    Pius XII, 128–29, 131, 134, 140, 252
    Sixtus IV, 16
    Urban VIII, 95–96
positivism, 229–30
postmodernism, 13
presentism, 4
primary and secondary causes, 55, 145–47, 158–59, 162
pseudoscience, 138, 157
Ptolemy 62, 65–69, 71–72, 77

quantum mechanics, 27, 104, 139–40, 194, 219
Quran, 15, 106

reductionism, 149, 191, 215, 220, 236, 252–53

relativity, theory of, 9, 27, 43, 104–5, 128–29, 144
renaissance, 1, 56, 147
Riccioli, Giovanni, 61–64, 74–75, 87, 92, 100, 244

Sagan, Carl, 19, 60
Saturn, 39–41, 63, 65, 71, 124, 243
Schaeffer, Francis, 13, 18, 250
Schrödinger, Erwin, 7, 48–49, 189
scientism, 14, 34, 229–33
social Darwinism, 168, 170
Solzhenitsyn, Aleksandr, 20, 258
soul, 115, 151, 153, 203, 212–15, 250–53
spontaneous creation, 104, 114–16, 246
stardust, 39, 41
steady-state theory, 137–38
Steno, Nicolas, 119–20, 149
Stott, John, 256

teleology, 49, 148–49, 152–53, 162, 189
Tertullian, 29
theistic evolution, 248, 254

thermodynamics, 46–49, 58–59, 125–26, 235
Thirty Years' War, 63, 82–83, 95–96
tidal theory, 65, 88–90, 97
tough problem, 214, 218
truth,
   true, 13
   two ways to, 13–14, 16–17, 227, 236–37
two-book metaphor, 12–18, 28, 37, 84–85, 130, 241

uniformitarianism, 120, 123–25

Voltaire, 97, 229

Waage, Peter, 2–3, 160
Weinberg, Steven, 19, 154, 188–89
Wigner, Eugene, 8–9

young earth creationism, 112–13, 190–91, 243–44, 247, 249, 254

Zu Chongzhi, 3, 210

www.ingramcontent.com/pod-product-compliance
Lightning Source LLC
Chambersburg PA
CBHW071237230426
43668CB00011B/1471